Imre Nagy on Communism

IMRE NAGY

ON

COMMUNISM.

IN
DEFENSE
OF
THE
NEW
COURSE

FREDERICK A. PRAEGER · *Publishers*

NEW YORK, N.Y.

First published in the United States of America in 1957
by Frederick A. Praeger, Inc., 15 West 47 Street, New York 36
Copyright © 1957 in the United States of America
by Frederick A. Praeger, Inc.

Library of Congress Catalog Card Number 57-13457
Printed in the United States of America

PUBLISHER'S NOTE

This is the complete text of what the author calls a "dissertation," written during Imre Nagy's forced retirement in 1955 and 1956 after he had been ousted from his position as Premier and expelled from the Central Committee. It was directly addressed to his former colleagues on the Central Committee and indirectly to Hungary's Russian overlords. A copy of the original mimeographed document was smuggled out of Hungary in the spring of 1957. It is unquestionably authentic. In July, 1957, it was also printed clandestinely in Hungary by Nagy's friends and distributed throughout the country.

The book is a statement of principles, policies, and plans—set forth by one Communist for consumption by other Communists —that is meant to justify Nagy's "New Course" program and to establish the need for liberalization within the framework of Communism. What is most significant, as revealed in this book and in the events in Hungary which followed its writing, is that the power-mad oligarchy of Communist rulers denied the Hungarian people the measure of freedom Nagy sought to give them, and that Nagy, the idealist, his faith unshaken, writing as a devoted Communist calling upon the words of Marx, Lenin, and even Stalin, to support his tenets and programs, clinging to Communist theory as the only salvation of mankind, was himself repudiated and crushed, denounced as a heretic by his associates who, as practical and genuine Communists, obeyed only their own motivation of ruthless application of power.

Imre Nagy is best remembered in the West as the Premier-of-a-week in revolution-torn Hungary last October; the last hope of a Hungarian Communist Party desperately seeking to placate the rising tide of the people's demand for freedom. At that moment in history he emerged as a symbol of liberalism within the Communist movement. The precedent for this had been established earlier, during Nagy's less well known Premiership, when, from July, 1953, to March, 1955, he had introduced a new set of liberalizing policies which became known as the "New Course."

The tragic irony of the book and of Nagy's position is that his program, though couched in Communist terminology, buttressed with the Communist scriptures, and proposed as the only "correct" application of theory as opposed to Rákosi's "deviations," is in direct opposition to all the realities of Communism, and Nagy cannot see this. More clearly than any document or statement that has come out of the Communist world, Nagy's argument reveals the insoluble contradictions besetting Communist dogma and practice.

Nagy's book is a crushing indictment of the policies of a satellite government imitating and sometimes even refining the total slavery practiced in the USSR. Unfortunately, Nagy's picture of Hungary under Rákosi is also the picture of Hungary under Kadar, whose government and its political police is replete with the same power-drunk bureaucrats and callous murderers who previously served Rákosi. It has reverted very quickly to the methods and fabrications of the Rákosi period.

Frederick A. Praeger

FOREWORD

by HUGH SETON-WATSON

The author of this book, Imre Nagy, is a veteran Communist. The Hungarian Communist Party was founded at the end of 1918, largely from Hungarian soldiers captured by the Russian Army between 1914 and 1917 who joined the Bolsheviks and were indoctrinated by them. In March, 1919, the Hungarian Communists were able to seize power, but by August they had been driven out by a Rumanian invasion. The Communist Party had had a good deal of support at first, chiefly among the Budapest workers but partly also among nationalists of all classes who hoped that Russian help would enable them to defend their country against the territorial claims of neighboring states—Czechoslovakia, Rumania, Yugoslavia. The military collapse of August, 1919, ended these hopes, there was a general revulsion of opinion against the Communists, and the minority of workers and intellectuals who remained loyal to the Party were finally persecuted by the police of the very conservative government that now ruled in Budapest. During the following decades the leading Communists were in exile, either in Central Europe (Austria, Germany, or Czechoslovakia) or in Moscow. Fifteen of these years Imre Nagy spent in Moscow, where he studied agricultural problems, wrote propaganda articles, and broadcast to Hungary.

In 1944-1945 the Soviets, pursuing Hitler's armies in retreat, occupied Hungary. In their baggage train came a small band of Hungarian Communists. Their leader was Mátyás Rákosi, who had been a junior minister in the 1919 government. Among them was Imre Nagy. As a specialist on agrarian problems, he was given the post of Minister of Agriculture in the postwar government. In this capacity he was responsible for carrying out the Land Reform of 1945. This was an important measure, for in prewar Hungary nearly half the cultivated land had belonged to a small number of great landowners, and more than three million Hungarians were either landless farm laborers or owners of tiny plots of land too small to support a family. Ever since the end of the nineteenth century Hungarian democrats had been urging a redistribution of land, but without success. The 1945 Land Reform put an end to the estates and gave land to hundreds of thousands of peasant families. The Reform was strongly supported by all the democratic parties that in 1945 formed a coalition government with the Communists (Social Democrats, Small Farmers', and National Peasants). But by giving the Ministry of Agriculture to a member of their Party, the Communists were able to claim more than their share of credit for the reform. Recently (in the summer of 1957) the Soviet puppet rulers of Hungary have claimed that the reform was really the work not of Imre Nagy but of Marshal Voroshilov, who headed the Soviet occupation administration. Curiously enough, there is some truth in this assertion. The Land Reform was in fact prepared by the Soviet authorities and rushed through in an arbitrary manner for political reason, without regard for economic conditions. Nevertheless, there is no doubt that the principle of agrarian reform was very close to the heart of Nagy, and that he considered its achievement a culmination of his career to that time. Also, though the Hungarian peasants were for the most part not deceived by Communist Party demagogy, they remembered the name of Nagy with gratitude.

In the autumn of 1945 a general election was held, and in spite of the presence of Soviet troops the vote was free. The Hungarian people refused to be intimidated, and 57 per cent of their votes went to the moderate Small Farmers' Party, only 17 per cent to the Communists. Marshal Voroshilov however refused to allow the Small Farmers to form a government alone, as was their undoubted constitutional right. He had only agreed to the vote being free in return for a promise that the coalition would be maintained, and that the Communists would share in power. After the election he went further, and demanded that the key post of Minister of Interior, which controlled the police, should go to a Communist. The person chosen for this post was Imre Nagy. He did not however hold it for long. He was replaced by Laszlo Rajk, a tougher and more cruel character, who carried through the establishment of a one-party Communist dictatorship. In the first months of 1947 the Small Farmers' Party was broken. Several of their parliamentary deputies were arrested in connection with a frame-up "plot," tortured, and made to confess treason. The General Secretary of the Party, and its most fearless and able leader, Béla Kovács, was arrested by the Soviet security police and deported to the Soviet Union. By the summer of 1947 the Party was led only by complaisant individuals who took orders not from the Party membership but from the Communist leader Rákosi, and mobilized their freightened remnant of parliamentary support to do his bidding. During the same period Communist pressure on the Social Democrat Party was tightened. In February, 1948, the independent-minded leaders of their original left wing (Anna Kéthly and Antal Bán) were expelled on Communist orders, and in June the leaders of the rump party solemnly voted it out of existence by "fusion" with the Communist Party. The Party now changed its name to the Hungarian Workers' Party, but it was entirely controlled by the Communist *apparat,* headed by the four former Muscovite exiles to whom Nagy, in the present work, frequently refers as "the foursome"—Mátyás Rákosi, Ernö Gerö, Joseph Róvai, and Mihály Farkas. Of these four, however, the undoubted boss was Rákosi.

A new period began in 1949. In that year the Communist leaders openly proclaimed their intention of collectivizing agriculture—that is, of taking away from the peasants the land that the 1945 reform had given them, and subjecting them to unlimited economic pressure in the interests of the Communist Party's general plans of total power. In the summer of 1948 Moscow had broken with the Yugoslav Communists, and Hungary, like the other East European satellites, was obliged to sever all economic relations with Yugoslavia in 1949. The excommunication of Marshal Tito and his colleagues by the infallible high priest of Marxism-Leninism, Marshal Stalin, led to a fierce campaign against "nationalist deviation" in the Communist Parties of Eastern Europe. This gave Rákosi the opportunity to rid himself of the only member of his Party who could challenge his power by virtue of his position and his fighting record—Laszlo Rajk.

In 1948 Rajk was transferred from the Ministry of Interior to the much less powerful post of Minister of Foreign Affairs, and soon afterward he was arrested. After a long period of both torture and persuasion, Rajk was "ready" for a short trial, carefully modeled on the Soviet examples of 1936-1938. According to a most circumstantial account by refugees from the 1956 revolution, who were personally acquainted with members of the Central Committee of the Party, Rajk was promised his life and liberty, under a new name in another country, provided he would confess in public to a long list of wildly improbable crimes. The man chosen to persuade Rajk to do this was a close friend, Janos Kadar, who succeeded him as Minister of Interior. Rajk kept his part of the bargain, but Rákosi betrayed him, with or without the previous knowledge of Kadar. It is typical of Rákosi's character that he arranged that Rajk should be hanged under the window of the cell in which his wife was imprisoned, so that she could hear the whole proceeding.

During the years 1949-1952 tens of thousands of members of the Party were arrested. They included friends of Rajk, but for the most part had little connection with him. Among them were former Social Democrats, of two types—weak dupes who had surrendered to Communist pressure or believed Communist promises, like the former President of the Republic, Arpad Szakasits, and active traitors to Social Democracy, who had systematically undermined their party, like Gyorgy Marosan, who survived to reappear as traitor for the second time in 1956 together with Kadar. Many of these arrested Communists and Socialists, factory workers or intellectuals, were subjected to physical and mental tortures designed to turn them into frightened animals deprived of human dignity or personality.

Plenty of evidence of the bestialities and humiliations perpetrated by the security police (AHV) was revealed during the
1956 revolution. Perhaps the most astonishing part of the
whole story is that so many survived, not only physically but
mentally and morally as well.

But suffering was of course not confined to members or
fellow travelers of the Party. Mass collectivization, which by
1952 had affected about one-third of Hungary's peasants, was
accompanied by much brutality, injustice, and robbery against
the farming population. The forced industrialization, imposed
by the Five-Year Plan that began in 1949, laid heavy burdens
on the factory workers and miners. In 1951, as a result of the
Soviet demand for still more heavy industry and more military
expenditure in connection with the international dangers
brought on by the Communist aggression in North Korea, the
industrial targets were still further increased. The years 1951
and 1952 were the worst of all for the Hungarian people. To
all their other sufferings were added mass deportations of families from Budapest to miserable quarters in villages or to
forced-labor camps. This measure was directed chiefly at members of the prewar middle classes or landowning gentry, but it
gave the security police ample opportunity of paying off personal scores against their enemies of any social class. Those
who took over the apartments and houses of the deported were
the members of the new privileged elite, especially Rákosi's
praetorian guard of torturers from the police and slave-driving
factory managers.

In 1952 Hungary had a full-blooded totalitarian regime,
closely modeled on the Soviet prototype. In one respect it was
closer to its original than any other East European satellite
regime. As the Soviet regime was a personal autocracy of Stalin,
so the Hungarian regime was a personal autocracy of Rákosi.
The party leadership was very thoroughly purged so as to leave
in it only the servile creatures of the boss. This can be clearly
seen from a study of personnel at the Central Committee level.
Of ninety-two persons who were members of the Central Committee between 1949 and 1954, only forty-six were still members in 1954. About half of these were removed between 1949
and the Second Congress of the Party in 1951, and half in the

following period, probably in 1952. This rate of turnover—50 per cent—was exceeded only in the leadership of the Czechoslovak Communist Party, where in approximately the same period it was nearly 60 per cent. On the lower levels of the Party apparatus information is insufficient. The personal ascendancy of Rákosi in the Hungarian Party was however far greater than that of his opposite number, Klement Gottwald, in the Czechoslovak Party. When Gottwald died in 1953, second-rank men were available to take over as a "collective leadership." But in Hungary there was no one except Rákosi. His supremacy ensured the advantages of ruthless leadership, but the Party's complete dependence on one man was a source of weakness.

The death of Stalin in March, 1953, was a decisive event for the history of Hungary as well as of the other satellites. His successors fumbled toward a milder policy. The combination of mass discontent with uncertainty as to future leadership caused the violent demonstrations by Czech workers in Plzen in early June, and the much more widespread workers' rising in Eastern Germany two weeks later. This in turn, by discrediting the Soviet security police, provided the occasion for the overthrow of Beria in Moscow. The whole future of policy in the satellite countries was uncertain. The Soviet leaders decided that economic concessions, a "New Course," were urgently needed, and the country in which they decided to go furthest was Hungary. The instrument of the new policy was to be Imre Nagy.

From 1947 onward Imre Nagy had retreated into the background. Though he had continued to hold a high position in the Party hierarchy and had never been under arrest, he had not been given any important governmental duties. He had certainly disapproved of the Rajk "trial" and of the breach with Yugoslavia, but it seems that he was prudent enough to hold his tongue. One of the most interesting revelations of this book is that his selection in June, 1953, as Prime Minister in place of Rákosi was made by the Soviet leaders themselves. "It must be stated that it was not Mátyás Rákosi but the Soviet comrades, Malenkov, Molotov, and Khrushchev, who recommended what Rákosi and all members of the Hungarian delegation [in Moscow—ed.] accepted with approbation. Thus, Rákosi . . . bears no responsibility at all for my nomination." The separation of the Premiership and the First Secretaryship of the Party of course followed the recent Soviet model. Stalin had held both offices, but his successors, after a significant gap of a few days, had decided to divide them, giving the first to Malenkov and the second to Khrushchev. In Hungary, where Rákosi held both offices, he had to give up one. He decided to keep the First Secretaryship, but a Premier had to be found. Imre Nagy's account of the Soviet leaders' comment on Rákosi's attitude at this time is interesting. Malenkov, he claims, said, "We asked, 'Whom do you recommend as your deputy?' He could name no one. He had objections to everyone whose name was mentioned; he had something against everyone. Everyone was suspect except him alone. This appalled us very much." Molotov said of the same discussion with Rákosi, "He wanted a Premier who would have no voice in the making of decisions."

Appointed by the Soviet leaders, Imre Nagy introduced radical changes. The peasants were to receive far more economic help, and they were to be allowed to leave collective farms. Where a majority of the members of a collective farm wished to dissolve it, this was to be permitted. The pace of industrialization was to be reduced. Police terror was relaxed, deported persons were gradually allowed to return home (though they did not recover their former dwellings), many arrested persons were released. Nagy also called for better treatment of intellectuals and for toleration of religion. During the next year and a half he did his best to put these policies into practice. But though Rákosi accepted them in principle and in public, he opposed them in practice. Already his speech of July 11, 1953, by its different emphasis and tone, suggested disagreement with Nagy's speech of July 4. This impression of Western observers at the time is now confirmed by Nagy. He also confirms the belief then held by Western observers that the apparatus of the Party, still firmly controlled by Rákosi, sabotaged the Premier's work. Among other things, Rákosi was able to ensure that the June, 1953, resolution of the Central Committee, which strongly criticized previous policies, was not made public.

Rákosi bided his time. In February, 1955, Malenkov was

removed from the Premiership of the Soviet Union. Whether
(as seems possible from internal evidence) Nagy enjoyed some
personal protection from Malenkov, or whether it was merely
that Rákosi shrewdly used a moment of uncertainty in Moscow
to reassert his autocracy, it is certain that he acted quickly and
to good effect. He was helped by the fact that Nagy was then in
poor health. In the spring of 1955 the latter was removed from
his office, his "errors" were publicly denounced in resolutions
of the Central Committee, and he was expelled from the Politburo and the Central Committee. In November he was expelled
from the Party. However he was not arrested. A return to the
unlimited terror of 1951-1952 was no longer possible. The
Soviet leaders were now determined to reconcile themselves
with Yugoslavia, and Marshal Tito was determined that part
of his price was to be the disgrace of his bitter enemy Rákosi.
The Hungarian boss was thus on the defensive. Khrushchev's
denunciation of Stalin at the Twentieth Congress of the Communist Party of the Soviet Union in February, 1956, weakened
Rákosi still further, and on July 18, 1956, he was forced to
resign as First Secretary. This, however, was not the end of
the story. The weakness of the Party, hitherto concealed by the
impressive figure of Rákosi, rapidly became apparent. In
October the whole regime collapsed.

The present work was written by Imre Nagy in the period
between his disgrace in the spring of 1955 and the fall of Rákosi
in July, 1956. It is especially interesting in relation to its
author's views on four subjects—industrialization, agriculture,
foreign policy, and the problem of police terror and dictatorship.

He defends himself vehemently against the accusation that
he was against industrialization in general or the priority of
heavy industry in particular. In this he is obviously correct.
No intelligent person could doubt that Hungary needed and
needs industrial development, or that there must be a certain
emphasis on the production of capital goods. But Nagy rightly
objected to the absurd exaggeration of Rákosi's industrial
policy. This concentrated not only on production of capital
goods, but specifically on capital goods designed to produce

other capital goods. There was thus a shortage not only of consumer goods but of capital goods required for the later production of consumer goods. The workers' standard of living was ruthlessly sacrificed to the achievement of heavy-industry targets. "Economies" were made at the expense of workers' wages and of social services. As Nagy points out, Rákosi promised during the Five-Year Plan (1949-1953) to raise the workers' standard of living by 50 per cent. In fact, however, though industrial output doubled during this period (from 150 to 300, if the level of 1938 be taken as 100), and labor productivity increased by 63 per cent, wages remained approximately at the 1949 level, and the standard of living thus steadily fell until 1953. Nagy claims that under his New Course policy it rose by 15 per cent, but this of course, as he realized, was far less than the rise in output or in productivity. Thus on the one hand the working class was impoverished, while on the other hand dangerous maladjustments were created between branches of industry, which gravely distorted the whole Hungarian economy. The Hungarian rulers pursued a policy of autarky, competing needlessly with neighboring countries rather than pursuing a specialization in certain fields, which would have been economically far more profitable. This policy was generally characteristic of all the satellite states in these years, and was caused partly by the priority for military needs after the outbreak of war in Korea, partly by considerations of prestige, and partly no doubt by the personal obsessions of Stalin (though Nagy prudently refrains from mentioning this factor). It is however most interesting that he records that after Stalin's death the Soviet leaders themselves expressed thir dismay at Rákosi's industrial policies. In June, 1953, in Moscow, he writes that Mikoyan spoke of "a certain adventurous spirit" in Hungarian economic planning, and criticized "the excessive development of your own iron-smelting industry. Hungary has no iron ore, no coke. All this must be imported. No one in Hungary has figured out yet exactly the price of a ton of iron ore and steel in Hungary. Hungary is building foundries for which no one has yet promised to supply the ore. In 1952, for instance, there was a shortage of 700,000 tons of coke." In 1954 Kaganovich declared, at a conference in Moscow with Hungarian leaders, "Earlier mistakes in economic policy have not yet been corrected completely. The proportion between heavy and light industries is almost the same as in the past. You wanted to build socialism, on which we have been working for thirty-five years, too rapidly. The situation is entirely different in Russia than it is in Hungary, and you do not want to recognize this fact."

Nagy tried to remedy these errors. But he was not helped by Soviet trade policy. Trade conferences with the Soviet Union and the other satellites in the second half of 1954 revealed that in 1955 Hungary would get from these sources only 50 per cent of the raw materials and other essential goods that she had had in 1954. But as it had already been decided to reduce imports from the "capitalist" countries in 1955, Hungary required more from the Soviet Union and the satellites than she had had in 1954. Nagy's policies were made still more difficult by the interference of an Economic Policy Committee of the Party, over which he had no control. It was managed by Rákosi's close collaborator Gerö, and took action without consulting the Prime Minister. Even within the Council of Ministers, matters of foreign trade were removed from the Premier's jurisdiction and entrusted to Gerö, in his capacity of First Deputy Premier.

Agriculture was Nagy's special field. On assuming office, he found a desparate situation here. Agriculture had been neglected by the government except as a source of revenue. Investments had been negligible, and forced collectivization had driven the peasants to passive resistance. As a result, in the spring of 1953 approximately one million acres, more than 10 per cent of the arable land of the country, remained untilled. This situation Nagy resolved to remedy by giving the peasants strong material incentives, by reducing violent pressure upon them, and by persuading them that the government no longer regarded them as its enemies.

Nagy strongly defends himself against the accusation, made in the resolutions of March and April, 1955, that he opposed the development of cooperative farming and favored individual peasant ownership of land. He even goes so far as to claim that the Danish system of agricultural cooperatives, which he describes as "capitalist," had ruined "Denmark's working peasants." Whether he really believes this nonsense, or merely put it in his memorandum as a ritual slogan to show his orthodox respectability, is not clear. In general, Nagy shows ingenuity in defending his views by quotations from Stalin, mostly taken from the period 1924-1928, when Stalin defended the interests of the peasantry against the "Left Opposition" critics Trotsky, Zinoviev, and Kamenev. Stalin's later attitude is of course well known to Nagy, but he here ignores it. He prefers to compare Rákosi's supporters, whom he describes as "pseudoradical 'left-wingers,' " to the defeated Opposition in the Soviet Union in the 1920's. He maintains that he is strongly in favor of cooperative farming but is against prematurely and violently forcing the peasants into collective farms. He insists that it is not possible *simultaneously* to develop a vast heavy industry, to collectivize agriculture, and to raise the output per acre of agriculture. But this last aim is essential if Hungary's trade is to be developed and her economy to prosper. To attempt the first two aims at the same time, at forced pace, is to abandon the third. In fact, he claims, "in Hungary the 'left-wing' deviationists, despite a 30 per cent social sector, have kept agricultural production at the prewar level though it should exceed that by at least 25 to 30 per cent."

Nagy's arguments, which are most interesting, must be considered at two different levels, one economic, the other political. There is much to be said for the view that small farmers cannot prosper as separate individuals but must be joined together in cooperatives. As a convinced Marxist, he inclines to underrate the possibilities of intensive farming on private small holdings. Nevertheless, quite irrespective of Marxist dogma, the experience of the East European peasants between the world wars showed clearly the weakness of unaided small farms and the necessity of cooperatives. Indeed these were strongly recommended by the democratic peasant parties, such as the Hungarian Small Farmers' Party, over whose ruthless destruction by the Communists in 1947 Nagy has no tears to shed. A strong case can be made, on empirical economic grounds, not only for marketing and credit cooperatives but also for cooperative farming, including the pooling of machinery, in areas of large-scale cereal production, which was of course highly developed in Hungary before the war. The peasants themselves to a large extent favored cooperatives, and could certainly have been persuaded to go still further if approached by the authorities in a tactful and intelligent manner. They could be expected to resist only if they were to be deprived of the ownership of their own holdings.

It was of course the intention of the Communists to deprive the peasants of their holdings. But it would be a mistake to regard the conflict between the Communists and the peasants, in Hungary or elsewhere, as primarily a conflict about ownership. This is of course the impression one gets from the literature on the subject that is inspired or influenced by Communist sources. These present the problem as economic. They stress the advantages of large-scale production and deplore the reactionary narrow-mindedness of peasants who cannot see, or be made to see, their own interests. When the problem is put in this way, Western students, though disliking the violence used by the Communists against the peasants, are inclined to sympathize with the Communists' general argument.

But this is not the essence of the problem. The essence is not economic progress but political power. The collective farm, as it developed in the Soviet Union from 1929 onward, was an instrument of political coercion in the hands of the ruling Communist Party. The collective farm, or kolkhoz, was managed by a chairman, who was chosen by the local Communist Party leadership and exercised autocratic powers over the peasants who had nominally "elected" him. The collective farms were controlled by the Machine Tractor Stations (MTS), which monopolized all large agricultural machinery, and which in the 1930's supervised about thirty collective farms each. The MTS in turn was controlled by its Communist Party branch, whose title was changed from time to time—"Political Section" in 1932-1934, "Assistant Director (Political)" thereafter until recent times. In the last years, Khrushchev has considerably modified the apparatus, but the essence of the control by the Party over the peasant masses through the hierarchy of MTS and kolkhoz remains unchanged. This control is far more effective—more centralized, more positive, better designed to mobilized rural man power for the government's purposes—than any old-fashioned dictatorship, as in Russia under the Tsars or in Hungary under Horthy.

The purpose of the control is to obtain from the peasants a high proportion of what they produce, at a price far lower than they would obtain in a free market. The Soviet government has thus been able to supply food to the growing urban population comparatively cheaply, and even so to make a vast profit on the deal. The policy has been extremely successful in so far as it has subjected the peasantry to the government's will. Where it has not been so successful is precisely in the field that Communist propaganda has most stressed—in raising agricultural output. The peasants have been unable to resist the government by force or to prevent it from taking the crops that they have raised. But they have been able to refrain from producing more than a minimum. This passive resistance of the Russian peasantry has produced a critical situation in the Soviet Union. The urban population has not only increased but has begun to exert pressure for better standards of living, for more varied food of better quality. The Soviet government can no longer ignore the pressure. But it cannot provide the better and more ample supplies unless agricultural yields are increased. Khrushchev has tried to do this mainly by bringing new lands into cultivation. He has had some success, but it cannot suffice. He will solve his problem only if he improves output in the acres already under cultivation. This means that he must give the peasants material incentives to produce more, that he must cease to treat them as a hostile conquered population to be exploited as a colony in the interests of the ruling Party.

The policy of collectivization introduced by Rákosi in Hungary after 1949 followed the Soviet model and had the same aims, though it must be admitted that it was not carried out so quickly or so brutally as in the Soviet Union from 1929 to 1933. Nagy does not mention the horrors of Soviet collectivization: for understandable tactical reasons, as he is in fact appealing to Khrushchev in 1956, he seeks to show that Hungarian policy is much worse than Soviet policy, and that its exponents have failed to learn the lessons taught by the wise Stalin. But of course Nagy, who lived long in Russia, must have been well aware of this when he wrote this work.

The arguments used by Nagy in favor of peasant cooperatives are not unconvincing, but they are quite unrealistic, as they bear no relation to realities either in "People's Democratic" Hungary or in Soviet Russia. Undoubtedly Hungarian peasants would benefit from agricultural cooperatives. But the essence of a farming cooperative is that it should be managed by the farmers, in their own interest. As long as the Communist Party rules a country, this is impossible. The best example of success-ful cooperatives run by farmers is precisely that very Denmark that Nagy affects to scorn. The significant difference between Danish cooperatives and any conceivable Hungarian kolkhozes is not that the former are "capitalist" and the latter "socialist" —this is mere mumbo jumbo—but that in the former the peas-ants manage their own affairs and in the latter they are exploited by the Communist Party bosses. Actually there are few coun-tries in the world where the Danish type of cooperative could flourish better than Hungary. If large-scale cereal farming were increasingly supplemented by intensive crops, by the production of vegetables, fruit, and animal products, all of which are of unusually high quality in Hungary, a vigorous canning industry and export trade could develop, which would be of far more benefit to the Hungarian economy, and would do far more for the Hungarian workers and peasants, than many of the megalo-maniac heavy-industrial enterprises pursued for reasons of prestige or dogma. Development of this sort requires above all cooperatives managed by the farmers themselves. But Marxist dogma, as interpreted by Stalinist bosses, was bound to reject this promising perspective.

Of all this Nagy, as an agricultural expert and a true friend of the peasants, may well be aware. But in the present context he could not say it. He is thus driven to combine quite concrete and valid criticism of Rákosi's policies with quite unrealistic and abstract considerations about the advantages of cooperation.

In discussing political conditions under Rákosi, Nagy allows himself greater freedom of expression. He denounces the "cult of personality," "Bonapartism," and "Führerism" that flourished under Rákosi. To bring this about, "the Party's leading cadres had to be exterminated, and the AVH [security police —ed.] had to be made the supreme power." The result is that "most of the workers have come to believe that they are at the mercy of illegalities and abuses, that there are no laws that protect their rights as human beings and citizens," and "the spread of the theory that a People's Democracy is synonymous with the anarchy of law and order." At the time of writing (late 1955 and early 1956) "the number of persons imprisoned is greater than ever before. . . . But the most alarming fact is that the majority of those convicted come from the ranks of the working class, the industrial workers." The execution of Rajk and the mass arrests and tortures of 1949-1952 were simply criminal actions, and it is intolerable that those who committed them should remain in power, using the disgraced head of the Soviet security police, Beria, and the former Hungarian security chief, Péter Gábor, as scapegoats on which to unload their own sins. In this connection he even claims to quote a remark of Khrushchev (date not stated) : "In June, 1953, we correctly passed judgment on the Hungarian Party's leadership, and that judgment is entirely correct today too. They cannot hide behind Beria, as Rákosi is trying to do." One may observe that this comes curiously from Khrushchev, who tried precisely this gambit when trying to ingratiate himself with Marshal Tito on Belgrade airfield in June, 1955. However there can be no doubt of Nagy's sincerity in the following statement, which though coming from a Marxist has a strong flavor of what Communists contemptuously describe as "bourgeois morality": "It is not compatible with public morality to have in positions of leadership the directors and organizers of mass trials, those responsible for torturing and killing innocent men, organizers of international provocations, and economic saboteurs or squanderers of public property who, through the abuse of power, either have committed serious acts against the people or are forcing others to commit these acts." The Rákosi clique "have made virtues of self-abasement, cowardice, hypocrisy, lack of principles, and lies." The growth of servility and careerism is often explained away by the apologists of the regime as a survival from the past, a state of mind fostered in the prewar bureaucracy by the Horthy dictatorship or by "capitalism." This easy explanation Nagy rejects: "Unfortunately, it is not simply a question of remnants from the past, but derives from the stifling of criticism, intimidation, and retribution against candid speech that are in evidence now in leadership methods and that unavoidably lead to the spread of opportunism." Nagy also rejects the constantly invoked argument that injustices have to be accepted in the interest of Party unity: "They forget that the Party is not a den of criminals, the unity of which must be maintained by making a secret of crimes. What kind of unity is it that is held together by knowledge of and participation in crime?"

But perhaps the strongest argument invoked in favor of terror, in Rákosi's Hungary as in Stalin's and Khrushchev's Russia, was the danger of foreign capitalist intervention and of war. Nagy clearly states his belief that this danger has been exaggerated. This caused him to be denounced by his enemies as a pacifist, a charge that he here indignantly denies at some length. But in his chapter on foreign policy he sails dangerously close to the wind. He denies that he is a nationalist or a chauvinist. On the contrary, he stresses that he has always favored, and actively pleaded for, friendship between Hungary and the Soviet Union, and between Hungary and her territorial neighbors—Czechoslovakia, Rumania, Yugoslavia, and Austria. At the same time he proudly asserts his devotion to his own country, his Hungarian patriotism. All this, to a Western reader, seems reasonable and convincing. But in the context of a satellite country such arguments are highly risky, and one marvels at Nagy's courage, or perhaps his temerity. For it is clear, when he speaks of the necessity of Hungarian independence and even of an independent Hungarian foreign policy, that he can be thinking only of independence from Soviet domination. Even to advocate, as he does, close friendship with the other Danubian countries, rather than close bilateral ties between these countries and the Soviet Union, is heresy: one recalls the severe rebuke administered in 1948 to the Bulgarian Communist leader Georgi Dimitrov for recommending a Federation of Eastern Europe. It is a dogma in the Soviet world that no substantial concentration of power may exist in any part of the world that can be controlled from Moscow. The world outside the borders of the Soviet Union consists of two types of states: enemies and slaves. The existence of enemies is to be tolerated until the Soviet Union is strong enough to destroy or enslave them. But where Soviet power is effective, only slave status is permitted. Yet Nagy takes so seriously the "five principles" of peaceful coexistence, as proclaimed at the Bandung Conference of "Afro-Asian" states, that he writes of the necessity to "liquidate the power groups." By this phrase he is putting the "camp of peace" (the Soviet Union, China, and their satellites) on an equal footing with the "camp of imperialism." But this is sheer heresy. It is one thing for a "peace-loving" (consciously or unconsciously Soviet-inspired) citizen of a Western or a free Asian country to urge the abolition of "power groups." This means a demand that such alliances as NATO and SEATO and the Baghdad Pact be dismantled. Such a demand is "objectively progressive," because it strengthens the military power of the Soviet bloc. But it is quite another thing for a citizen of a satellite state (a member of the "peace-loving" or "democratic" camp) to urge the liquidation of all "power groups," including the Soviet and Chinese systems of military alliances. Such a demand is "objectively" nothing less than "warmongering" or "kowtowing to imperialism." One recalls the rage of the Soviet leaders when Marshal Tito spoke of the Soviet Union and the Western Powers as power groups on a footing of equality.

Nagy was undoubtedly influenced, when he wrote these pages, by his sympathy for Tito's Yugoslavia and his belief that, now that Khrushchev had made his peace with Tito, Yugoslav ideas on foreign policy had become respectable. But it must be noted that Nagy goes very far in this direction. He writes that Hungary "must avoid becoming an active participant in any of the clashes between power groups." He mentions Hungary's neighborhood to Austria and Yugoslavia as factors affecting foreign policy. He asserts: "It is the sovereign right of the Hungarian people to decide in which form they believe the most advantageous international status will be assumed, and in which form they think that national independence, sovereignty, equality, and

peaceful development will be attained." In the Soviet empire
such words are sheer blasphemy.

Nagy's views on political problems are both limited and
daring. His denunciation of the terror, torture, murder, and
defamation practiced by Rákosi against Communists and
against workers is sincere and moving. But there is not a
word of the cruelties exercised against non-Communists, no
denunciation of the methods used by the Communist Party
to seize power in 1947-1948. He even finds is necessary to
express, in stale and conventional rhetoric, his pride in the
Party's record up to 1949. This has to be stated, though it
is also only fair to admit that Nagy could not have done
otherwise in 1955. Moreover, it was no doubt correct tactics
to make a noble martyr of Rajk, who had on his hands the
blood of countless tortured and murdered people, even if
he was innocent of the crimes for which he was executed. What
Nagy's innermost beliefs on these matters are, we cannot tell.
But the Western reader must be warned not to accept his
statements at their face value. On the other hand the boldness
of Nagy's conception of foreign policy is astonishing. Here we
have already the essence of the policy that he tried to carry
out during the October revolution—neutrality based on the
Austrian model.

This work was essentially addressed to Khrushchev. But when
Khrushchev finally decided to sacrifice Rákosi, as a necessary
price for Tito's friendship, he replaced him not by Nagy but
by Gerö, the closest collaborator of Rákosi. Moreover he persuaded Tito to give his blessing to Gerö. The Yugoslav leader
met Gerö in the Crimea in September, 1956, when both men
were Khrushchev's guests, and he invited him to Belgrade
in October. In fact it was from Belgrade, flushed with self-
importance and confident of Tito's approval, that Gerö returned
to Budapest on the historic October 23, to make the venomous
broadcast speech that turned the incipient revolution into a
blood bath.

The choice by the Soviet leaders of Gerö to succeed Rákosi
is superficially similar to their choice in Poland of Ochab to
succeed the dead Bierut, for many years previously the boss of

Polish Communism. But closer examination shows that the differences were not only more important than the similarities, but were of great historical significance. Bierut had been a faithful executant of Moscow's policies, but he had not been a sadistic and vainglorious autocrat like Rákosi. Ochab had been a loyal collaborator of Bierut, but he retained some Polish patriotic emotions. During the summer the demand for the return to leadership of Gomulka, the "Titoist" or "nationalist deviationist" of Polish Communism, disgraced in 1948 and arrested in 1951, grew irresistibly within the Polish United Workers' (Communist) Party and within the Polish working class. Ochab and his colleagues decided to yield to this demand. Gomulka was elected First Secretary of the Party in October, and when the Soviet leaders arrived in Warsaw they found the majority even of the Central Committee, including Ochab, united behind Gomulka. They accepted the facts, and the Polish revolution was carried out without bloodshed. During the same period a similar pressure grew in Hungary for the return to leadership of Nagy. But Gerö ignored it, and when the students' demonstrations of October 23 grew into a mass movement in the streets of Budapest, he ordered the security police to fire. Bloodshed began, and shortly afterward Soviet troops intervened. Whether the intervention was requested by Gerö or decided independently of him in Moscow remains obscure. The United Nations Special Committee were unable to make up their minds on this point. But certainly there is nothing in the known character of Gerö that would prevent him from inviting Soviet soldiers to kill Hungarian workers. There is also a further difference between the Polish and Hungarian events. In Poland the security police for some time had been deprived of its special powers, and in the summer of 1955 a "nationalist" Communist, General Komar, was placed in command of its paramilitary formations, the Security Corps (KBW). In Hungary the security police remained undiminished in power during the last months of Rákosi's rule and under Gerö, and its paramilitary formations, commanded by loyal Rákosi men and practiced torturers and executioners of the people, fired unhesitatingly on the crowds.

It is these differences between the actions of Ochab and Gerö, not any difference between the personal characters of Gomulka and Nagy, that explain the different courses of events in Poland and Hungary.

It is often asserted in the West that Nagy is a weaker man, a less gifted leader, than Gomulka. This may or may not be true: the present writer has no information on which to base such a judgment. But this view is often combined with another, and undoubtedly unjustifiable, view: that whereas the Poles showed themselves sensible, realistic fellows, the Hungarians, poor misguided heroes, made a sad mess of their affair. Unfortunately this morally convenient explanation does not accord with the facts. The Hungarians were not reckless, nor the Poles prudent. The Poles were given the opportunity to stop halfway, at "national Communism," without bloodshed. The Hungarians were denied this chance. They were given only the choice of surrender to Soviet aggression or resistance. If they chose to fight, they cannot be rebuked.

The reason why the Poles had a chance, and the Hungarians none, lies in the difference between the patriotism of Ochab and the panic-stricken fanaticism of the Soviet puppet Gerö.

As for Nagy, he too had little freedom of movement. He was proclaimed Prime Minister on the morning of October 24, after the Soviet troops had gone into action. A series of proclamations and appeals, alternately threatening and panic-stricken, was published in his name. But during the first days he was a prisoner at Communist Party headquarters, unable in any way to influence events. To the outside world he appeared to be behaving as an obedient Soviet puppet. It was therefore inevitable that Western broadcasts in the Hungarian language should represent him to the Hungarian audience in an unfavorable light. It is indeed possible that Western attacks on him in these critical days contributed to lessen public confidence in him, to accelerate the political movement away from any sort of Communism, and to increase the general confusion. It can also be argued theoretically that it was unfortunate that the diplomatic representatives of the Western nations were not in close contact with Nagy and did not exercise a moderating influence on him. Yet all these regrets are purely academic. While Nagy was detained at Party headquarters, no contact was possible and no clearer picture of his political attitude was available. The results may indeed be regretted, but the fault does not lie with Nagy, with Western broadcasting stations, or with Western diplomats: it belongs exclusively to Gerö and his Soviet masters.

When Nagy did become a free agent, in the last days of October, he saw that the situation had moved beyond any sort of Communist dictatorship, however "nationalist," and that the people would not accept less than full freedom to choose their political leaders. He realized that no social class insisted more strongly on this than the industrial workers in whose name the Communists had professed to speak. He thus had to choose between serving the Hungarian people, at the cost of Communist defeat, and serving the Soviet regime, at the expense of the Hungarian people. That Nagy chose the first is to his credit: it shows him not as a weak man but as a good patriot. Gomulka had been more fortunate than he. He had been allowed a bloodless victory. He had the confidence of his people. He was able to persuade them that they must do without the freedom they desired, and must be content to advance from slavery to half-slavery. Nagy did not have this opportunity.

During the few Days of Liberty, political development in Hungary was very rapid. Several of the victims of Communist dictatorship in 1947-1948 re-emerged, pre-eminent among them Béla Kovács of the Small Farmers' Party and Anna Kéthly of the Social Democrats. The general trend was toward a coalition of two main political groups, the one socialist and based on the industrial workers, the other Christian Democratic and based on the peasantry—in fact toward the pattern that is familiar in neighboring Austria. In foreign policy also the government of Imre Nagy modeled itself on Austria, seeking neutrality in the great world conflicts and friendly relations both with the Soviet Union and with the West. In Austria this internal and foreign policy has hitherto been successful. There is no reason to doubt that it would have been successful in Hungary too if it had been permitted. But the Soviet leaders decided otherwise. Khrushchev did not justify the hopes that Nagy had placed in him. Marshal Zhukov, the hero of Berlin in 1945, did not hesitate to use against the workers of Budapest the army that he had once led to victory over Hitler, in order to introduce in occupied Hungary a regime similar to that of Gauleiter Koch in occupied Ukraine fifteen years earlier. General Serov, the organizer of the mass deportations of Balts and Caucasians in the 1940's, the author of the treacherous arrest of Polish resistance leaders in 1944, came to Budapest to perform similar acts of treachery toward free Hungary's military leader General Maleter and toward Imre Nagy himself, and to restore to their previous privileges the torturers of the AVH security police.

As the United Nations Special Committee's report clearly shows, the counterrevolution that took place in Hungary occured on November 4, 1956, and was the work of the invading Soviet army, which suppressed the revolution of the Hungarian people.

The fate of Imre Nagy himself is unknown. But he remains one of the few outstanding figures thrown up by the East European Communist system of the last decade. He has neither the heroic glamor of Marshal Tito nor the penetrating political vision of Milovan Djilas, and he has not been so fortunate as Wladyslaw Gomulka. But he has shown himself a brave and honest man and a true patriot, unusual qualities in a leading Communist. He will have his place in the history of his own country and of Europe.

Introduction

I wish to state by way of introduction that I wrote this dissertation prior to the Twentieth Congress of the Soviet Communist Party, mainly during the summer of 1955, and I had practically finished it by September of 1955. I expected my case to be discussed by the Central Committee of the Hungarian Workers' Party * during the fall of that year, after my recovery from my illness.

Hoping for this, I was prepared to hand my dissertation to the Central Committee as a justification of my principles and as a detailed reply to the accusations made in public against me since March of 1955. As is well known, my case did not reach the discussion stage, and I was not granted any kind of opportunity to expound my views or to refute the baseless accusations and slanders spoken against me. My dissertation was not placed before the Party forum at that particular time. I was expelled from the Party without having had my views clarified within the framework of the ideological battle or by legal Party procedure.

Since then, events of great significance have taken place before our eyes, among which the Twentieth Congress of the Soviet Communist Party is the most outstanding. This convinced me that stating my views in writing, in order to refute the accusations made against me and the baseless slanders,

* Communist Party.

would not be in vain—just as it was not in vain, after I was expelled and after the Twentieth Congress, that I added one or two chapters to bring the dissertation up to date. (I have indicated the date of writing separately at the end of each of these chapters.) Preparing this dissertation was not in vain, because when I reread it after the Twentieth Congress it strengthened my earlier conviction of the correctness of my stand on basic questions of principle.

The events of recent times have gradually led me to the decision to place this dissertation—if circumstances permit—before the Party members, and to let the Party membership ponder my replies to the accusations made against me.

So far I have kept quiet because I was silenced. But I now feel that it is my duty to the Party to speak up. Several circumstances have led me to do this. First, the just demand of the Party membership at past meetings that my case should be taken before the Party publicly, thus granting me an opportunity to explain my views.

Another circumstance that causes me to speak is the unprecedented amount of lying, slander, and abuse—in total contrast to Communist tendencies, morals and principles—by the so-called leadership, who shift the "ideological battle" so often mentioned since the Twentieth Congress from the ideological to the personal sphere through this slander and these barefaced lies. I wish to prove in my dissertation that I will not follow them along this path, which is so diametrically opposed to the Lenin party system and to Communist morals. I will stay within the limits of an ideological battle fought by arguments.

Lastly, I was induced to make this dissertation public by the fact that the Party and the Hungarian press—newspapers and magazines—gave me no opportunity for publicizing my views. Thus I was deprived of all means of acquainting the party membership and the general public with its contents.

The smouldering political, personal and ideological differences within the Party leadership since the June, 1953, resolutions of the Central Committee came to the attention of the Party membership and the general public in a one-sided fashion, i.e., in the form of accusations raised against me. I will disregard the personal questions, although they have a significant role in the political persecution being carried on against me. One of the reasons for this is that the settlement of intra-Party differences, debates and exchanges of views have been shifted to the field of personalities. The clarification of problems arising from differences in principles is therefore all the more important. The battle being waged for the purity of the teachings of Marxism-Leninism and their proper application to the Hungarian situation is, in the last analysis, the battle to keep power in the hands of the people. This is the underlying question of these ideological-political differences. These questions clearly cannot be solved and clarified through resolutions brought about by one-sided accusations. An indispensable prerequisite is that all ideological-political differences that may arise must be solved through debate on the basis of principles, with valid arguments and the widest possible publicity. This is absolutely necessary, because this is the only proper Marxist, scientific method, and the Party method of clarifying ideological questions. There is a need for this because these are basic questions with regard to Party life and to building socialism. And lastly, the debate is necessary because the accusations were made against the former President of the Ministers' Council, and the Party membership as well as the people of the nation are plainly justified in wanting to see clearly what actually happened.

Mátyás Rákosi, at one of the sessions of the Communist meetings held in Somogy county, stated among other things the following:

> In the Communist Party there cannot be two separate organizational rules, two kinds of laws: one for the leaders, let us say the members of the Political Committee, and one for others, the ordinary members. In this regard there cannot be any differences between Party members. One who makes a mistake—this was stated by the third Congress—regardless of the position he holds in the Party or simply as a personality—must answer for this before the Party. . . . The Party was right when it took this question to the masses of the hundreds of thousands of Communists and the millions of working people. Thus we have shown that we have no problem that we cannot place calmly before the judgment of the working people.

All this is proper and true. Therefore there should be no difference among party members: everyone should answer for his own mistakes—without regard to personalities—whether he be Imre Nagy or Mátyás Rákosi. I wish to avail myself of the rights outlined in the organization's rules, which assure me of the possibility of placing before the Party the responsibility and the mistakes of Mátyás Rákosi in the same manner that he used against me. Let the Party membership and the workers judge from this and from the accusations which he has raised against me what kind of mistakes were committed by whom, and who is responsible for what. I agree with the contention that there is no question that we cannot calmly take to the people for their judgment. But let us weigh things equally, on the basis of the equality of party members, and take not only Imre Nagy's actions, but also Mátyás Rákosi's actions to the people for their judgment. The justification of this demand was established by Mátyás Rákosi himself. I hope that he will not disclaim this when it comes to a question of his own person being judged.

In the question of intensified ideological differences between November, 1954, and January, 1955, I presented my views to the Political Committee on several occasions. This is what I reviewed briefly in a memorandum submitted to the Central Committee at its March meeting.

There were serious differences of opinion in the evaluation of the political and economic situation in the fall of 1954. After the October 1954 session of the Central Committee, as a result of the initial implementation of the resolutions then made, the strained situation prevailing prior to the meeting improved without a doubt. The confidence of the Party membership in the leaders grew, as well as their self-confidence in their ability to solve successfully the many problems then existing. The confidence of the masses in the Party and in the government also improved, and the masses looked to the future with hope.

This is indicated by the fact that the figures for production in the final quarter of the year were more favorable than the previous figures. There was a significant increase in the execution of the export plans (1950 million forints) which was well above the quarterly average. The balance between purchasing power and consumer goods indicated that in this period we were able to reach a peak volume, almost without a problem. By the end of the year, compared to the year 1953, our domestic trade showed a 15 per cent increase. The constant and significant increase in currency circulation since July, 1953, had ceased to some extent in the final quarter of 1954. Certain improvements were evident in the better showing made by industry and the rising productivity of labor. Therefore, after October—except for the collections made in the agricultural sphere, where the results remained bad—there was clearly a certain tendency toward improvement, which it would have been wrong to overestimate and equally improper to disregard.

The policies of the Party were significantly successful, as set forth by Party documents, in calling to life the Patriotic People's Front Movement and in promoting its effective development. Despite growing pains, which had to be corrected as they went along, the Patriotic People's Front Movement could give important support to the policies of the Party and of the government in all areas followed by us since June in this new period in economic, political and cultural fields.

The Patriotic People's Front Movement strengthened the political activity of the masses on a nation-wide basis with regard to local, national, and international questions. This successfully added to the increase of local economic opportunities and to new work activities in the field of many social reforms.

A similar picture emerged after the second national political event in October: the election of the local councils, which had a decisive significance with regard to the political course of the Party and the government. Party documents state that the council elections of November 28, 1954, were a distinct success for the Party and the People's Democratic system. The Party's connection with the workers was strengthened, and the prestige of the executive branches grew. An impressive and intimate political atmosphere developed, where the great majority of the citizens professed their faith in the basic aims of building socialism, indicating that they were willing to follow the Party and the government in realizing its goals during this new political period. The success of the elections symbolized the failure of the internal and external enemies of our People's Democracy.

This is the manner in which the Party, in official documents, evaluated the situation that evolved after October. Naturally, there were mistakes and deficiencies during this time, and dangers developed against which it was necessary to fight. To sum up: the period after October 1954, was characterized by the growth of the People's Democracy, the strengthening of the Party, the widening and stabilization of the bases for building socialism. Exaggerating the difficulties and mistakes, the frightening picture that Mátyás Rákosi painted of the situation in the country and the Party produced extraordinary dangers: it tended to discredit the policies carried on since June, to drive the Party and the country from the path taken in June, and to support the view that it was better to return to the old system.

It was from this viewpoint that the question of "rightist danger" arose. I did not concur in his exaggerations then, nor do I do so now. It must be admitted that the fight against "leftist" views and dangers had been carried on in a one-sided fashion for more than one and a half years, and that we had neglected the fight against the danger from the right. This was without doubt a mistake. This had to be changed all the more because in the Communist Party one cannot fight against only one deviation or danger, and because in the situation that arose the danger of rightist deviation grew. From this it follows that the attention of the Party had to be directed to this danger, and that it was necessary to use all the Party's means, agitation and propaganda for making more effective use of our ideological work against the danger from the right. I feel that this is what would have been proper, and that this would have been understood by the Party membership. But I could not approve a course that greatly *exaggerated* these internal troubles and dangers, or the hurling of these unexplained and unjustified charges into the ranks of the Party membership with explosive effect, thereby causing the greatest confusion.

Later the chief danger seemed to be that of increasing rightist danger. The uncertainty of the Political Committee, which it showed on this question, reveal the insufficient attention and work devoted to this serious problem. And if such a serious danger as this from the right was said to be, had arisen in the Party, allegedly drowning the Party and the country, why was this problem not taken to the Central Committee?

This was a far-reaching question, particularly in view of the fact that the October session had taken place only four to six weeks previously. This session had called attention to the fight against the danger from the right, but directed its real fire against the leftist deviation and danger. During that time the Political Committee, but primarily Mihály Farkas, was following a line differing from the resolution of the Central Committee, and did not ask for appropriate resolutions from the central leadership.

And it was not proper then, nor is it proper now, that the battle against the rightist danger (which was absolutely necessary) was not carried on by Party methods or regular Party procedures, but primarily and chiefly through administrative directives, by terrorization, vilification, dismissals, etc.

To sum up: in my March petition I established that the Party could not fight only on one front and carry on a battle exclusively against the "leftist" or the rightist dangers and mistakes, as has been the practice until very recently. Ideologically and politically, the Party must be prepared to fight against those rightist mistakes and viewpoints, but in such a manner as not to disable the Party from dealing with the mistakes and dangers of the left, which probably have deeper roots in our Party than elsewhere.

In my opinion the Party must definitely be oriented toward directing the closest possible attention to the danger from the right and fight on *both* fronts against all the dangers and mistakes that present themselves. Meanwhile attention must be paid to any deviation or danger showing up simultaneously in the work of the Party or in the various spheres of life.

In wide circles within the Party the fear has formed—and I too have had fears of a similar nature, which have since been proved correct—that what happens at present is not designed to correct the mistakes made in carrying out our policies since June on the economic, political, and cultural fronts, but to revise the June policies themselves and to revert to the policies in existence prior to June. I will carry on this June policy myself with all my strength, as I undertook to do in the declaration that I signed. The revision of the June policies and the reversion to those prior to June are what is being discussed now.

Events prove this. And this is a catastrophe both for the Party and for the country. As a most serious consequence the Party will break away from the masses, which, from the internal standpoint of the country and considering the impact it might have on the international situation, might have almost unforeseeable results.

In consideration of all this, I felt it necessary to emphasize in a resolution that the Party and government policies, from an economic, political, and cultural standpoint, cannot in substance be anything else than the application of the teachings of Marxism-Leninism to the concrete Hungarian situation, a re-formation and redevelopment of the socialist people's economy on the objective and lawful basis of building up socialism through this temporary transition period. This policy had to contain in itself socialist industrialization as the chief means and basis for socialist re-formation, with main emphasis being placed on heavy industry producing implements for necessary production, as well as the re-formation of socialist agriculture. In the economic policy of the Party the controlling factor must be production and the lowering of the cost of such production. To this, completely improperly, we have not paid enough attention thus far. This must now be remedied by serious exertion on our part.

I stressed in my petition that the June policies of the new period were not a deviation from the principles of Marxism-Leninism. This must be clarified because the danger exists that mistakes and difficulties in the economic and political situation and in literature, especially because of this exaggeration about the rightist danger, make it appear to Party members as though the June policy had been a rightist deviation. And this would inevitably lead to the abandonment of the June line and to the return to the old wrong policies.

That is why I emphasized that the Central Committee should declare that the actual mistakes that had earlier been revealed before it would be corrected. Meanwhile, let us go ahead in the spirit of the June resolutions along the path of building up socialism.

The views that I outlined in my petition I uphold, because I am convinced that those serious mistakes that were apparent in our Party's policies took place prior to the June resolutions. They sprang from exaggerated "leftist," sectarian, anti-Marxist views, whose chief representatives in our Party was the "foursome" under the leadership of Mátyás Rákosi, which was seriously branded by the resolution of the Central Committee in June. Lenin's statement characterizes them perfectly:

> For the true revolutionary the greatest danger—possibly the only danger—is the exaggerated revolutionary spirit which forgets within what confines and under what circumstances it is proper and effective to apply revolutionary tactics. The true revolutionaries most often "broke their necks" when they tried to write "revolution" with capital letters, and almost canonized it as an immortal concept. They lost their heads and became unable to soberly weigh circumstances under which one must revert to reformist action. True revolutionaries can be destroyed only if they lose their ability of right thinking. They are destroyed not by external defeat, but by the internal failure of their cause, in this case most definitely, since by losing their ability to think straight they take it into their heads that "the great world revolution" can and will solve all manner of problems, under any circumstances, by absolute revolutionary methods.

Those who take such things "into their heads" are lost, because they have accepted an utter nonsense on a fundamental question. During the time of merciless war (and a revolution is the most merciless war of all) stupidity is punished by defeat.

From what does it follow that the "great, victorious revolution" can use only revolutionary methods, and that only the use of these is permitted? There is no precedent for this. And it definitely and undoubtedly is not true. That it is not true is clearly apparent on the basis of theoretical viewpoints, presupposing that we do not leave the area of Marxism. That it is not true is also proved by the experiences during our revolution. Concerning the theory: at the time of a revolution stupidities are committed just as they are committed at any other time, stated Engels—and "he stated the truth," wrote Lenin.

Prior to June the mistakes of our Party were without a doubt caused by "leftism," by sectarianism. Such mistakes have deep historical roots in our Party. At the same time we must know that "leftist" mistakes give birth inevitably to rightist mistakes. Since the announcing of the policies of June and the opposing of leftist mistakes, such mistakes have shown up in the national people's economy, in culture, and in the ideological field as well as in some phases of social life.

From this it clearly follows that one must fight with all the possible means of an ideological battle to eradicate these deviations, against that petit bourgeois frame of mind and the influence exerted by the lower middle class upon the worker. However, one must not for a single moment lose sight of the fact that the reasons that brought about sectarian "lefticism" and that have had such deep roots in our country are still there. That deviation is always most dangerous against which we do not fight with the necessary determination. And this at present is the danger from exaggerated sectarian "leftism." Therefore one must fight ceaselessly against *both* rightist deviationism and against "leftist" mistakes and deviations.

However, in weighing all this, it must be established that the present difficulties in our economic, political and social life reach back to the time prior to June. Although we were successful in alleviating a major part of the difficulties in the process of realizing our June policies, inevitably as a result of past policies and partly through our own mistakes, new difficulties arose.

Taking all these into consideration, the Central Committee of the Hungarian Workers' Party was informed in a letter that I sent under the date of May 4, 1955, that I concur in the guiding principles and the practical objectives of the March resolutions made by the Central Committee. This is summarized as follows in the introduction to the resolution:

The Central Committee establishes that the resolutions made at the session of the Central Committee in June, 1953, were correct, that they remain in effect and, together with the resolutions made by the Third Party Congress, even today comprise the basis of our Party policies. In the spirit of these resolutions our Party still feels its main objective to be the systematic improvement of the welfare of our workers, an ever increasing rise in the social and cultural requirements on the basis of a widened socialist production and growth in productivity. The chief aim of our Party can be attained first of all through stressing heavy industry, in addition to socialist industry, and on the basis of developing our agriculture.

Our Party will continue the socialist rebuilding or agriculture and the policies for further developing of the farmers' cooperatives on a voluntary basis. In addition to this it will further continue to assure support for the individual working peasantry and to enforce the principle of financial aid in order to increase their production and above all reach a greater degree of productivity. Communist criticism and self-criticism remain in effect in the interest of establishing collective leadership, and so do the resolutions made to insure its legality.

I agree with this completely even today, and similarly with the contention that in the successful fight waged to carry out the proper resolutions there were mistakes made and there were deficiencies. I consider it a mistake that the opportunist distortion of the true character of the June resolutions is not pointed out in either the March or the April resolutions made by the Central Committee. For this very reason the matter must be given the widest publicity in the Party press (since, as Mátyás Rákosi stated in the speech at Kaposvár, we have no secrets before the people), so that in comparing the June, 1953, resolutions of the central leadership with the measures taken for carrying out the directives, everyone should have the opportunity of establishing where, when, and by whom these Party resolutions were "distorted." This is the correct Party method of clarifying this question, and not one that simply states accusations without proof.

It would also be worth while to examine what kind of political and economic bankruptcy was left behind by the "leftist" exaggerators—what kind of a legacy we had to take over from them when in June, 1953, they had finally led the Party and the people's economy into a blind alley. Since June, 1953, for almost two years, the whole country's workers have been working to correct the serious damage brought about by the "leftist" exaggeration in all branches of the national economy. The Party and state leadership headed by Mátyás Rákosi in the financial sphere alone cost the nation two years of intensive work.

It can be figured, and it must be figured, what this meant in billions of forints. But who can judge in figures and in billions the political, cultural, and moral damage that was caused to the Party and to the nation? The political and moral capital that the Party resolutions and the government program represented was for two years used up to rehabilitate the country. If all the material, political, and moral strength that had been used to eradicate the damage which the so-called "foursome" had caused, had instead been used for building socialism, Hungary today would be a cheerful country, living in plenty and prosperity. However, we inherited a very heavy burden.

In the name of Marxism-Leninism, the "leftist" deviationists made promises they could not fulfill, with which they discredited the prestige of Marxism-Leninism. What did the "leftists" promise? They promised that during the period of the First Five-Year Plan they would raise the living standards of the workers by 50 per cent. On the other hand, between 1950 and 1954, industrial production (1938=100) grew from 150 to 300, while living standards decreased until 1953 and then increased by 15 per cent only as a result of the policies of the new period. The workers, in comparison to 1949, doubled industrial production, increased the productivity of labor by 63 per cent, and decreased the cost. Despite this their wages were in general comparable to 1949 levels.

They promised the upsurge of agriculture. Instead, as a consequence of the exaggeration of the "leftists" as regards peasant policies, there was a serious decline in agricultural production and a decided decrease in the number of livestock. It is well known that the area of untilled land in the spring of 1953 was approximately one million acres, which is more than 10 per cent of the arable lands of the country. The "leftist" exaggerators promised an abundance of consumer goods; but they created a scarcity that had no parallel since the liberation. If we now examine the 1955 program of the "leftist" exaggerators in detail, we again find the same promises, which again they cannot fulfill, because they have not taken into consideration objective facts, the laws governing social-economic life. One must no longer make promises that one cannot fulfill. We must not shatter the faith of the masses in the Party, the truthfulness of the Party, or the correctness of Marxism-Leninism.

The honor of the Communists will be lost if they are considered chatterers. This danger is seriously apparent at the present time. This in turn shatters the political power of the working class, the federation of the working peasants, and thus weakens the status of the Communists. Not every mistake and sin can be rectified by self-criticism. The criticism of the masses, as has been pointed out by the classicists of Marxism and with special emphasis by Lenin, is a weapon powerful enough to sweep away power. We need a criticism by the masses that will strengthen this power. However it seems that the "leftist" exaggerators keep forgetting this.

It is well known among other things that the Hungarian "leftist" exaggerators caused a great decline by their policy of forced collectivization in the development of Hungarian agriculture. This had and still has a decisive influence upon the fact that production volume in Hungarian agriculture on the average is approximately what it was prior to the war. This is why there are serious faults apparent in the Worker-Peasant Federation without which the working class cannot uphold its power. This power is the basic decisive factor in every revolution, ours included. In the last analysis, however, those differences of opinion that have arisen within the Party in connection with the charge of rightist deviations are primarily not related to economic policies but concern the fate of political power. Because when the "leftist" exaggerators with their scatterbrained attitude endanger the basic indispensable requirements for building socialism—the power of the proletariat—they are jeopardizing that power built upon the faith and confidence of the working masses without which the building of socialism is impossible. The pseudo radicalism of the "leftists," their opposition to the masses, endangers this power of the proletariat, because it denies the Leninist teaching that keeping and solidifying the power of the working class is a task transcending everything else. The "leftist" crackpots have caused a deep political crisis among the working masses and have risked their power in our country. The main question of the differences of opinion in the ideological battle therefore is the question of retaining political power, and which of the differences are mirroring the existing differences in principles.

The "leftist" exaggerators during the years 1949 to 1952 were guilty of grave mistakes in carrying out their political line, and in practice experienced failure. This was proved most tangibly by the necessity for the June resolutions, and by life itself. Yet they did not relinquish their anti-Marxist, anti-Leninist theories. The Marxist-Leninist theory teaches us that if in practice, in life, a theory is disproved, this theory should be re-examined. But the "leftist" deviationists are resurrecting their "theory," which has been shattered by life. They are again trying to mold the practical work of the Party and the country to this faulty theory. They are trying to mold economic policies above all else, meanwhile justifying all this as a battle against rightist deviation. The "leftist" deviationists, with the above resolutions, have created such chaos in political concepts that it cannot be established what is the correct Marxist-Leninist viewpoint; what is "leftist" deviation or rightist deviation; and who is what kind of a deviationist. Those who are doing this try to cover up their own deviation by hypocritically alluding to Marxism. That is why they avoid debates, and instead of engaging in honest arguments vilify their opponents. But can one carry on a debate over differences in principles and politics and the various views regarding them? I absolutely think so.

The central leadership should have no other standpoint, therefore they should assure the possibility for such debate. One cannot escape this. The charges and accusations demand an answer. If we want to assure in the Party that unity on principles which is nonexistent today, we must end the ideological and political chaos. And for this there is only one possible road to follow: clarification of differences of opinion by debates on principles and by free exchange of views.

It was for this reason that this lengthy dissertation was written. I have tried to prove the contention that the March resolutions of the Central Committee, to the effect that "rightist views had become so dangerous in our Party and state, because Imre Nagy supported in his speeches and articles these anti-Marxist views, and in fact primarily was the one who proclaimed them," is an unjustified and baseless accusation.

I am trying to prove with facts and arguments that there is no basis for the April resolutions of the Central Committee which declared:

Comrade Imre Nagy, as a member of the Political Committee and as the president of the Minister's Council, represented political opinions which were sharply opposed to the over-all politics of our Party and inimical to the interests of the working class, the working peasants and the people's democracy. Comrade Nagy tried to throttle the motor of socialist building, socialist industrialization, and especially the development of heavy industry, and in the provinces the movement of the agricultural cooperatives, which is the decisive method of socialist rebuilding of the villages. He tried to obscure and force into the background the Party leadership, and he attempted to pit the goverment agencies against one another, and the Patriotic People's Front against the Party. Comrade Imre Nagy by all this prevented the building of a solid basis for increasing the welfare of the people.

These anti-Marxist, anti-Leninist, anti-Party views of Comrade Imre Nagy form a composite system, an attitude which spread to the various fields of political, economic, and cultural life. The activities of Comrade Imre Nagy have caused serious damage to our Party, our People's Democracy, and our whole socialist structure.

Comrade Nagy in the interests of realizing his rightist, opportunist policies resorted to un-Party-like, anti-Party and even factional methods, which are completely incompatible with the unity, the discipline of the Marxist-Leninist Party.

All this is without any proof, facts, or arguments. I do not follow this path. My standpoint, my rights, the correctness of my views, my Marxist-Leninist faith I shall prove with theoretical and practical facts. It is possible that on one question or another my standpoint is incorrect. The Party debate can clarify all this. Let them prove by Marxist-Leninist teachings and methods that I am wrong. In my dissertation I have expounded my convictions, which I will uphold until the time that they can prove the contrary through the scientific means of Marxist-Leninist arguments and methods.

For my convictions and views I am ready to accept stupid

slanders, political persecution, social ostracism, and deep humiliation, as I have in the past. I also take the responsibility for the mistakes that I really committed. I will not accept responsibility for one thing: giving up my conviction on principles.

It was with these thoughts that I began to work on my dissertation. I have tried to accomplish a useful task for the benefit of the Party and for my country. The Central Committee can help to realize this aim by arranging the widest possible debate on this dissertation.

Contents

Imre Nagy on Communism

Chapter 1. A Few Timely Questions Regarding the Application of Marxism-Leninism

In our time, which is also called the "atomic era" in view of the discoveries in the natural sciences, but chiefly because of the revolutionary discoveries brought about through splitting the atom, economic trends and technology change at a tremendous pace and scale. These changes are manifested in the relationship between the various countries and peoples, as well as in the relation between the two existing systems.

One must take into consideration such developments and changes, and Marxism-Leninism must keep in step with these changes. Marxism-Leninism cannot rigidly adhere to its present ideological tenets within the framework developed by the genius of its great masters, nor can it confine itself merely to renewing its old theories, as there are no eternal, never changing teachings which remain applicable regardless of time or space and independently of concrete situations. The masters of Marxism-Leninism did not bind the hands of future generations with their theories. The Talmudists and exegetists, those who regard Marxism and the various conclusions and theories of Marxism as a compendium of dogmas that are independent of the various changes taking place in social development, think that if they commit these theories and conclusions to memory, and keep quoting and reiterating them ad infinitum, they can apply these conclusions and theories for all time, to all countries, to every phase of life. However, those who can think only in this fashion see the letter of Marxism but not its substance, and they memorize the text of the conclusions and theories of Marxism but do not understand its contents.

Marxism is a science that cannot remain static but must develop and become more perfect. It is impossible that Marxism in its development should not become enriched with new experiences, new knowledge; therefore certain Marxist theories and conclusions must necessarily change as time passes. There must be changes by adding new theories and conclusions to conform with the new historical demands of the times. "Marxism does not recognize unchangeable conclusions and theories that are binding for every era and time," Stalin wrote in the Marr debate.

One must keep in step with the rapidly changing economic, social, political, and cultural situation. As a matter of fact Marxism-Leninism must be the first to point out the further development of vital, basic needs in international relations, in revolutionary transformation, in the future of socialism.

Therefore Marxism-Leninism has not been completed with the scientific theories and results attained thus far. The further development of Marxism-Leninism and its enrichment through the additions of new theories did not cease with the death of Marx, Engels, and Lenin.

The scientific theories of Marxism-Leninism, its theoretical statements, their further development in conformity with changing social-economic trends on the basis of the teachings of the masters—there is the historic role and duty of every Communist and Workers' Party. The forms, methods, and means of attaining this were not prescribed by Marx, nor did he tie the hands of the leaders of the socialist revolution or himself in attaining this goal. He foresaw that during the period of development the ever changing situation would bring about new problems. It was from this that the Lenin directive sprang: that the science for which Marx laid down the cornerstone through his teachings about the dictatorship of the proletariat must be expended in all directions, in order that it keep pace with life. The theory of Marx—as Lenin stated—gives general guiding principles, which must be utilized in Britain in another fashion than in

France, in France differently than in Germany, and in Germany in another way than in Russia.

The further development of Marxism-Leninism has two serious obstacles, which are becoming increasingly more difficult:

A. Dogmatism, "exegetist Talmudism," that rigid adherence to the old theories and their mechanical application;

B. The monopolization by Stalin of explaining Marxism-Leninism based on the cult of the individual, which inescapably brought about dogmatism, the crippling of courageous and pioneering theoretical work, the disregarding of the particular characteristics of the various countries, and the applying of the old, sometimes antiquated scholastic theories—whereas the further development of Marxism-Leninism must be based on many-sided, characteristic situations and their solution through scientific-theoretical methods.

Without a doubt it would be a mistake to apply and consider Marxism-Leninism as a "dead letter," a trite saying, or a dogma. It cannot be doubted that in every country there exist differences in class struggles, in economy and culture, which are characteristically different from that of any other country, which came about through the various phases of social development. Moreover it cannot be doubted that the proper application of Marxism-Leninism can and must be done only by recognizing these characteristics in the field of history, social development, and the like—and not independently of time and space. At the same time it is clear that Marxism-Leninism as a teaching about the legitimacy of developing society remains always applicable in all social questions.

Since the death of Lenin a rigid dogmatism has been the rule, based on the application and further development of Marxism-Leninism and upon the theory of scientific socialism. This has caused serious theoretical mistakes, which have had repercussions in social development on a world-wide scale as well as on the struggle between the two systems, and finally on the fate of socialism itself.

As a result of the Stalinist monopoly over the science of Marxism-Leninism, ideas became prevalent in Communist and Workers' Parties that the only way of building socialism through "proper" methods, ways, and means, were those practiced in the

Soviet Union. Leninist teachings dealing with the application of Marxism-Leninism to characteristic situations in the Soviet Union were forced into the background. The existence of the Soviet Union, its development and strengthening, have had a decisive historical significance on the development of socialism all over the world. This is the basic theory of scientific socialism. Of course it cannot be denied that the Communist Party of the Soviet Union has had the most experience in the pioneering application of Marxism-Leninism, which means that the Communist Party of the Soviet Union is the one that is destined to play the most important role in further development of Marxist-Leninist teachings. But from all this it does not necessarily follow that the application of Marxism-Leninism to Soviet situations should constitute a general law, which would be everywhere applicable, regardless of characteristic Soviet situations, as the only correct and binding theory. This could cause serious difficulties in the development of socialism on a world-wide scale.

"All nations will arrive at socialism—this is inescapable—but they will not arrive there in a completely identical fashion. Each will lend its own characteristics to one or another form of democracy, or one or another form of the dictatorship of the proletariat, or to the changes and the pace at which socialist life will be finally accomplished," stated Lenin.

The great importance of these individual traits is especially pointed up by the following words of Lenin:

As long as there are national and governmental differences between nations and peoples—and we know that these differences will be apparent for a very, very long time to come, even after the attainment of the dictatorship of the proletariat on a world-wide scale—there will be a need for the tactical unity of the international movement of the world's Communist workers. This will not demand the elimination of various differences, or the end of specific national characteristics, but the validation of basic Communist theories (soviet power and the dictatorship of the proletariat), in conformance with national and governmental differences. It is necessary in each individual country to seek out, to study, find, and recognize those national characteristics, those characteristic elements which, from a national standpoint, may lead to the concrete solution of the central international problem, to the victory over opportunism and leftist doctrinairism, to overthrowing the rule of the bourgeoisie, and to the creation of the Soviet Republic and the dictatorship of the proletariat: this is the chief aim in the leading, (and not only the leading) countries at the present time.

Lenin is speaking of the same thing when he says that the road leading to socialist economy is generally well known, and he rounds out this declaration by the following:

But the concrete ways and means of achieving this change are necessarily very diverse and they must so remain, since they depend upon conditions upon which the creation of socialism and progress toward it begins. All these local differences, as well as the characteristics forms of the economy, the way of life of the population, the degree of their preparedness, and all plans directed toward realizing the road to socialism, must be reflected in the attempts for bringing socialism about.

Lenin brought this to the attention of Hungarians during the first days of the Soviet Republic, when he told us in a direct radio message:

It can not be questioned that under the characteristic conditions of the Hungarian revolution it would be wrong merely to imitate our Russian tactics in every detail.

Serious damage was done to the ideological preparation of the Communist and the Workers' Parties as well as to the further development of Marxist-Leninist theories by those methods which, since the death of Lenin, have tried to "solve" arising difficulties and various viewpoints with drastic rules, branding of people, with terrorism, and by enforcing the autocratic rule of dogmatic voluntaryism stemming from the monopolization of Marxism-Leninism, instead of through scientific debates and exchange of views. This is clearly proven by the sharp political-theoretical differences which have cropped up in the Hungarian Party, and by the method through which these have been "settled."

A People's Democracy is the only characteristic form that has thus far been recognized by the dogmatic explanation of Marxism-Leninism in attaining socialism through the transition from capitalism to socialism. But the People's Democracies are treated as similar, utilizing identical methods, prescribing for their development identical forms and pace, not recognizing the diversity of differences in conditions, although it is clearly apparent that socialism is different in its development in the Soviet Union, China, Yugoslavia, or Hungary.

Such rigid, dogmatic interpretations of Marxism-Leninism and its application prevent the "working out" of the characteristic forms of socialism. According to present accepted precepts the People's Democracies are a type of proletarian dictatorship. The nonclarification of this theory, the absence of scientifically processed data, has had the deleterious effect that the People's Democracy as a type of proletarian dictatorship under the mechanical interpretation of Marxism-Leninism, and the copying of Soviet methods under completely different internal and international situations, have resulted in the loss in its essence of the people's democratic character in all People's Democracies. Serious contradictions have arisen between the form and the substance of these democracies.

The historical circumstances surrounding the birth of the Soviet Union, the October Revolution, the civil war and imperialist intervention, the building of socialism in a country under a hostile atmosphere, being left to its own devices, had lent to the dictatorship of the proletariat in the Soviet Union special substance and form until the time of the Second World War. This demanded other methods than that of the People's Democracies which could rely on strength and help from the Soviet Union and each other.

A People's Democracy is a democratic type of dictatorship of the proletariat. If in a People's Democracy methods used by the Soviet under entirely different circumstances are imitated (as we have observed it to a lesser or greater degree in all People's Democratic countries and to the greatest extent in Hungary), then the People's Democracy ceases to be a type of proletarian dictatorship and loses the characteristics demanded by the situations existing in that particular country. This has been experienced in the People's Democratic countries to a great degree, and it has been a serious obstacle to the stabilization of the system and the building of socialism.

It is also an improper, anti-Marxist, anti-Stalinist viewpoint that regards the People's Democracies as a type of the dictatorship of the proletariat advocating force. Development in building a socialist society is not attained by large-scale use of force, but by eliminating antagonistic interests in the social and economic spheres, by systematically decreasing the use of force to eliminate existing differences, and utilizing democratic forms and methods in the interest of close cooperation on the widest possible scale with the masses of working people.

Only within the framework of this general theory and in the interest of assuring and stabilizing the People's Democratic system and insuring a socialist victory over attempts by the exploiting classes to put into operation their reactionary, counter-revolutionary plans is it necessary and timely to utilize the more drastic methods of a dictatorship.

This question has not been clarified as a theory in the People's Democratic countries, and this is the reason for the uncertainty and the sharp changes, and the reason why in certain Communist and Workers' Parties regarded as the special character of a People's Democracy is a deviation from Marxism-Leninism, a viewpoint damaging to the Party, "rightist" and antipopular.

The Soviet form and methods of building socialism, its mechanical application, disregarding the special characteristics of various individual countries, raise serious obstacles in the path of international revolutionary workers' movements, primarily and especially to the work of the Communist and Workers' Parties in the Western capitalist countries in *their* battle for socialism. For Central and Eastern European countries, and last but not least for us, it is necessary that we find and use such forms and methods in building socialism in all phases of social, political, economic, and cultural life, and we must realize such a rate of progress that it will make socialism acceptable and desirable to the widest possible masses in the capitalist countries and to all strata of the working classes.

Our social, economic, and cultural situation from which we proceeded to build socialism is in many ways very close to the situation that prevails in the capitalist countries of the West. Therefore the similarities in the situations of the Western capitalist countries and the present People's Democracies in Central and Eastern Europe make it possible that by the application of a creative Marxism-Leninism, taking into consideration the special character of the transition period and the situation in the various countries, as well as the new road to socialism, one can extend immeasurable aid to the Communist and Workers' Parties of Western Europe in gaining the support of the working masses in their struggle for socialism. Our conspicuously proper or improper standpoint on principles, our good or our bad work, our success or our failure, can promote or impede the cause of socialism in Western Europe.

Chapter 2. The Peaceful Coexistence of the Two Systems

The rigid, mechanical interpretation of Marxism that disregards the necessity for exchange of views and debates within the Party, so prevalent in Stalin's era, was a prime factor in the role assumed by the Cominform in its stand against Yugoslav Communists. This stand caused such serious conflicts that it paralyzed for years the cooperation of the socialist and People's Democratic countries with the Yugoslav Communist Federation, in the face of Lenin's theory of international proletarianism.

The speeches of Comrade Khrushchev in Belgrade and in Sofia, and the July 4 and July 17 issues of *Pravda,* unmistakably revealed the motives behind the sharp attacks against the Yugoslav Communists and the conflict in the Cominform. It was established that the conflict was sparked by the enemies of peace and of international workers' groups. It was established that upsetting friendly connections with Yugoslavia would serve only the forces of imperialist reaction and of the aggressors. Therefore the campaign against the Yugoslav Communists was a large-scale international provocation.

Soviet and other sources have established that Yugoslavia, despite the difficulties it had to endure because of the disruption of connections between the Cominform countries, did not renounce its sovereignty, but preserved its national independence completely, in face of the imperialist camps.

Yugoslavia is a country building socialism through stressing basic production methods in light and heavy industry, in banking, in transportation, in commerce and the retail trades. The working class and the peasantry are the basic classes of the country.

Politically, the working class and the peasantry are in power. Yugoslavia is developing through building socialism and through its cooperation with the socialist camps of other countries. From the standpoint of its continuing development, it is most important for Yugoslavia to develop this cooperation and the strengthening of friendly ties with other countries.

The principle has been established historically that, in addition to the unity accepted in the chief and basic questions of insuring the victory of socialism, various forms and methods may be applied for solving concrete problems in the building of socialism—independently of historical and national characteristics. "As long as there are national and state differences between peoples, the tactical unity of the world's Communist worker movements demands that the basic principles of Communism (Soviet power and dictatorship of the proletariat) be enforced in such a way that they will be carefully remolded to meet the different requirements of the various national states, to solve concretely the universal international problem," writes Lenin.

The Soviet Communist Party now finds it desirable to make contact with the Yugoslav Communist Federation on the basis of Marxism-Leninism. This will be greatly aided by the joint declaration issued in Belgrade, according to which internal order, the differences in social structure and the different methods of building socialism are strictly matters for the people of the specific nation to decide.

The Belgrade announcement has historical significance. It leads the international revolutionary movement back to the road shown by Marx-Engels-Lenin, making possible the unfolding of its powerful, all-inclusive, scientific principles and teachings; providing for a flexible application of these principles and teachings according to the specific requirements of the various countries, thus making possible the principle of peaceful coexistence; and eliminating the monopoly of Marxism, by repression of dogmatism all over the world in the interests of a victorious socialism.

On the basis of the principles laid down in the Belgrade announcements and subsequent commentaries, "Titoism"—so called in an effort to designate the political principles of Yugoslav Communists for building socialism—cannot be regarded as a deviation from Marxism-Leninism or as a bourgeois ideology or as a detrimental viewpoint of imperialist agents, but as the creative application of Marxism-Leninism to building socialism under the specific, characteristic social and economic conditions of Yugoslavia. The charge of "Titoism" and "Yugoslav socialism" (when applied to me it was called "new Titoism" and "Hungarian socialism") sprang from the already discredited anti-Marxist, anti-Leninist viewpoint, according to which the only and the exclusive method for building socialism was that used by the Soviet.

That platform of political principles which considers all deviation from rigid dogmas as a stand to be prosecuted, which does not permit even an exchange of views within the Party, has carried on a ruthless campaign against all Party efforts that seek to find new ways of building socialism by paying particular attention to characteristic local situations. Efforts that try to apply Soviet methods mechanically instead of critically evaluating them are in reality merely a continuation of the battle against Titoism in a disguised form.

Lessons of great historical significance can be learned from the Belgrade declarations, lessons that can be learned only from an intensive study of principles and a wide exchange of experiences.

A. In applying Marxism-Leninism, one must discard everything that is superannuated, antiquated, outworn, and create new scientific principles in conformity with the times, thus developing scientific socialism further.

B. To apply Marxism-Leninism to other countries by upholding its principles without modification can cause only the distortion or stagnation of Marxism. It is therefore an improper, unscientific and anti-Marxist method to copy or mechanically ape the application of scientific socialism. By enriching Marxism-Leninism with new tenets and applying them practically on the basis of experiences gained in the various countries, after careful and intensive examination, these principles can be utilized bravely in conformity with the characteristic local situations.

C. In this sense, "Hungarian socialism," which was meant to be a disparaging label for the independent application of scientific socialism, is in effect nothing else but a type of Hungarian socialism, in other words, the application of Marxism-Leninism to specific Hungarian situations.

D. The scientific development of Marxism-Leninism on the basis of experiences gained through theoretical and practical work is the primary problem of the Communist Party in every country. Renouncing this obligation, neglecting it, shifting it to someone else, placing certain Communist Parties under an ideological guardianship, or acceptance of such guardianship, creates great danger for the fate of socialism and is foreign to the teachings of socialism and to the ideals of the founding geniuses.

The conflict in the Cominform was a provocation of the greatest magnitude, with the most serious consequences in the history of the international revolutionary workers' movements. It created a schism between the Communist and the Workers' Parties; disrupted the internal unity of the Parties; put the countries of the socialist camp into sharpest opposition to Yugoslavia; disrupted the economic cooperation of the Comecon countries; increased international tension; increased the danger of war. All of this caused immeasurable political and moral losses.

The civil war was carried on in the international workers' movements through unprecedented means and methods. Political propaganda utilized every means of a "cold war," not shrinking even from the use of slander, incitement, disparagement, threats, and the most ignoble, contemptible means. Political pressure, economic blockade, military threats had made the conflict extraordinarily serious, threatening, and dangerous, so much so that for almost seven years it paralyzed the endeavors of the international revolutionary movement and aided the forces of imperialism.

In this civil war, in this international provocation, a serious role was played by the Hungarian Party, whose "foursome" leadership, with Mátyás Rákosi at the helm, excelling even the activities of the Soviet Union, and the Communist and Workers' Parties of other People's Democracies in this field was in the forefront of the attack against Yugoslavia and its Communist Party and leadership, and in organizing international provocation. The Rajk trial; the executions, all built up on the *"conception"* method, which have since been completely unmasked as lies; the mass imprisonments; the persecutions; the unbridled, inciting speeches and writings of Mátyás Rákosi, Mihály Farkas, Ernö Gerö, Joseph Révai, and others: all of the anti-Tito, anti-Yugoslav literature, the pamphlets, the declarations, the activities of the press and radio, as well as a long, long line of economic, political, and other measures taken against Yugoslavia—all these are well-known, irrefutable facts.

Serious responsibility rests on the leadership of the Hungarian Party during that time for the role it played in this civil war—and on Mátyás Rákosi first of all. The vitally urgent duties in the leadership of the Hungarian Party, stemming from international proletarianism and the best interests, economic and political, of the Hungarian nation, demand that the serious mistakes that have been committed should be revealed; the necessary conclusions drawn; the responsibility established; the obstacles that stood in the path of the civil war and their deleterious effects removed. Thus compensation can be made for the mistakes of the past, and all the necessary requirements created for establishing Yugoslav-Hungarian friendship on a brotherly basis between these two neighboring countries.

The most stable basis for this is the political and economic interdependence of the two countries. The construction of the national economy of the two countries, the direction of their development, the supply of raw materials, the geographic location, the transportation lines, the pathway to the sea, moreover the political and internal security angles and other mutual points of interest, make it imperatively necessary that the Hungarian Party should work out the questions, forms, and methods of political, economic, cultural, and other types of cooperation between the two countries.

These have become necessary through the experiences of the

seven-year conflict with Yugoslavia. The experiences have convinced us that in addition to the political damage done and the
economic harm to Yugoslavia, there were also serious economic
repercussions to our country and our people, in addition to the
irreparable harm to the good neighborly feeling. Calculating
the damage to our peoples' economy must be done as soon as
possible. Simultaneously with rectifying the damage done to
Yugoslavia by the economic blockade and the stoppage of transportation facilities, our people must be made aware of the magnitude of the damage done to our own country, and of our responsibilities for the active participation in this conflict of the
Cominform.

Creating a mutual basis of principles and policies for friendly
connection between the two countries and the two parties can
be done on the basis of the policies set forth in the Belgrade
declaration. This opens up a new era of furthering Marxism-
Leninism in the international revolutionary movement and the
reciprocal relationship of the Communist Parties. In the interest of re-establishing political and organizational connections
between the Hungarian and the Yugoslav Communist Parties,
we must start the liquidation and elimination of all anti-Marxist views that belong to the category of "Titoism," on the basis
of the principles of the Belgrade declaration and in the spirit of
Marxist-Leninist teachings. Action initiated by the leaders of
the Soviet Communist Party to end the conflict in the Cominform is an event of historical significance in the international
revolutionary movement. It means the beginning of a new era
in the countries building socialism and in the connections between the Communists and the Workers' Parties. Following the
example of the Communist Party of the Soviet Union, our
Party must sincerely and as soon as possible also step on this
road. All the more because, following the example of the Communist Party, the People's Democratic countries, along state
and party lines alike, have done much more in the interests of
restoring friendly connections with Yugoslavia than we have.
In our case, a part of the leadership played a role that was overly
compromising, and because of the serious personal responsibilities, apart from a few hackneyed, stereotyped phrases did not

aid by one single step or do anything toward restoring friendly connections between the two countries.

In addition to numerous facts and occurrences this is indicated by the speech of Comrade Tito on July 27, 1955, at Karlovac, in which he established that the endeavors of certain leaders of the Hungarian Party and of Hungary were to prevent the restoration of good relations and to continue the old detrimental policies. The problem of leadership of the Hungarian Party was to clear away the obstacles in the path of resuming mutual friendly relations, end all the scheming, maneuvering, time-wasting, wait-and-see policies, as well as the double-dealing, which indicated the continuation of the old, obscure, detrimental policies against Yugoslavia and the Communist Party of Yugoslavia, serving only the interests of the enemy. Attempts like those in the articles by Béla Szalai about the development of Hungarian-Yugoslav friendship must be discontinued as inimical to the best interests of the country and Party. Such activities, instead of revealing and correcting mistakes, mean to "solve" the question by falsification of facts, unprincipled "covering up," and in reality trying to take the question of Hungarian-Yugoslav friendship into a blind alley. From all this one must conclude that to the degree to which the Hungarian leadership participated at the time in the Cominform conflict, at least to that same degree it should participate in the *elimination* of the damaging results of this conflict—primarily in the restoration and stabilization of Hungarian-Yugoslav friendship and brotherly-friendly connections. The Rákosi speech at Csepel, which in its essence was a repetition of the tactics proposed in the Szalai article, was an evasion with regard to disclosing and rectifying mistakes, and did not give the slightest indication of a Rákosi type of self-criticism. It did not advance the satisfactory solution of the Hungarian-Yugoslav question by one single step: a solution that is necessary from the viewpoint of both parties and both countries, as well as from the standpoint of the international situation. This is necessary and inescapable. I do not know whether the Central Committee discussed or at least saw the article written by Béla Szalai, entitled "Lasting Peace," dealing with settling the Yugoslav-Hungarian problem, and the statement made by Mátyás Rákosi at Csepel on this same question. Either way it is the duty of the central leadership to put an end to the allusions to "Péter Gábor and his band" in connection with the breaking down and degeneration of Yugoslav-Hungarian friendship. Péter Gábor and his fellow conspirators, who have been called to account and convicted by the Hungarian courts, had committed a long series of despicable crimes against the Hungarian people. But to declare that Péter Gábor and his fellow criminals were to blame for the "evil situation" through which Hungarian-Yugoslav relations worsened is a distortion of facts. It is also a lie that the hostile, provocative activities of Péter Gábor and his band "misled" the Party leaders, Rákosi, Gerö, Farkas and Révai, and that not they but Péter Gábor and his accomplices slandered the leaders of the Yugoslav people. This is a lie, which underestimates the memory of the workers. To take this attitude on the question of restoring friendly relations between the two People's Democratic countries and two Communist Parties is only a revival of the cursed past. A stop must be put to this before it is too late. It may be assumed that shirking responsibility in this fashion had a serious effect upon the breaking off of the conferences in Belgrade on Hungarian-Yugoslav financial matters. The Party leaders must accept the responsibility for these serious consequences. Hungarian Communists, especially the central Party leadership, must take to heart very seriously the following declaration by Marx concerning the duties of the proletariat, which he sent as a message to the first International Workers' Federation:

> They must take up the cudgels in defending the simple, basic laws of morals and justice, which must rule the relations between private individuals, and which must also be the chief laws governing the contacts between nations. We must not permit the country and the Party to be diverted from these basic principles.

Hungarian Communists must regard this as their honored cause: that on the basis of the mutual principles established by the Soviet in the Belgrade declaration, they immediately take a stand to restore relations between Hungary and Yugoslavia. It is unforgivable that in the midst of decreasing international tension the relation between two countries building socialism should continue to worsen instead of becoming the closest co-operation for stabilization of friendship. Therefore, the central leadership of the Hungarian Workers' Party should urgently discuss the question of settling Yugoslav-Hungarian relations; make the proper resolutions; and direct the competent Party and state authorities—the Political Committee and the government of the People's Republic—immediately to take up the establishment of friendly relations between Hungary and Yugoslavia, and to start to eliminate radically the serious mistakes committed in the past. It is the moral and political duty of the Hungarian Communists, following the example of the Communist Party of the Soviet Union, impregnated by the spirit of international proletarianism, to eradicate the causes of tension, thus assuring the brotherly cooperation of the peoples and the Communist Parties of Yugoslavia and Hungary.

One may certainly rest assured that if the relationship between the two countries is based on mutual trust and sincere friendship, then understanding will not be found wanting on the part of Yugoslavia: for this there is an especially great need under present circumstances.

Chapter 3. The Five Basic Principles of International Relations and the Question of Our Foreign Policy

During the past one or two years, we can safely say that we have been eyewitnesses of extraordinary events in world politics. These new and extraordinary events are: the five basic principles that were first explained at the Bandung Conference by the representatives of the Chinese Republic and India, Chou En-lai and Nehru; following that, the announcement at the time of Tito's visit to India, and later the joint Soviet-Yugoslav communique issued at Belgrade, declaring these principles to be the basis for settling international relations. Since then the five principles have traveled a long, long road, going around the world. The conference of the heads of state at Geneva, the Assembly of the United Nations, the trip of Khrushchev and Bulganin to Asia, the visit of Tito to North Africa, gave added emphasis to the international significance of these five basic principles. During recent times there have not been governmental declarations that did not propose to settle relations between countries and peoples on the basis of national independence, sovereignty, territorial inviolability, noninterference in internal affairs. Not a single declaration has been made that opposed or even questioned the justice and correctness of the five basic principles. From these facts we must arrive at conclusions of utmost importance: that these will have a decisive influence on the great changes that are taking place in the field of international relations.

The five basic principles are designed to regulate relations between the various countries. If, however, we try to analyze them more thoroughly, we can see that although these principles are apparent in international relationships, their significance goes much further: they include national existence, social development, and many basic questions of human freedom. If these aims are not realized, the countries and peoples will remain in slavery, at the lowest rung of social development and human civilization, emergence from which can be attained only through the principles of national independence, sovereignty, equality, noninterference in internal affairs, and the assurance of self-determination. Losing, limiting, or renouncing these rights must result in the dissolution and destruction of nations, peoples and cultures.

The five basic principles may be considered the goal of any national liberation movement, of any transformation of colonial or semicolonial peoples. In principle the problem of national liberation movements and transformation of peoples is to bring about victory for the cause of national independence, to eradicate every form of national dependence and subordination. Attaining nationhood, national independence, sovereignty, and equality are not always realized by various peoples simultaneously, or through the same means or similar processes.

The centuries-old battles for national ideals and national independence, the struggle for economic, political, and cultural nationhood, was carried out in Hungary under characteristic local circumstances, despite the survival of a dependence stemming from the feudal system and foreign subjugation.

Nothing could be more erroneous than to feel that, since national independence, sovereignty, equality in an era of social progress were problems of internal transformation, national principles and ideals are also antiquated.

The nation's bourgeoisie, which could prosper only by oppressing the working class, established its rule and subordinated the great national interests, for which it had also fought at one time, to its own selfish class interests. Thus the interests of the ruling bourgeoisie clashed with the interests of the nation, to the great detriment of the country.

The historical events of the last decade prove most convincingly that the ideals of national independence, sovereignty, equality, and self-determination, which from a historical standpoint became the ideal of the masses through the national liberation movements, the social transformation, and development were most important factors in the period of change from capitalism to socialism. The emergence into the forefront of international life of the five previously mentioned basic principles during the last two years prove this most convincingly. These obvious facts also indicate other things, above all, that the world is now living in an era of socialist transformation, by peaceful methods or revolution; that the five basic principles are not proving completely effective in practice, and that therefore the development toward socialism, the transition from capitalism that we are facing in the present era, is increasingly significant.

Moreover, facts indicate that the five basic principles cannot be limited to the capitalistic system or the battle between the two systems, but must extend to the relations between the the countries within the democratic and socialist camps.

The five basic principles do not spring from differences between the two systems—capitalism and socialism—they do not express this difference, but they are factors independent of social and political relationships in the international field. Therefore these five basic principles cannot be interpreted in a one-sided fashion, as meaning that one must fight for their realization only in the battle against the imperialist endeavors of the capitalist great powers. It must not be assumed that these principles are antiquated and therefore unnecessary in the countries within the socialist camps.

There exist erroneous views to the effect that clinging to these five principles and enforcing them in the relationships between the countries belonging to the democratic and socialist camps is contrary to proletarian internationalism and nationalism, and indicative of a deviation toward chauvinism, and thus weakening the democratic and socialist camps.

On the contrary: they strengthen them, because the socialist camp can become the rallying point of independent sovereign countries possessing equal rights, respecting the principle of noninterference in each other's affairs. Moreover close cooperation within the socialist camp in the economic, political, and cultural fields can insure a healthy relationship if the five basic principles are mutually respected. Therefore close cooperation among the countries of the socialist camp and realization of the five basic principles do not contradict one another. At the same time, however, these connections are based on new principles which conform to the demands of a development toward socialism. It cannot be considered accidental that these five basic principles became apparent and greatly significant in connection with laying the foundation for the relationships between countries belonging to the democratic and socialist camps. It must also be taken into consideration that the five basic principles were put forward by the economically under-developed countries who participated in the Bandung Conference. For them the adoption of these principles was the prime requisite for their economic, political, and cultural development and for the assurance of their national existence.

The principles that govern the relationships between countries and peoples do not touch the interests of only one or another social stratum, but affect the fate of the entire nation; therefore they are considered the basis of all-inclusive national policies. Such national policies can be carried on only by a nation that possesses national independence and sovereignty, and thus can protect its liberty and equality against other peoples and does not permit interference in its private affairs. National independence, which is the most important factor of all in the five basic principles, has as its basic requirement national unity, creation of national loyalty, and winning the support of the masses for the cause of national independence. In such a way, the support of the widest possible masses is won to participate actively in the solution of decisive national problems. These events are taking place before our very eyes, not only in certain countries but on entire continents. This is the role of people creating history, carrying on the battle that is based on the ideals of the five basic principles.

The noble traditions of these five basic principles have roots in our country also, which were formed during our historical development. There were periods in history when the light of these principles and ideals of ours shone brightly in all of

Europe. The noble traditions of battles for independence are still alive today, and have their effect, nurturing these principles as our greatest national virtue. Attaining national independence and sovereignty where it is nonexistent, or preserving it, has always been the greatest national problem in past periods, as it is today and will be in the future, even under the socialist system's development. While nations and national states exist—and on this score we face an entire historical era—the five basic principles will remain the motivating power of the development of the socialist system. That is why the nation clings to its independence, sovereignty, and freedom. That is why it cannot and does not yield to force or "voluntary" relinquishing of these ideals. There were and are difficult times in the life of a nation, when those in power alluding to the best interests of the people and the nation, accept dependence, subordination, humiliating slavery—betraying the cause of national independence. There are many instances in history that show that the former ruling classes accepted slavery for the nation, instead of independence, sovereignty, liberty and equality, to ensure their own specially privileged status. However, according to the lessons of history, these betrayals of the nation do not end with the destruction of the nation but with that of the traitors, following which the ideals of freedom and independence burn with a stronger and brighter flame in the hearts of the masses.

The ideals of national independence and sovereignty that in our time have been so emphatically set forth by the five basic principles—which in the old Hungary had never been fully realized—were left as a legacy to the working classes. The working class must become a more consistent fighter for the ideals of independence and freedom than were the bourgeoisie. The working class cannot clash with the cause of national independence, sovereignty, freedom and equality. It cannot subordinate the universal interest of the nation to its own class interests, because the working class can liberate itself and has done so only in conjunction with the other working classes, and can stabilize its power only by cooperating fully with them. Thus the interests of the working class and the nation are identical and cannot come into conflict with the universal national interests. Historical developments have made the working class the supporter and guardian of the future fate of the nation and the embodiment of national ideals.

With the emergence of the five basic principles, the greatest problem in the development toward socialism came to the forefront. So far, in the transition from capitalism to socialism, little was said about these principles, as though the road to socialism had outstripped these principles. The scientific theory of Marxism-Leninism, the foreign policy of the countries in the socialist camp, applied these five basic principles only to the imperialist great powers and capitalist relationships. Neither from the theoretical or practical political standpoint is it correct to view the five basic principles as a schism between the two systems, limiting it exclusively to the capitalist world. This would not agree with the Marxist-Leninist viewpoint either. The five basic principles are undoubtedly powerful motivating factors in the struggle against imperialist, capitalist conquest and its efforts to subjugate. But they are also a powerful factor in the building of a socialist society. Minimizing this or denying this may have serious consequences, and as facts show, the danger does not recede but grows. These situations arise from improper anti-Marxist views which declare that socialism supersedes nationalism, denying the national characteristics of socialism, falsifying international proletarianism—in reality this means a cosmopolitan distortion of Marxism. The working class, if it wants to fulfill its historical role and accept, as it must, the burden of solving national problems, must above all insure its independence and sovereignty. In this it will inescapably find itself in opposition to those cosmopolitan views which declare that the dogmas remaining from the ideological, autocratic rule of Stalin are binding principles of socialism in general. By this they place obstacles to the spreading of socialism in all parts of the world. It is understandable that under these circumstances the five basic principles play such an important role, gaining ground so swiftly in those countries that are taking their first steps toward socialism. The remnants of ideological, autocratic rule, the binding dogmas and patterns, are in sharp contrast to the realization of the five basic principles, making it more difficult for the working class to fulfill its leading role. Through such actions the working class is separated from the workers' movements of the world. Its international character, stemming from its class role, becomes limited, and as a result proletarian internationalism is falsified. The working class is hindered in creating national unity and prevented from lining up the majority of the nation to support and accept the aims and leadership of the working class. In carrying out this goal, acceptance of the five basic principles is inescapable. Only through such acceptance can national ideals and problems be solved. The working class cannot be international, in the interpretation of the idea by Marxist socialism, if its internationalism does not lie in devotion and faithfulness to its own nation—and if it does not rest on accepting responsibility for its own national independence, sovereignty, and equality.

The dogmas remaining from the ideological, autocratic rule of Stalin interfere with the harmony of the working class as well as with its unity in attempting to realize its historical role. They mean disruption of unity and harmony on the international and national level. They mean that accepting the national ideals expressed in the five basic principles, the imperative task of the working class in building a socialist society, is opposed to proletarian internationalism. The only proper way of eradicating these differences is to discard the anti-Marxist views regarding the dogmas and patterns declared under the ideological, autocratic rule of Stalin as binding and generally applicable, and to replace his view with the Marxist-Leninist theory of locally characteristic socialism; the five basic principles of national existence, and the principle of noninterference. In Hungary, the Party labels the application of the five basic principles as an opportunist, nationalist, anti-Soviet view, opposed and contrary to the only proper—that is Marxist—viewpoint. Under such circumstances the working class cannot become the standard-bearer of the five principles or embrace the cause of national independence. The party renounces acceptance of these principles, thus isolating itself from the majority of the nation—because it does not take into consideration national characteristics, traditions, and other factors. As a result it comes into contradiction with itself. This in turn creates a social crisis in economic, political, and cultural affairs alike. Therefore this road is impracticable and impossible for Hungarian Communists to follow.

The question arises: can the working class be at one and the same time the chief pillar and vanguard in building socialism *and* in putting national ideals and aims into practice? Can the ideals of socialism, proletarian internationalism, and national independence be reconciled? These questions must without doubt be answered by an unqualified Yes. The national ideals embodied in the five basic principles do not point toward a separation between nations, but indicate the drawing together of nations that are speeding up and smoothing the course toward socialism. The five principles are guarantees that while advancing together inside the socialist camp, and continuing social, economic, and cultural development under nationally specific situations, the independence, sovereignty, and equality of the individual nations can be preserved.

This circumstance makes it possible for countries and peoples in which there are Marxist workers' parties, other progressive nationalist parties or patriotic forces, to approach and develop socialism, which is impossible along Soviet lines. It opens up wide vistas of possibilities with regard to developing socialism along specifically national roads. These are based on the past unequal development of countries under capitalism, a logical result of which is unequal development under socialism. Since the five basic principles are so closely connected with this theory, we find that this view is diametrically opposed to ideological dogmatism. In answering the questions that have been posed here, one cannot ignore the fact that, under situations that govern the building of socialism, the working class which is in power as the embodiment of national aspirations *can* become the true fighter for proletarian internationalism *only* on the basis of nationalistic principles.

There are serious mistakes and errors from the ideological and practical viewpoint in the transition from capitalism to socialism on such decisive questions as are expressed in the five basic principles, which cannot be reconciled with Marxism. The concepts expressed in these principles under their original interpretation cannot be narrowed down or limited in their development toward socialism. If they are *modified,* they become more perfect, more complete, more general, and more comprehensive. In the process of realizing a socialist society, therefore, the principles of national independence, sovereignty, freedom, equality, self-determination, noninterference, and a socialist national existence become more perfect and inviolable if added to other basic factors.

Only thus, along the only correct basic Marxist principles and upon the principle of peaceful coexistence of countries having different social and political systems, can there evolve a socialist society that consists of countries traveling different roads under particular national patterns, but independent, free, and equal. It cannot be doubted that it is more difficult to enforce these five principles against the imperialist great powers than between countries of a democratic and socialist type. But from this it does not in the least follow that among the latter these guiding principles have become "superfluous," or that they should be interpreted differently. On the contrary, there they are more easily realized and offer wider possibilities for application. The decisive question is: who does respect these basic principles, and who does not?

The concepts outlined in the five basic principles have become very apparent to us, and have come to the forefront in relations between nations after the Soviet-Yugoslav declaration made at Belgrade. These five basic principles and the Belgrade Soviet-Yugoslav declaration, which directly concerned us, created great ideological and political opportunities for us. They depicted the clear and concise outlines of a Marxist platform, on the basis of which the Communist or other Marxist workers' parties could work out the political and theoretical method of cooperation and harmony along proletarian internationalist lines, as well as the guiding principles governing their realization.

The leadership of the Hungarian Workers' Party as evidenced by many manifestations, regards—completely incorrectly—the Belgrade declaration as a temporary compromise and a sacrifice which the Soviet Communist Party was obliged to make in order to tear Yugoslavia away from the influence of the imperialists. This is the explanation why nothing has happened so far in our camp to put into operation the principles enunciated in the Belgrade declaration or to use the opportunities which it has created. It is clear that the five basic principles and the Belgrade declaration are not temporary compromises. They were a historic necessity, even though there are people who attempt to use them for covering up their political machinations. As to the historical necessity: from the events of two decades of the Communist International, from the activities of the Cominform, from the damaging legacy of the autocratic, ideological rule of Stalin, and from the proven political interdependence of the Communist and workers' parties, emerge rich international experiences. The Hungarian Party's leadership does not want to learn anything from these experiences. Although they could have learned from their own difficulties, they did not draw any conclusions and behave as if nothing had happened. For them so far the Belgrade declaration has remained a scrap of paper. In order that it should become a living reality, the still-existing strong remnants of Stalinist autocratic rule must disappear. Those principles that have become rigid dogmas and hackneyed phrases, the talk about enforcing the Soviet example and about the binding nature of certain principles, which have created the crisis in the cause of international socialism, can now be replaced by the application of the Belgrade declaration.

Every vestige of the manifestation of Stalinist autocratic rule must be liquidated all the more because the dogmatism emanating from it monopolizes the interpretation of Marxist-Leninist theory, the methods of its practical application, while all other views or interpretations are branded as opportunism. Those who do not accept it, approve of it, or who consider the methods injurious, who want to enforce in their own countries the true Marxist-Leninist theories brought forth by the Belgrade declaration and forgotten during the Stalin era, are considered opportunists.

A change is necessary also because autocratic ideological rule is opposed to the spirit of the Belgrade declaration and its special provisions, which consider all interference as unforgivable, including ideological interference, which prevents and excludes in the Party an exchange of views, debate, the battle of opinions, the democratism of Party life, and instead raises to the level of virtue all slavish copying, obscures and devalues ideology, degrades the Party, and insults the self-respect of the Hungarian Marxist.

This also applies to the creation and stabilization of lasting friendly relations with all other countries. But since, within the socialist camp, the relation of individual countries with the Soviet Union and the relationships of the Communist or Workers' Parties to the Soviet Communist Party is also a decisive question, the chief problem lies in placing these relationships on a firm and lasting basis.

The Soviet Communist Party and the Soviet government took a huge step forward to liquidate the serious mistakes of the past by the Soviet-Yugoslav declaration. One must hope and trust that the practical application of these principles in the relationships between countries and parties is not too far distant. It is the destiny of the Soviet Communist Party to develop and spread future socialism, further develop and apply it in practice. In consequence of the rigid dogmatism of the Stalin era this became the fountainhead of many and serious mistakes, was, and has remained up to the present time, the great obstacle to any wide-scale evolution of socialist forces and societies.

The problem of the Hungarian Communists is to insure in their own country the requisites of a policy that, in the spirit of Marxism-Leninism, will place the relations and the political connections of the countries and kindred parties on the basis of national independence, sovereignty, and noninterference.

Today in Hungary the Party and the country are led by those who with their anti-Marxist, sectarian, "leftist" policies have moved into opposition to the majority of the Party membership and to the widest strata of the country's population. Lacking mass support, they cannot stand on their own feet, nor can they enforce the basic principles in relations with friendly countries or kindred parties. These are the people who because of their cowardice and their spiritual poverty cannot do without the Stalinist autocratic rule and the dogmas that outline for the Party and the country the policies and directives that must be followed in international and internal politics, as well as in the economic, political, and cultural life of the nation. They not only voluntarily accept such a dependent and humiliating role but cling to it, because this is the only solid support to insure their power. But the more they try to enforce the application of these dogmas and schemes and their imitation here at home, the further away they get from Hungarian reality, the Hungarian peoples' aims and national aspirations, which cannot be disregarded.

The leaders of the Party and the country must understand that the fate of the nation and that of the people are identical. The people cannot be free if the nation is not independent, if it does not possess complete sovereignty, if foreign influences prevail in its internal affairs, as no nation can be independent and sovereign whose people do not possess completely the right to freedom.

National independence and freedom of the people can be realized together under socialism. Independent and sovereign national existence and freedom of the people are equal factors in the development of a socialist society, just as important as economic and political factors, or the peaceful coexistence of nations and the theory of economic rivalry on the international level. If a nation does not possess its sovereign rights or is unable to attain them, the dependency and subjugation of the country will result in the rule of poverty and backwardness for the nation. Only in an independent, sovereign, and free country are the people rich and prosperous. Therefore the fate of the people depends very much on the way in which national independence develops. In a country lacking independence, prosperity is nonexistent. People do not struggle ceaselessly for national independence, sovereignty, and equality merely for the sake of economic well-being or merely because of their enthusiasm for ideals. These two ideals are closely intertwined in the national aspirations of the people.

We are living in an age, and we are facing times, when the realization of the five basic principles in countries having different systems and those having identical systems will be crucial for the future of nations possessing national independence, sovereignty, and equality. The country and Party must be led by those who are completely reliable and able to lead the country along democratic lines and attain the greatest possible national support, in order that the country may be assured of complete possession of its sovereign rights.

The five basic principles of peaceful coexistence and the mutual relations of the great powers—and of the economically backward small nations as well—is of primary importance from the standpoint of preserving peace and the formation of power groups. The policies of the power groups are contrary to the ideals of national independence and sovereignty that are based on the five principles, as well as to the ideal of peaceful coexistence between various states. The separation of states into various power groups must lead sooner or later to armed conflict. For this reason the only feasible path for peaceful development and the avoidance of war is not the creation of power groups but the liquidation of such groups as may exist. For small countries, such as Hungary, it is a question of vital importance to decide properly on our position in relation to the various states. The country must strive to uphold the peace in every possible way. It must avoid becoming an active participant in any of the clashes between power groups or becoming embroiled in war, to serve as a field of battle or an area of troop passage. It must also assure that in all such questions the nation will decide for itself, in full possession of its sovereign rights. Our country, as an independent nation, must align itself with the countries and peoples who are fighting for peace. But can a small country exist without belonging to a power group? Peaceful coexistence of nations demands the liquidations of power groups. In the fight against aggressive power politics the most potent force is the great and solid strength of the socialist nations, headed by the Soviet Union, which at present constitutes the basis of the greatest antiwar group in the world. The five conditions of peaceful coexistence, which are the basis of cooperation of the small and economically backward countries and of the fight against the power groups—and they are the general rules of international coexistence—can therefore become the guarantee of realizing socialism peacefully.

The liquidation of the power groups is in the interest of all progressive mankind, the socialist camp included, transcending national interests. Therefore the countries of the socialist camp must endeavor to liquidate the policy of power politics. Their foreign policies must be carried on in this direction by aiming for the liquidation of all power groups as soon as possible. Gaining a socialist victory is possible only in this way. For this reason, taking a stand against such power groups, whether that of neutrality or active coexistence, will mean the realization of consistent representation of the basic principles of cooperation within the countries of the socialist camp. The correctness of this principle cannot be denied. However, in regard to the policies of putting this into practice, there are serious considerations. The main question is: which is the most practicable way of liquidating the power groups and power policies? According to present experiences the rivalry of the power groups and their battle against each other will hardly lead to the cessation of power politics and will hardly be responsible for attaining peaceful coexistence. It is more likely that differences will be aggravated and international tensions will increase. The most practicable plan, seemingly, is the active coexistence of progressive democratic socialist or similar countries with those other countries having a different system, through a coordinated foreign policy and through cooperation against the policies of the power groups, through neutrality or active coexistence. This path is made easier for Hungary by its geographical location through its neighboring states, neutral Austria, and countries building socialism, among them the Soviet Union, and neighboring Yugoslavia, which stands on the principle of active coexistence. It is the sovereign right of the Hungarian people to decide in which form they believe the most advantageous international status will be assured, and in which form they think that national independence, sovereignty, equality, and peaceful development will be attained. Joining forces with the five basic principles of peaceful coexistence is most advantageous, because the Soviet Union has already accepted these principles as guiding principles in international politics. Hungary must choose this path all the more, because historical experience decisively proves that economic, political, military, and other power groups are built on quicksand and cannot entice the masses of the people into the service of their cause or win their allegiance. The Hungarian people have become convinced by the terrible experiences of the two world wars that they cannot and must not become participants in the rivalries of free power groups. The country cannot undertake obligations that transcend its capabilities, that will draw away its forces or divert its attention from solving its own national problems, or that endanger the independence and sovereignty of the country with the possibility of a new war and its devastating consequences.

On the basis of all these logical assumptions, the Hungarian nation must keep in mind the particular national interests and the general interests of the socialist countries. The Hungarian nation must follow the policy of active coexistence in the field of international politics, which is in the national interests of Hungary and of the successful spreading of socialism and the peaceful coexistence of the two systems, including economic competition. This policy would create a much firmer and more lasting basis for Hungarian-Soviet relations and would make the connections between the socialist countries a closer one. For this reason it is our duty, which cannot be postponed, but is the command of history. On the basis of the experiences and lessons learned during the long, stormy, centuries-old battle for the independence and sovereignty of our nation, we must lay the foundation of an independent national foreign policy that will, despite the buffeting received through political tactics, show for our country the way and the clear goal and will preserve us from again becoming the plaything of historical storms. Hungary has for centuries stood in the focal point of hostile world forces, and thus could not find for itself a place in the family of nations. For this we have paid a very heavy price in a series of national catastrophes. After our glorious freedom fight was crushed, our great national genius Louis Kossuth summarized the great historical lessons—unhappily too late—and designated the path to be followed. He envisioned the assurance of an independent, sovereign, self-governing Hungary, not through alignment with a great power or through joining a power group, but by close cooperation with neighboring peoples within the framework of a federation of free and independent nations.

We must return to the ideals which have been revived under new historical circumstances, of the peaceful coexistence of peoples and their cooperation—the true conditions for which are created by the realization of socialist ideals. The ruling classes in Hungary did not follow the ideals of Kossuth in the sphere of international relations. Their realization, together with so many other great national problems—among them national independence and reallotment of land—was left as a legacy to us Communists. Since the Hungarian nation for the first time since 1849 has become again a factor in forming history and in the relations and cooperation between nations, the forms and framework of political law—the Kossuth ideals—must be accepted. And we do accept these ideals, taking into consideration the changed historical situation for building socialism. The peace of independent, sovereign, and free peoples, their friendship and their dependence on each other, as well as their common desire to create a socialist society, is a firm and lasting basis upon which an independent Hungarian national foreign policy can be formed—one that would point toward the future and open up wide vistas for establishing an independent national foreign policy. Absence of this makes the internal and external situation of our country very precarious and wavering. No lasting harmony can be attained in internal and external policies, nor can any decided line of direction toward various countries or relationships to power groups emerge, if a clear stand is not taken in regard to the various important international problems. The main reason for this is that on these questions the Party and the government is not guided by its own particular circumstances, but by dogmas. Such a situation is unworthy of a free, independent, and sovereign country.

This situation, which did not develop in the Marxist-Leninist spirit of proletarian internationalism or in the relations between independent, sovereign, and equal socialist countries, must undoubtedly be changed—all the more as this is not a question of an isolated occurrence, but one that must be solved *generally* within the socialist camp. In fact the problem is even more far-reaching. Occurrences that are repeated often in the Communist parties of the capitalist countries—the cleavages in the international socialist movement, the disunity of forces, the disorder in relations and cooperation between the socialist and social democratic parties within the international and national framework, etc.—all show that the principles laid down at the

Bandung Conference and the Soviet-Yugoslav declaration at Belgrade are of historical importance. Their realization cannot be deferred without serious consequences for the Communist parties and the cause of socialism.

It is encouraging that in international politics the Soviet Union deviates from the Stalin attitude and the rigid dogmas, which had limited the possibilities of international cooperation, but now upholds the Lenin ideals of coexistence. But despite the fact that in recent times this Leninist principle of peaceful coexistence of countries with varying social and political systems has been receiving more emphasis, and although the application of the principles shows great promise for mutual cooperation, practical realization is still in the primary stages.

Nevertheless, the isolation of the countries building socialism from the other parts of the world and from the family of nations is detrimental to the countries that have accepted socialism or those countries which are planning to do so. This situation cannot prevail for too long, especially in the ranks of the more culturally and economically developed countries of Europe. It cannot be continued because it would create tensions between individual countries, and in the international arena, which would sooner or later lead to serious repercussions. One can not completely disregard a country's national traditions which have evolved through history; they are not a Gordian knot that can be simply slashed in half. The world will rush past us, and our country will be left behind, if we do not step out of the narrow framework of Stalinist dogmas, if we evade the challenge of peaceful rivalry between the two systems and shut ourselves off from it with the idea that this will insure greater momentum and exertion or a more infallible way of success in outdistancing capitalism. This is a very narrow-minded policy, in opposition to Marxism, and stems from the fact that we do not trust the forces of socialism and their superiority, although we never for a moment stop stressing it. We must lay the foundation of a policy of international cooperation for our country which would end our self-imposed seclusion, end our isolation, and make possible our progress toward socialism in peaceful coexistence with the family of nations, definite economic competition.

Now, since together with other democratic countries Hungary also became a member of the U.N.—this great community of the world's nations—we have to take steps according to the basic principles of the Charter to further the development of connections between the countries practicing different political systems. This will strengthen healthy, friendly connections between the socialist countries also, all the more so because these connections must be based on new foundations. The principles stated in the Charter of the U.N. and those principles that govern the cooperation of the socialist countries—even if they are not identical—cannot be in opposition on fundamental questions, since the majority of the socialist countries are members of the U.N., acknowledging the Charter and supporting it. The fact that we belong to the socialist group, with all the obligations which this entails, means that our internal and external policies cannot be opposed to the basic principles of the U.N. On the other hand, the fact that we are a member nation of the U.N. cannot hinder our close connections with the nations of the socialist group. The two must be brought into harmony in principle as well as practice, if we intend to widen and finally make universal the peaceful coexistence of nations—in which aim the countries of the socialist group must be the pioneers.

In order to make this task easier, the oppressively heavy inheritance of the Stalin era must be radically liquidated, including all the remnants of subordination and dependence. In this way we can increase the respect and confidence of the socialist group; we can dispel the doubts, suspicions, and prejudices of those countries where peoples and parties of the workers would not like to see their independence, their sovereign and national rights and special interests endangered by closer connections or active cooperation with the socialist group, or by the monopoly of one political ideology and the slavery of dogmas and uniformity.

The complete disappearance of the remnants of Stalinist political and ideological dictatorship and of subjection to uniformity and dogmas could destroy those obstacles that prevent other countries and peoples from moving closer to the socialist group and prevent the socialist group from approaching the other countries in order to develop closer contacts, to liquidate power blocks among the nations, and to bring about a realization of universal, world-embracing peaceful coexistence.

A correct evaluation of the international situation and a correct estimate of its possible developments is very important from the viewpoint of Party politics, and affects the tactics of the Party.

Our own experience proves that a superficial, unscientific, and therefore incorrect evaluation of the international situation, an erroneous assessment of its possible developments, might bring about very dire results: incorrect estimation in planning the proportions, methods, and rhythm of socialism, sharp changes unjustifiedly executed in the life of the Party, uncertainty and groping which discredits the leadership of the Party and state.

The scientific Marxist evaluation of the international situation and the objective deductions derived in relation to the internal and external politics of the country so far have not been considered to be the task of the Party leadership. We never examined the international situation thoroughly in the light of our own country's interests nor from the viewpoint of its effects on our country. Our own activity in the field of international politics was restricted to some equalizing efforts, which were deemed necessary to insure homogeneity inside the socialist group. For this reason questions of the international situation and external policies played an insignificant role in the politics of the Party and the government, especially where these questions touched on the problems of our own country. In general we used the international situation only to prove an economic or political aim, which was determined beforehand, and ignored the actual situation or often distorted it. We always explained it arbitrarily as the given situation happened to require it.

This was the reason why changes in the international situation often clashed sharply with internal politics. In the years 1949 to 1952, incorrect evaluation of the international situation, overemphasis on the war danger, and the actions resulting from these assumptions played a very serious part in those grave mistakes that were made by our Party leadership with regard to the economic activities of the people. These mistakes were made public by the resolution of the central leadership in June, 1953.

In consequence of these mistakes the country was brought to the brink of catastrophe. The events in June, 1953, in East Germany, Czechoslovakia, Hungary, and elsewhere clearly show how an incorrect evaluation of the international situation and a resulting unsound foreign policy brought about grave crises in the internal life of the countries mentioned. The great importance of the June policy, the policy of the New Era, and of the political changes that occurred in 1953 in the Soviet Union and in the People's Democracies, is that it has brought the objective international situation into harmony with internal and foreign policy.

During the fall and winter of 1954, as a consequence of the mistakes committed in the field of foreign policy in the countries of the Socialist group—and in our country also, which overshot the mark—the Party leadership aimed at the liquidation of democracy and the sharpening of the dictatorship of the proletariat. The deterioration of the internal situation, and the allegations about the increased danger of war played the main roles in those attempts, which aimed at the liquidation of the June policy and at the return to the old policies.

In his speech delivered in May, 1955, at the Party college, Mátyás Rákosi still called it one of the chief mistakes that "Imre Nagy overestimated the easing of the tension in the international situation." Since then the internal situation has eased to an even greater degree, which—after several events in between —was lately evidenced by the results in the foreseeable effects of the Geneva summit conference. Yet, in spite of the further easing of international tension, the Party leadership in internal politics is using the more oppressive methods of the dictatorship of the proletariat.

The higher leadership of the Party is carrying on the same policies at a time of lessened international tension as it had during the alleged increase in the danger of war. This shows on the one hand how irresponsible and unreliable the Party leadership is in dealing with international problems, and on the other hand indicates the extraordinarily serious effects that their dangerous playing with international questions and loud demagoguery have on the situation of the country and the living conditions of the people. But it also indicates that Rákosi is carrying the Party leadership along a dangerous path, which is equivalent to speculating on war tension in foreign policy and on the increasing use of the force of proletarian dictatorship in internal policies.

It is the urgent duty of the Party leadership to examine the background of these policies and their motivating force, because Rákosi's pursuit of such directions cannot be considered accidental.

Hungary at present is a weak unit in the socialist camp. It is an uncertain factor which contributes to the deterioration of the united socialist front, because in the midst of lessening tension in the international situation, internal tension is rapidly growing in our country. Partly because of this, and partly because of the serious mistakes of the past and the rigid rejection with regard to the liquidation of mistakes, and also because of the general distrust with which we are regarded in international life, the present policy of Hungary is a serious obstacle to the rapprochement between the West and the East, and especially between socialists and Communists.

The inner tension of Hungary, which is chiefly political, is caused by the fact that the leadership is opposing the ideals of national independence, sovereignty, and equality, as well as Hungarian national feeling and progressive traditions.

This growing tension must be weighed from the viewpoint of the security and defense of the socialist countries, because the unrest of the masses undermines our ability to defend the country.

The contention that to change the present policies and leadership would cause internal shock and strengthen reaction is not true. As a matter of fact it is not true that there is danger of a counterrevolution. On the contrary, the country and the cause of socialism are being brought to the brink of a catastrophe if radical political and personal changes are not carried out quickly. Nothing will aid international imperialism more than the policies of the present leadership, which drives the people into the arms of reaction. The lessening of tension in the field of international relations makes possible the radical liquidation of this inner tension without having to fear the consequences of the political machinations of international reaction.

On the contrary, they would lose ground as a result, all the more because the Communist and People's Democratic forces are standing firm in Hungary. They have every political and personal basis for finding a solution in a new policy based on the Belgrade declaration. This would make it possible for the country to progress toward socialism on a path compatible with the particular Hungarian situation, on the basis of national independence, sovereignty, equality, without any type of interference. Such a change would make Hungary a firm supporter of socialism and close brotherly cooperation within the socialist camp.

Our country cannot progress toward socialism in a vacuum of social development. Around us in the world, near and far, there are countries of varying social orders, in various stages of development, which show their diversity in their language, traditions, economy, culture, and their whole way of life. We are one of the countries within this circle. We must therefore recognize that we are members not only of the socialist camp but of the great community of nations, to the countries and peoples of which we are bound with countless ties, which we cannot and indeed must not sever, because we do not want to be disbarred from the great community of nations, and also because we could not then successfully progress toward socialism through social and economic improvement. The barriers between the countries of the socialist camp and the great community of nations must be torn down, and the ties that bind them together must be developed.

This Marxist-Leninist lesson must be learned as a consequence of the experiences of the past ten years.

It is the historical mission of the Soviet Communist Party to liquidate the burdensome legacy of the Stalinist era, to which task the Hungarian Communists and the Communists of all other countries, as well as the progressive democratic and socialist forces, will in all probability add their far-reaching support.

Proletarian internationalism, national independence, international solidarity, in harmony with national feeling and deep patriotism, together with the unity of ideologies and principles, will widen the path for all mankind toward creating a socialist society. We Hungarian Communists will faithfully cultivate and always profess the historical Marxist Communist motto: "Workers of the world, unite!"—to which we will also add the motto expressed in the "Szózat", representing deep national feeling and love of country: "Oh Magyar, keep forever thy native country's trust." For us Hungarians in the great struggle for the victory of socialism, and in our daily work and lives, these two mottoes have been welded together indissolubly. The principles and ideals which they express will serve as the guiding principles for our activities in internal as well as foreign policy.

(January, 1956.)

Chapter 4. Ethics and Morals in Hungarian Public Life

The party of the working people that stands at the head of the nation and leads it toward socialist society must be the embodiment of social ethics and morals, and must encompass within itself all the moral virtues and values that our people developed in the course of their history and that constitute our heritage. The eternal moral precepts and laws of progressive mankind are adopted on the same basis by our society, which is developing toward socialism. The new and higher morals and ethics of socialist society unite within themselves the moral ideals and ethical principles common to mankind as a whole and peculiar to the Hungarian nation; they develop and perfect these ideals and principles while preserving their characteristic features.

In addition to the change in our political, economic, cultural, and legal structure, a crucial factor involved in our becoming a socialist nation is the level of social ethics and morals that must prevail in all aspects of public life and individual activity. However, we cannot become a socialist country until we ourselves have become new socialist beings who have been elevated to a higher plane of humanity, not only by our material welfare, knowledge, and culture but also by our superior moral point of view and pure ethical principles. The evaluation of this new, socialist type of being is influenced in the first place by the social transformation that is in progress in the field of economy, politics, and culture. Beyond all this, however, the evaluation of this new type of man must be influenced by the new and loftier socialist ethics and morals, which must influence the economic foundation and permeate other phases of our social structure, our entire political, cultural, and scientific life, and our laws, legislature, and courts.

The transformation taking place in economic foundations and in economic relationships are prerequisite to the development of the new social ethics and morals. However, this is not an instinctive but a scientifically established process, which requires purposeful work and direction. Consequently one of the causes of the ethical and moral crisis in social life is the attitude of the leading organs of government, of society, and of the Party, all of which during the past ten years flouted, underestimated, and failed to do anything about this matter which is so vital to our social development. Under their leadership, the building of socialism was reduced to the socialization of the instruments of production, the establishment of the economic basis of socialism, the transformation of the economy and the class relationships depending thereon, and the acquisition and consolidation of political power. They completely forgot about living society, about man with his manifold, complicated, individual and social relations, at the crux of which are ethical and moral problems, or rather, the rules and principles that have been or are to be evolved. The cultural revolution that began in science, art, literature, teaching, etc., also bypassed the serious ethical and moral problems of society, and this undoubtedly contributed to the intensification of the moral and ethical crisis in social and Party life. However, the roots of the trouble are much deeper than this. Ethics and morals, which are a vital and integral part of the social structure, are a reflection of the substructure, so that in discussing the moral crisis of social life now, we must seek and find its cause in the social economy, in the system of material production. The moral crisis indicates that we got off on the wrong road in laying the basis of the social economy and the social system. The political and economic crisis that occurred in the spring of 1953 showed plainly where we had gotten off the road. The first task of the policy of the New Course was to steer the country out of the economic and political crisis, to place the building of socialism on a new basis, and to lead the country toward socialism along new roads and through new methods. The sudden shift and the profound changes initiated by the New Course saved the country from the more serious consequences of political and economic shock, tremors of which were felt at Csepel, Ozd, and Diosgyor at the time of the June, 1953, events in Berlin, Pilsen, and Prague. The New Course gave new meaning to socialism and helped to develop the unity of the economic foundation and structure of society on a new basis and to establish harmony between the economic system of socialism and its moral and ethical laws. In other words, it laid a firm moral basis for socialist society. Today it is easy to see that the ethical and moral aspects of the New Course were of no less significance than its political and economic aspects. There is not better proof of the political significance of the New Course, of the fact that it expressed the will of the masses and that it truly represented the newly born society together with its economic basis and structure, than the fact that within a brief year and a half it generated moral forces of such tremendous power that they are operative even today, and constitute positive proof that the ever deepening crisis will be resolved despite all setbacks. The March, 1955, resolution of the Central Committee that initiated the liquidation of the New Course, and the subsequent resolutions that completed this work and had such serious effects on the fate of the country, broke the harmony that had developed between the basis and the structure of society and brought the building of socialism to the brink of crisis in the fields of economy, politics, and culture alike. This inevitably led to an ethical and moral crisis in Party and social life as well. Because of the directive role of the Party in our society, it follows that the entire blame for this situation devolves solely upon the Party leadership. It devolves upon the leadership because this leadership, by ignoring the ethical and moral norms of socialism and by its erroneous and incorrectly implemented policy, is undermining ever more seriously the moral foundations of socialism and those rules and principles without which no modern human society can exist, much less a socialist society, which needs them to thrive and become stable. The leadership is undermining the rules and principles that form the basis both of peaceful coexistence and of economic and cultural competition between differing social systems. This is what has led to the ethical and moral crisis which is assuming ever more critical proportions in the life of society and the Party and which, combined with the preceding political and economic crisis, is shaking the Party and society to its foundation.

What are the symptoms of the current ethical and moral crisis in society and Party life? This question merits close attention and profound study, so that the serious omissions in this field can be remedied. At present, for the purpose of reviewing the matter, I must limit myself to listing rather than analyzing these symptoms; to deal with them on a theoretical and practical basis requires much more preparation, and there are others better qualified to do it than I.

The lofty ideals and principles of socialism, which have great appeal to a large sector of the people in our country, are increasingly losing their true significance in the public consciousness due to the people's experiences in their everyday life, their social life, and their working conditions since the liquidation of the June policy. The violent contrast between words and deeds, between principles and their realization, is rocking the foundations of our people's democracy, our society, and our Party. This contrast, of which the people are becoming more and more aware, is leading to dissension and to loss of faith among the masses, who hope for a better, happier, and more peaceful life, and for the realization of the truly high ideals of socialism. The working people are unable to reconcile the rapid progress of socialism with the deterioration, or at least stagnation, of their standard of living. The people cannot understand how it is that, the greater the results they achieve in the economic, political, social, or cultural field, the greater their burdens become. They feel more and more that the immeasurable sacrifices they have made in working harder or accepting a lower standard of living are not commensurate to the results achieved. They are beginning to doubt ever more seriously whether this road, which consumes all their work and most of their material and spiritual wealth without bringing them any closer to the fulfillment of their hopes through the attainment of socialist ideals, is indeed the true road to socialism. These doubts are entertained not only by the petty bourgeoisie or by vacillating intellectuals, but by the working masses, and this means an increasing renunciation of socialism. Not only the non-Party, untrained working masses are involved. Party members, even Party old-timers, are frequently voicing their misgivings about the faulty policies of the leadership and the impermissible, antisocialist methods and devices that have been used to implement these policies. And their answers are ever more frequently and emphatically a denial of present methods. This doubt, this loss of faith in the ideal, this compromising of socialism through the mistaken policy of the Party leadership, is a consequence of the stupid and harmful political recklessness that was a result of the March resolution. The paths, methods, devices, and forms of socialism that the Party leadership is attempting to force upon the members, and to present with their help as a desirable goal to the workers and the government, are receiving less and less support from the masses. This is because these paths to socialism and these methods ignore man, the greatest asset, with his many desires and needs, all of which demand a standard of living higher than was attainable under the preceding capitalist system. The Hungarian people reject the old system and its masters, and they will crush all attempts to bring it back, no matter in what form. The Hungarian working people, who made many sacrifices in the struggle against the old system and for the establishment of the new socialist system, do not desire to risk or bargain away the fruits of their victory, but want to increase them. They want to follow that path to socialism which is better, easier, more tolerable and humane, and more in keeping with Hungarian conditions, circumstances, potentialities, and traditions: they desire to follow the path of development set forth by the June resolution and the policy of the New Course, rather than that catastrophic policy which has already bankrupted the country once, compromised the ideals of socialism, and proved that its goals and tasks were untenable. Fear of a repetition of this is giving rise to serious doubts among Party members and the working masses. Furthermore, the danger of a repetition has been growing and becoming ever more pronounced since the March resolution and the subsequent Party resolutions. The policy of insistence on the March "principles" has become a tension-creating, undermining force which is as destructive to our economic and political life, to the basis of our society, and to our official morals and policies as the political goals, the humanism, the superior moral and ethical purity of June and of the New Course were creative. In their blindness, the leaders fail to consider public opinion; they do not realize what a powerful political and moral factor it has become; and they either do not see or prefer to ignore the fact that the public opinion of the nation is increasingly condemning and turning against the activities of the Party and the government. Let them realize at last the consequences of making an empty phrase of the slogan: "With the people, for the people, through thick and thin." In the interests of the people, the country, and socialism, let them depend not on bayonets but on the people.

The danger of the Party leadership's policy, which serves personal dictatorship, lies in the fact that it attempts to frighten Party members and the masses away from the June policy by predicting that the June policy will result in a return of the old system. But by condemning the policy of the Party leadership and the goals for the March resolution, by rejecting that road to socialism which already came to a dead end once, the majority of Party members and workers are not trying to return to capitalism; they are trying to return to the other road to socialism, the June way. The danger inherent in the Rákosi type of policy is that by opposing the policy of the New Course it deprives the Party members and the workers of the prospect of socialism. By its stupid and dishonest way of branding the popular policy of the New Course harmful or calling it an attempt to return to the old system, the present Party leadership is actually benefiting the old system. Anyone who claims that the New Course is a degenerate form of capitalism, and that the present policy of the Party leadership is the only road to socialism, is actually making capitalism seem desirable in the eyes of the masses. This stupid policy, which reckons without the opinion of the Party members or the workers, and which cannot tolerate any criticism of the policy of the Party leadership in word or deed, is actually driving the masses to accept enemy propaganda. For no good reason, the Party leadership prefers to alienate the people rather than give up its already bankrupt political concepts. No enemy propaganda, no Christmas or other "message," will destroy more completely the people's faith in socialism and in a better, happier, and more human future than a forced return to the old, mistaken, antipopular pre-June policy. It is undoubtedly this accursed blind policy that is strengthening the forces of reaction and counterrevolution, and increasing the danger of capitalism. The Party membership and the Hungarian people, those powerful supporters of the New Course and the June policy, do not want a return to capitalism. They want a people's democratic system in which the ideals of socialism become reality, in which the ideals of the working class regain their true meaning, in which public life is based on higher morals and ethics; they want a system that is actually ruled not by a degenerate Bonapartist authority and dictator but by the working people through legality and self-created law and order. They want a People's Democracy where the working people are masters of the country and of their own fate, where human beings are respected, and where social and political life is conducted in the spirit of humanism.

Today, probably a return to the policy of the New Course and the application of the June principles to the economic, political, and social life of the nation could still check the growing crisis and avert catastrophe. But it is doubtful whether a return to the June principles would suffice as a solution tomorrow. Today, the effects of the June policy are still strong; there is still great confidence in it, and the people and the Party members would joyfully welcome it, with its members and a Communist Party rejuvenated through the June principles. However, if this does not happen soon, there is a danger that the masses, having lost their faith, will reject both the June way and the Communist Party, and it will become necessary to make a much greater retreat in order to keep the situation under control. The senselessness and political blindness of the Rákosi type of Party and government leadership makes it less and less certain where we will be able to stop. The currently mistaken policy and inhumane tactics of the Party leadership have aroused doubts and uncertainty in practically all sectors of society. Anyone who goes through the country with open eyes and ears can see and hear how political hooliganism is driving the people to despair and how the workers are falling prey to dissension.

The degeneration of power is seriously endangering the fate of socialism and the democratic basis of our social system. Power is increasingly being torn away from the people and turned sharply against them. The People's Democracy as a type of dictatorship of the proletariat, in which the power is exercised by the working class and depends on the partnership of the two large working groups—the workers and the peasantry—is obviously being replaced by a Party dictatorship which does not rely on Party membership, but relies on a personal dictatorship and attempts to make the Party apparatus, and through it the Party membership, a mere tool of this dictatorship. Its power is not permeated by the spirit of socialism or democratism but by a Bonapartist spirit of minority dictatorship. Its aims are not determined by Marxism, the teachings of scientific socialism, but by autocratic views that are maintained at any cost and by any means.

The degeneration of power—the appearance of Bonapartism—is not new in Hungary. It dates back to those times when the clique headed by Rákosi, which came into power in the Party on the basis of charges that have since been proved false and through intrigues and crimes, together with reactionary forces, crushed the basis of Hungary's young democracy and liquidated our people's democratic forces and the democratic partnerships of socialism, thus isolating the working class, the principal power of socialism. It was then that power began to slip away from the people. The isolation of power and its use against its own supporters led to the dissolution of that pillar of strength, the worker-peasant alliance. Political guidance, the persuasion and winning of the masses, was increasingly replaced by the use of force and the devices of power, all of which raised the AVH * above society and Party and made it the principal organ of power. National unity, the People's Front, the policies of the worker-peasant alliance, and democratic principles, all of which symbolize progress and the development toward socialism in state and Party life, diminished progressively, and the organs of force became the masters of social, economic, political, and

* The Secret Police.

cultural life. In the monopolistic realm of power, the leadership clique no longer felt the need of winning the trust and support of the working masses through a Party and government policy truly representative of national and popular interests, or of ensuring popular support for itself through its everyday tasks. This policy was already not that of a People's Democracy, but the road to Bonapartism. The degeneration of power and the rise of Bonapartism could not have occurred without the degeneration of Party life, which means that the leadership clique at the head of the Party became a personal dictatorship. Rákosi made himself independent of the will and opinion of the Party membership and of the decisions of the Party. He subjugated the Party to his will, and by dictatorial methods—primarily with the aid of the AVH, which became predominant in the Party—forced it to execute his wishes.

Bonapartism, individual dictatorship, and the employment of force did not become predominant in state and Party life automatically. In this field, serious responsibility rests on the policy of Stalin, which gave far-reaching aid to the liquidation of anti-Bonapartist forces within and outside the Party. Without this aid, depending merely on his own power and influence, Rákosi would have been unable to achieve individual dictatorship. To bring about the triumph of Bonapartism, the allies of socialist democracy had to be destroyed. To bring about individual dictatorship, the Party's leading cadres had to be exterminated and the AVH had to be made the supreme power so that it could carry out assigned tasks. This is all historical fact. Such degeneration of power and of Party life inevitably sweeps the nation and Party toward catastrophe. The June resolution of the Central Committee and the policy of the New Course were required in state and Party life alike to avert this danger. In the life of the state, their principal task was the elimination of Bonapartism, the consolidation of the power of the working class, the assurance of its leadership role, and the revival of local councils and the People's Front through the development of a worker-peasant alliance. Validity had to be obtained for the rights and responsibilities of citizens and men as established in the Constitution; shaken law and order had to be consolidated; legality had to be restored; the role of the state had to be clari-

fied; and the relationship of the state and Party had to be put
on a new basis. In the interest of putting an end to personal
dictatorship and the elimination of Fuhrerism, the following
tasks had to be undertaken: the development of collective leadership in the Party; the development of criticism and self-criticism for assuring democracy within the Party; the restoration
of the Party membership's rights as assured by the organizational laws; and the restoration and further development of
the Party's prestige and its influence upon the masses. The series
of blows inflicted upon Bonapartism and personal dictatorship
after the resolution of June, 1953, are of immense significance
for our future development and for the fate of socialism. During the period of the New Course, powerful moral forces were
unleashed, which could not be suppressed by the March resolutions of the Party, by subsequent resolutions, or by terroristic
methods. However, these moral forces were unable to prevent
the return of Bonapartism and personal dictatorship in 1955.
After March, they were unable to prevent the degeneration of
power and Party life or those consequences that more seriously
are destroying the moral basis of our social and Party life today
than during the period prior to June, 1953; nevertheless they
show the way in which we averted a crisis once before. At the
same time we must recognize that the standard of social and
Party morals and ethics has sunk lower than ever before.

The predominance of Bonapartism, of the personal dictator,
and of the organs of force is not compatible with the constitutional legal system of the People's Democracy, with its legislature and government, with the democracy of our entire state
and social life. The two are in sharp contrast with one another.
A struggle between them is inevitable, because in our circumstances, with the destruction of Bonapartism and individual
dictatorship, the triumph of the People's Democracy and the
construction of socialist society can be assured on the basis of
constitutional law and order and legality that we ourselves establish. Bonapartism cannot comprise the state power and legal
system of the People's Democracy, and when Rákosi, in the
interest of individual dictatorship, took the road of Bonapartism, he plunged our socialist construction, achieved with
many great sacrifices, into an abyss. We must recognize as a fact

that Bonapartism has become predominant in our Constitution, in our legal system, and in the people's domain, as well as in the democratization of our state life. Thus the Constitution is no longer the basis of our legal system; legality as defined in the Constitution has lost its meaning; and the validity of the rights of men and citizens in everyday life is decreasing. The political, legal, moral, and all other concepts that made the Constitution the basic law of our social life are beginning to lose their original meaning and their compulsory legal force equally applicable to everyone. Thus, in crude violation of the legality of communal life, the law, its interpretation, and its implementation are being determined ever more frequently by the power interests of the Bonapartist dictatorship and by the momentary requirements of the personal dictatorship, rather than by the interests of society. This Machiavellianism, which is in conflict not only with socialism but with all the moral principles of progressive mankind, is gaining more and more ground in our government and in our social and Party life. Thus it can happen that although we have a constitution, a legal system, and laws that should ensure our socialist development, these things become mere devices for personal dictatorship over most of the people in the hands of the Bonapartist power.

The belief in socialist legality and in legality itself has been shaken. The abuse of power and the use of illegal devices reached alarming proportions in 1955 and exceeded even the malpractices of the period from 1950 to 1952. The situation has degenerated to such an extent that most of the workers have come to believe that they are at the mercy of illegalities and abuses, and that there are no laws that protect their rights as human beings and citizens. A striking and potentially dangerous consequence of the degeneration of power and the alienation of the people is the spread of the theory that a People's Democracy is synonymous with anarchy; that such a democracy leaves plenty of room for illegalities; that in such a democracy the life of the individual is characterized by constant insecurity and fear. The June, 1953, resolution of the Central Committee classified the violation of legality that it exposed as serious and dangerous, but the situation had not degenerated then to the extent that it has today.

The government and the Party leadership ignore completely the traditional or instinctive sense of justice of the masses, which developed in harmony with social morals. The legislature is insensitive in this regard also, while the enforcement of the laws and the execution of justice violate it crudely in every way. The administration of justice, which as a consequence of the degeneration of power cannot carry out the principle of socialist legality amid the conditions of Bonapartist dictatorship, is being crushed between the people and the rule; it is increasingly moving away from its moral and ethical moorings in the People's Democratic system, and from the people's sense of justice and feeling for Socialist legality; whereas, in the triumph of Socialism, as in all progressive social concepts, justice must play an exceptionally significant role, which together with the struggle of the working masses and everyday constructive work turns into a powerful material force indispensable to the establishment of socialist society. The judiciary must serve this social justice—this socialist social justice in our case—and the legal system of the People's Democracy. However, the Bonapartist dictatorship, which is separated from the working class and masses, is utilizing the administration of justice to serve its own assaults against the people. The degeneration of power and the moral crisis of social life are also evidenced by the fact that at present the number of persons imprisoned is greater than ever before; the number of those sentenced exceeds those imprisoned to such an extent that many thousands cannot begin to serve their sentence because of a lack of "space." But the most alarming fact is that the majority of those convicted have come from the ranks of the working class, the industrial workers. This, more than anything else, is evidence of the degeneration of power and economic and social conditions under which the working class is carrying on its task of socialist construction, and of the moral and ethical crisis that was brought about by these conditions.

Public morality is an indispensable requirement of socialist society. Its conditions include those upon which economic and political relations depend, and those moral and ethical principles that become valid in society. The morality or ethical conception of the public affects the formation of economic, political, and moral conditions. We can actually see their mutual effects here. The deterioration of the economic situation, the degeneration of power, the slackening of morals in social life, and the operations and structure of economic and political organs have become a source of grave problems as far as public morality is concerned. As a result of the degeneration of power, individuals whose actions went counter to the morals of socialist society and to existing laws acquired positions in important fields of public life. It is not compatible with public morality to have in positions of leadership the directors and organizers of mass lawsuits, or those responsible for the torturing and killing of innocent people, or organizers of international provocations, or economic saboteurs, or squanderers of public property who, through the abuse of power, either have committed serious crimes against the people or are forcing others to commit these crimes. The public, the Party, and the state organs must be cleansed of these elements.

There is a type of material dependence that forces men to relinquish their individualities and their convictions, which is not compatible with morality in public life. Unfortunately, this has assumed mass proportions here and must be considered virtually a disease of our society. Excessive centralization of the economic and political structure is the inevitable concomitant of personal dictatorship. What sort of political morality is there in a public life where contrary opinions are not only suppressed but punished with actual deprivation of livelihood; where those who express contrary opinions are expelled from society with shameful disregard for the human and civil rights set down in the Constitution; where those who are opposed in principle to the ruling political trend are barred from their professions —the journalist from his work in the area of the press, the author from his literary activities; and where a man is not only dismissed from his political office but from membership in the Hungarian Academy of Sciences and from his university teaching position as well; and indeed where all those activities whereby he might guarantee his livelihood are made impossible for him? What is this if not a shameful degeneration of political morality? Can one speak, in such a case, of a Constitution, of law and order, of legality; can one speak of the morality of public life when the "battle of opinions" is waged with such depraved tools, when they lie about freedom and at the same time deprive the brave representatives of freedom of the bare necessities of life? This is not socialist morality. Rather it is modern Machiavellianism.

This all-powerful material dependence, this anxiety for bread, is killing the most noble human virtues, virtues that should most especially be developed in a socialist society: courage, resolution, sincerity and frankness, consistency of principle, and strength. In their place, the leaders have made virtues of self-abasement, cowardice, hypocrisy, lack of principle, and lies. The degeneration and corruption of public life and the deterioration of character that takes place in society as a result thereof are among the most serious manifestations of the moral-ethical crisis that is taking place before our eyes. We must also see, however, that the deterioration of public life and of character has repercussions in every area of our social life, and that it hastens the decay brought on by the ever intensifying economic and political crisis. Falsehood and careerism are spreading dangerously in our public life and are deeply affecting human morality and honor; distrust is gaining ground; and an atmosphere of suspicion and revenge is banishing the fundamental feature of socialist morality, humanism; in its stead, cold inhumanity is appearing in public life. It is a shocking picture that the moral situation of our social life reveals.

The picture is no better in the Party or with regard to Communist morality. The weakness of Party morals is apparent from the trials, the rehabilitations, that have taken place, which reveal the degeneration of Party morality. The organs of the Party leadership have pronounced judgments that condemn not the criminals but their victims. Whatever has become of Communist morality, human respect, and honor, if there are Communist leaders according to whom the unjustly executed Comrade Laszlo Rajk was a coward because he admitted to false charges in order to deceive the Party leaders, leaders who act as if it were not they themselves who contrived the mendacious charges and the means for getting the confession? They who are thus making repeated accusations have not the courage and sense of responsibility to say openly, in connection with the baseless charges against Rajk, that our comrade Laszlo Rajk died a Communist martyr's death and did not "slip away from" execution before the Communist court of the People's Democracy; he "slipped away" from execution before the Arrow Cross blood court, not as a reward for his treason, as Mátyás Rákosi asserted with shocking cynicism in his speech before the Central Committee, but because, at the time, illegal Communists approached Laszlo Rajk's brother, an Arrow Cross state secretary, and asked him to intercede on behalf of his Communist younger brother. Therefore they know very well that it was not the intercession of the police or of the Arrow Cross Party that saved Laszlo Rajk's life, but the intercession of his brother. Rajk's brother condemned his Communist principles, views, and activities, and kept clearly aloof from them, but, as Rajk's brother, he undertook to save his life. Why do not those who still seek to besmirch Rajk's reputation by suppressing such facts and by charging Rajk with cowardice dare to make this public? Why do they outrage the memory of the deceased Rajk, and why do they protect and conceal the real criminals who are well known by name, i.e., the members of the clique, the so-called "foursome," Rákosi, Farkas, Gerö, and Róvari? Is this considered compatible with Communist morality, with human honor and dignity? They do it in the interest of Party unity—as they keep saying—but they forget that the Party is not a den of criminals, whose unity must be preserved by hiding their crimes. What kind of unity is it that is held together by knowledge of and participation in crime? Their answer is that "we do not moralize," and that this is a political question and not a moral one. They do not perceive that they have thereby condemned their policies and have admitted the loss of all moral ground.

This sort of view, and all views denying moral principles, views that seek to identify the Party with the clique of criminals, and Party interests with the interests of the clique, while ostensibly seeking to guard Party unity, actually protect the true criminals from exposure. Rather, real Party unity can be established only through the exposure of crimes. Without this, Communist morality will not prevail; without this, the Party will not escape from moral crisis; without this, there is and can be no talk about theoretical-political and moral unity. Why do they seek to clear the criminals at any cost, when these have admitted their own crimes, even boasted of them, before the country and the world? Neither suppression, glossing over, nor lies can undo the commission of the crimes. The question must be asked: On what sort of Communist morality do they base my expulsion from the Party ranks because of my theoretical differences with the policies of the Party leadership, while at the same time the accomplices in the mass executions of our comrades hold high offices in the Party? What kind of Communist morality is it in the name of which they now denounce Laszlo Rajk because, according to them, he confessed to the false charges raised against him because he was too cowardly to reject them, when in the name of this same Communist morality, the Central Committee condemned and expelled me from the Party because I was unwilling to assume responsibility for the false charges raised against me? What sort of political morality prevails in the leadership of the Party, where the truth is measured and Communist behavior assessed in such a manner? The foregoing, however, are only flagrant examples, only certain crude cases, of the deterioration of Communist morality. Much more perilous are the similar, all-too-prevalent occurrences that are spreading among Party officials and throughout Party ranks. As the dictatorship of the proletariat, because of the degeneration of its power into Bonapartism and personal dictatorship, is gradually losing its broad democratism, and raw power and reprisal are used more and more not only against hostile, reactionary, antipopular forces but also against the broad masses of the working people, similarly the Bonapartist spirit, personal dictatorship, regimentation, and slavish subordination are supplanting Party democracy, democratic centralism, and Leninist theories of Party life. In this atmosphere and confronted with such methods and means, Party life, debate, the exchange of ideas, and the cleansing of ideological deviations through the free battle of opinions, without which unity of principle in the Party cannot be created, are dying out. Among Party members, it kills initiative, spontaneous activity, and enthusiasm, which are being replaced by apathy and unconcern. The rapid spread of Bonapartism, of personal dictatorship, is destroying Leninist Party life. The liquidation of Party democracy and the introduction of dictatorship inevitably are accompanied by the dictatorial methods and techniques that have prevailed in the Party for the past six months. Intimidation and terror, insinuation and baseless charges, and the denunciation and branding of others as enemies have become mass method. They are the crux of the moral crisis in Party life.

But the most reprehensible procedure, and the one most destructive of Communist morality and character, is to exploit the existing material dependence of Party functionaries and members in order to influence their political views and personal behavior. There are those who, corrupted by their favorable material status and abandoning principled moral conduct, will do anything as servants of degenerate Bonapartist power and personal dictatorship. Many Party functionaries and members, however, with their Communist sense of honor and integrity violated through material dependence and their human dignity humiliated, are being compelled to deny their principles and political beliefs, to abandon their convictions, and to engage in falsehood and hypocrisy. These persons perceive and recognize the ignoble means, the untruth, the unprincipled un-Partylike procedure, and the prevalence of intimidation, revenge, and reprisal. Their Communist sense of honor rebels against and condemns such things, but the grave consequences of taking a courageous stand, of candidly expressing an opinion, and of adhering to principle, such as political ostracism, material losses and unemployment, all too frequently restrain them. Thus and therefore, one of the gravest manifestations of the deterioration of Communist morality—the conflict between Communists and Party morality, Party life, political methods, and themselves— has become a reality among Party members and officials alike. They are ashamed of their behavior which they know is incompatible with Communist morality; they are ashamed of mendacity, of two-timing; they are ashamed of their lack of principle and of their cowardice; they are ashamed that, despite their better convictions, they have become—through material dependency—blind, docile tools and have moved from their political opposition into passivity and indifference. Thus, servility, the serious malady of our social and Party life, is developing and spreading dangerously. The twins, Bonapartism—personal dictatorship—and servility go well together, but have no place in our society or in the Communist Party. The noxious weeds of servility must be pulled from the life of Hungarian society and the Communist Party, and from every walk of public life.

Another characteristic symptom of the deterioration of morality in public life, a symptom that has become actually epidemic in social and Party life, is careerism, the pushing and elbowing for favors, even alms, from above. If this were simply a remnant from the past, it would be easier to exterminate. Unfortunately, this is not simply a question of remnants from the past, but derives from the stifling of criticism, the intimidation, and the retaliation against candid speech that are in evidence now in the leadership and that unavoidably lead to the spread of opportunism. The careerists are sycophants, bootlickers; they have no principles or opinions of their own and will say without any compunction that black is white. In every case, they seek the favor of those who are in a position to assure them a better place in Party or state affairs, greater prestige, more income, broader authority, and, last but not least, a limousine. They go to any length to gain the favor of the leaders; they grovel and bow and scrape before them; they flatter them. The deterioration of morality in public life pleases the careerists, whom, unfortunately, we may encounter on all sides. The number of them tends to increase because, instead of denouncing them, the leaders tolerate and quite frequently even pamper them, since their kowtowing flatters the vanity of the leaders, as they will do anything or carry out any orders for them without reservation.

Opportunism is not an individual character deficiency but first and foremost a social symptom, which is found where an individual's position in society is determined not by his performance or ability but by those traits with which we have characterized the opportunist above. And if they seize a broad sphere of activity in our social and Party life and gain the chance to assert themselves over the tested, staunch, resolute, and steady Communists, if the opportunists become the spokesmen in public life, it shows to what depths political morality has sunk because of the wrongdoing of the Party leaders. It will, at the same time, give warning to take up the struggle against the opportunists on a broad front for the cleansing of the Party and the purification of Communist honor—a struggle in which the very roots of opportunism must be destroyed. A necessary condition to the success of the struggle is not only the moral but the political regeneration of the Party. This difficult struggle, undoubtedly involving sacrifices, must be fought by those individuals who, supported by solid foundations of social- ist morality and ethics, have the stability of principle, courage, and resoluteness to represent principles, the highest morality of the social order and of the Party, and who can undertake the struggle with all its sacrifices for not only the theoretical but also the moral purification of the Party. There are still such Communists; these are the majority of the Communists—mem- bers and officials—and their prize is the theoretical, political, and moral regeneration of the Party, a pledge that still should bring about a victory of socialist moral principles in society and in public life. In this struggle, the Communists who represent socialist morality without faltering must disassociate themselves clearly from the ever spreading deterioration that is now per- ceivable in the sphere of Party morality. These Communists must undertake the struggle to restore the reputation of the Party and of Communists, to reacquire, guard, and increase the faith and confidence of the people, and to represent fittingly that moral power and grandeur that the Hungarian people regard with appreciation and hold as an example to be followed, and that sooner or later will triumph over the moral decay pre- vailing in Party and public life. The real significance of this struggle is the benefit it will have for future generations, the new growing generation, which is the trustee of the future of our country, and which will continue and attain the construc- tion of the great works initiated by socialist society. Our present struggle is, therefore, of incalculable importance, because our successors, the generations following in our footsteps, can re- spond to their historic mission, the attainment of our national ideals, only if we leave them, as a heritage in human conduct and in public life, a higher order, a purer socialist morality, and an ethical outlook. This is the tremendous moral duty of the generation that is here today but will be gone tomorrow, principally of the Communists. We must avoid moral quagmires and fight steadfastly for the assertion of socialist moral principles in our social and Party life; we must represent courageously the virtues that our people have entrusted to us; and, last but not least, we must struggle, regardless of the difficult situation, to see that the future of the People's Democracy is in safe hands.

We have two ways in which to extricate ourselves from the disastrous situation brought upon the country by the Rákosi regime: we can either liquidate Stalinist policy ourselves in good time and lead the country back to the June road, by which we shall be able to avoid economic and political failure; or we can refrain from changing the course of events with the result that the increasing tension may bring the country to the verge of a grave crisis. In either case, the Hungarian Communists must become masters of the situation. In order to achieve this they have to make a definite break with Rákosi's disastrous policy and fight courageously for the June goals with the help of the masses of the people, to thwart the realization of the ambitions of the reaction. The Communists' most effective weapon against reactionary, counter-revolutionary attempts for the restoration of the old system is to inaugurate the June policy while the working masses still trust the Communists and the Party, and before this trust is irreparably undermined by the present regime through its campaign against the Hungarian people conducted with inhumane and lawless means.

"Clique leadership," and later the spirit of personal dictatorship, created a serious situation in other respects also. It destroyed those virtues that had gained popular respect for both the Party and the Communists and had increased their influence, and it destroyed the confidence that had given the people hope of attaining their goals. The virtues that little by little are dying out in Party life and in Communist conduct must be revived and developed. Such virtues include love and respect for the Hungarian people, close relations and unity with the people, loyalty to the people, and a true service to their interests. This is the moral dictate for the Party and for every Communist; this is the moral foundation on which all of their activities must be built. We must fight for the assertion of humanism, the principles of humanity in Communist activity, and we must renounce at every turn, and take energetic measures against, antisocial efforts, inhuman methods and means, and the anti-democratic spirit that is becoming more dangerously dominant in our state and Party life. Such a virtue is true patriotism; love of country, the noble ideal of loyal and unselfish service to the "homeland before all else," which inspires increased respect and popularity for the Communists in the broadest strata of the people. Without lessening the ideological-political struggle against excessive nationalism—chauvinism—and by fully using all ideological weapons against it wherever it crops up, we must nurture, in the spirit of proletarian internationalism and with the esteem of other nations, the virtue of love of country, which leaders alien to the Hungarian people are now seeking to defile and to identify with the vulgar instinct of chauvinism. They are so removed from the temperament of the people and the people's sense of Hungarianism, that they are perhaps unaware of how seriously they have wounded the national consciousness.

The Hungarian people are not chauvinistic, nor are they cosmopolites; they don't want to become so, and they will not. The stupid policy, alien to the people, which is simply national nihilism—i.e., a rejection of the virtues of patriotism and national sentiment—by its very nature stirs up this danger of chauvinism. Socialism should not deprive the people of their national character nor of their national sentiments and qualities; on the contrary, it is with these that people enrich the universal moral-ethical values of socialism. The unbreakable adherence of the Hungarian people to national ideals, to the concept of loyalty, freedom, and independence that has been the source of their strength in molding their history throughout the centuries, is not a nationalism to be condemned. Rather, it encompasses the most noble traits of the Hungarian people and the national virtues that must materialize in Communism if the Hungarian people want to be leaders. Whoever the men may be whom the Hungarian people are willing to follow on the rough road into future history, they must take cognizance of national self-consciousness and the feeling of national pride, to which small nations like ours are perhaps more sensitive than great nations. Both the past and the present of the gifted, industrious Hungarian people prove that they are capable of won-

derful contributions and achievements in the fields of science,
engineering, art, literature, music, and sport. Nor is their ability and strength to establish and maintain a state any less
developed. In every period of history, Hungary has produced
her geniuses, great statesmen, and military leaders, who have
guided the nation to the threshold of socialism through stormy
centuries of social change and development. Nor has the nation
now become immature or developed a need for tutelage; it is
still able to stand on its own feet, and it is still able fittingly to
represent and to advance the cause of national freedom and independence, together with the cause of socialism and human
progress, within the great family of peace-loving peoples. This,
however, can be attained only by leaders who spring from the
people and are of the people, and fight for them, working in
conjunction with the people. The base policy of our present
leaders seeks to progress toward socialism by way of denational-
ization, a policy that more and more supports the internal
enemy and pours oil on the glowing fires of chauvinism, because
the Hungarian people, like all other people, will accept socialism only if they do not have to sacrifice their national sentiments, consciences, and traits, which they seek to nurture within
the structure of a socialist society.

Other grave consequences of national nihilism exist in the
life of our society and Party, and it would be incorrect simply
to classify these consequences as only an injurious heritage from
the past. The problems are quite serious, or "touchy" as is
usually said. Therefore their only possible solution is to face
them courageously and to start liquidating them with vigor.
The weapons of anti-Semitism, anti-Sovietism, and chauvinism
must be struck from the hands of the enemies of the people
and of socialism, because such weapons destroy the moral foundations of our society, increase our difficulties, retard socialist
construction, and block our peaceful, fraternal coexistence with
other peoples. National nihilism is not, however, the way to
solve these problems; rather the solution lies in the political
and moral regeneration of state leadership, combined inevitably
with a changing of the guard.

Whoever observes the way the situation is shaping up with
open eyes, whoever approaches the problems taken up with

honorable intentions, cannot doubt but that a devoted and deep love for the people, the country, the Party and socialism, and an anxiety about the future, inspire these candid words and cause these thoughts to be put on paper. They are serious words, but true. However, the saying "Actions speak louder than words" applies here; therefore, the words await deeds.

(December, 1955.)

Chapter 5. Significance of the June, 1953, Party Resolution and Its Effect on Our Party

The key to the full realization of the historic significance of the Central Committee's June resolution may be found in the recognition of the extremely dangerous situation that had arisen in June.

The shocking situation was described by the key members of the Soviet Communist Party, who declared that the mistakes and crimes of the four-member Party leadership in Hungary, headed by Rákosi, had driven the country to the verge of a catastrophe, shaking the People's Democratic system to its foundations and that, unless prompt and effective measures had been taken to bring about a change, the people would have turned against them and, to quote Khrushchev, "we would have been booted out summarily." The chief purpose of the Central Committee's June resolution was to stave off the catastrophe and to counterbalance the effect of the disturbances in East Germany and Czechoslovakia, to ease the growing tension manifested in frequent mass demonstrations in the Great Plains, and in general to bring about a turn of the tide.

The resolution clearly revealed the seriousness of the situation and gave indications of the approaching catastrophe, the roots of which had sprung from gross violations of the laws and scientific principles of building Socialism and from an irresponsible economic policy. The significance of the Central Committee resolution lay in the fact that, simultaneously with a prompt

66

intervention and a sharp turnabout, a re-evaluation of the ideological basis of the transition period from capitalism to socialism took place in the spirit of scientific socialist teachings.

The basic difficulties in judging and evaluating the resolution arose from an incorrect appraisal of the economic and political situation of the preresolution period. Up to that point no systematic efforts had been made to expose the material damage, unprecedented in Hungary's history, which the irresponsible pre–1953 policy had caused, having swallowed up nearly 120 billion forints. The extent of the damage had to be determined in order to make possible an evaluation of the shortcomings and capacities of our people's economy; consider deficiencies in future planning, particularly in setting realistic goals for the Second Five-Year Plan; and last but not least, define the responsibility of the Party and government. In June, 1953, Rákosi and others did not concur with this evaluation of the situation; they considered it too pessimistic, claiming that the mistakes and difficulties were exaggerated, attributing this to lack of information and, after the Beria affair was made public, to the hostile activities of Beria. Obviously those who do not agree with the evaluation of the situation cannot accept the conclusions reached, nor the new objectives. From the very beginning, Rákosi's attitude toward the Central Committee's June resolution was characterized by duplicity and opportunism. From the beginning he had two irons in the fire. While he spoke *for* the resolution, he did everything to soft-pedal the measures aimed at the correction of mistakes. Rákosi's relation to the policy adopted in June, 1953, and his true attitude to matters of state and Party leadership became completely clear in connection with the March and April, 1955, resolutions.

From the beginning a distorted, arbitrary, Marxist interpretation of the June resolution was apparent in the Party leadership and within the Party apparatus, with Mátyás Rákosi the chief advocate. A mere two weeks after the June meeting of the Central Committee, on July 11, 1953, at a Budapest Party activists' meeting, Rákosi made the first open move to give a false interpretation to the June Party resolution, attempting to lessen the significance of the change, and trying to return to the old line. His speech was a call to opposition, and despite the slogans, like self-criticism etc., it was a clear indication that the Party apparatus was not standing behind the government program. The subsequent attitude of the Party proved that the hint was understood and acted upon.

Later statements by Rákosi gave further proof of his policy of duplicity and of the fact that the Party's policy was not identical with the policy of the government. By this attitude Rákosi and the extreme "leftists" converging around him hoped to achieve a double purpose: to maintain the political line and methods of the period preceding the June events, that would pave the way for a backswing at an opportune moment, and to drive a wedge between the Party and the government. The events that took place in the twentieth month of the June policy prove this.

By now it is a recognized fact that Rákosi, First Secretary of the Party, induced the Party, and primarily the Party apparatus, to assume a passive attitude toward the execution of the June resolution and the realization of the government program. In an attempt to turn the tables on me, he tried in the March resolution to create the impression that the government had sought to push the Party into the background. In reality the Party, by following the Rákosi-inspired passive attitude, have been pushed into the background, or rather had elected to assume such a stand, throwing extreme obstacles in the way of the June resolution and the government program.

One of the most frequently made yet completely unfounded statements is that the government program deviated from the June resolution. This slanderous accusation emerged from the March resolution. The June resolution and the government program were judged as fully integrated by the Third Party Congress, despite Rákosi's efforts toward a re-evaluation of the June resolution during the preparations for the Congress, as well as by Central Committee meetings before and after the Party Congress, for the last time in October, 1954. Consequently there was no contradiction between the government program and the June resolution; the deviation was created only by the deliberate distortion of the June resolution. The claim that in the government program I abandoned the course delineated by the June resolution is completely false and unfounded. On the other hand a series of facts prove that Rákosi and the extreme "leftists" turned against the June resolution and against the government program, which latter embraced the very Marxist-Leninist principles set forth by the Central Committee in the historic June, 1953, resolutions as the basis for the building of socialism.

The fact that Mátyás Rákosi and members of the Politburo felt forced to go back on their previous attitude and views concerning the June resolution, both in the March resolution and in the course of its execution, proves beyond doubt that it was not I who turned against the Central Committee's June resolution, but they. There is irrefutable factual proof that the June resolution had been given an entirely new interpretation, contradicting its original trend and spirit. The new interpretation actually invalidated the June resolution and stripped it of its historic significance to such an extent that it no longer constitutes the political basis of Party and government activities.

The pseudoradical deviationists use yet another angle to do away with the June resolution. They claim, with increasing frequency, that the June resolution did not represent a turning point, still less a change in the trend toward building socialism. This is refuted by the June resolution itself and the subsequent Party resolution, which acknowledged the turn and the decisive significance of the change of direction. At one time (June 23, 1953) in the course of the preparation of the June resolution, even Ernö Gerö was forced to admit that it entailed a significant *change of direction*. At the October, 1953, meeting of the Central Committee, the Politburo affirmed the fact that the June resolution *fundamentally modified the Party line*. Now they use these assertions of the Party resolutions against me, classifying them as right-wing deviations. They claim that the June resolution was not a turning point or a change of line, but merely the correction of discrepancies that had arisen in the course of developments. Yet, the June resolution was much more. It embraced, in the transition period, the most important ideological aspects of socialist development, delineating its various ways, methods, and forms under specific Hungarian circumstances. It was the first step toward the application of Marxist-Leninist tenets to fit specific Hungarian conditions.

Consequently, he who claims that the June resolution meant no changing of the line, he who tries to narrow down its significance by interpreting it as a mere adjustment of the unbalanced economy, denies the necessity of applying one of the basic Leninist teachings about the specific courses of building socialism: he advocates automatic emulation and schematism, thereby turning against the scientific teachings of socialism and representing an anti-Marxist, anti-Party stand.

Looking at the March resolution and the measures that followed in its wake, the question arises whether there is an ideological basis that proves that the March resolution was founded on the June resolution; whether it merely carried it further, rounded it out, or modified it to fit the changed circumstances. The June resolution was a necessity, theoretically justified and aimed to consolidate state power, improving the relationship between the Party and the state as well as between the Party, the government, and the people; to further the labor-peasant partnership, national unity, democratization of social and political life, the new economic policy, the gradual evolution of the people's economy, objective laws, socialist legality, democracy and criticism within the Party, and collective leadership. In other words, it was designed to place, during the transition period, the whole ideological complex of socialist building on the basis of scientific socialist principles, under the specific Hungarian circumstances.

The June resolutions successfully launched the Party and its leadership on the road to correctly solving the problems of the transition period, and laid the foundation of unity in the face of its ideological and practical problems. If we look at the June resolution from this, the only correct, point of view, it becomes obvious that the March resolution and the measures that followed in its wake are not consistent with the basic principles of the June resolution. The March resolution and the measures adopted subsequently by the Central Committee do not expand or fundamentally modify the basic principles of the June resolutions. Indeed, they are discarded and replaced by pseudoradical, "left-wing" theories which are in direct contrast to Marxist-Leninist teachings and which, on the basis of practical achievements and Marxist analysis, are inconsistent with the ideological and practical aims of socialist building, and are consequently unsuitable for the realization of these aims.

In the course of explaining and analyzing the March and subsequent resolutions, several attempts have been made to find an accord between the June and Third Party Congress resolutions and the resolutions passed by the Party and the state during the period following the March resolution, on the subject of the scientific evaluation of the transition period. However, this is an unscientific approach and one bound to fail. Just as it is impossible to bridge the sharp contradiction between the two political lines based on the June and March resolution, it is impossible to find a common platform between the two resolutions without repudiation and unprincipled falsification of Marxist-Leninist teachings and principles.

That is why the political line of Party leadership has not had and cannot have a uniform basis. That is why no ideological unity in Party leadership can be achieved. That is why ideological confusion arose in matters concerning socialist building and the theoretical and practical solution of problems concerning the transition period. There are two courses that may lead to a solution. One is the unreserved, sincere adoption of the principles of the June resolution, with an attempt to realize these and to follow the course delineated by the Third Party Congress and the October meeting of the Central Committee. The October resolution was a big step toward the realization of the June resolution, and it corrected the mistakes that had arisen in the course of progress and, with the change of circumstances, modified some of the aims. The October resolution, passed in the spirit of constructive application of Marxist-Leninist tenets, giving full consideration to the specific Hungarian circumstances and expanding the basic principles of the June resolution, looked far into the future and set new goals and aims. This would have been the one, and indeed the only, course.

The other one is the course that was followed during the period preceding the June resolution, which once before had driven the country to the verge of catastrophe and which had been proved erroneous and wrong, leading to a dead end and embarrassing the Party and the cause of socialism.

With the passing of the March resolution the Party leaders sought to return to the old, erroneous policy on the basis of the principles of the June resolution. They were soon forced to admit an anachronism there. However, from this realization they did not draw the only correct conclusion, namely that they must return to the policy outlined in the June resolution. Instead, they sought to establish a theoretical justification for the adoption of the pre-June policy that could be pulled off "satisfactorily" only through the distortion and falsification of Marxist tenets. This attitude is amply proved by a whole series of "theoretical" analyses and actual events. Several economists wasted their efforts on this useless endeavor, and to the ever-lasting shame of the science of economics, their activities involved perfunctory approaches and falsification, leading again to dogmatism and schematism.

The country and the people cannot watch with indifference which one of the possible solutions is being adopted by the Party. Despite the many propagandistic references to the June Policy, the March and subsequent resolutions have driven the country into an extreme "leftist" direction, causing immeasurable political, economic, and social damage.

It is the basic and most urgent task for the Party to return to the long-range course of socialist building delineated by the June resolution, the Third Party Congress, and the October meeting of the Central Committee. For this purpose, through a prompt revision of the March and subsequent Central Committee resolutions, the present political and theoretical confusion and lack of principles must be overcome.

Most of the charges of right-wing deviation and distortion are made in connection with the June resolution. However, a closer scrutiny of what is termed right-wing deviation and distortion in objective of the June resolution is branded either deviation or distortion, implying that essentially the entire June line was a right-wing deviation and distortion. This attitude is expressed in several articles and studies. Instead of a fair criticism of the June policy, the line followed during the whole last twenty months is that it was a right-wing deviation and distortion.

This is one of the methods used to liquidate the June resolution and the policy based on it. The other method is to charge that the government program distorted the June resolution. Both methods serve the same purpose: to invalidate the June resolution. The only difference is that while the first method condemns all aspects of the June policy, the second method is directed only against the government program, objecting only to the methods used in the implementation of the June resolution, thereby making opposition to the June policy justified while simultaneously placing the blame for all the mistakes on me, in an attempt to disclaim the collective responsibility resulting from collective leadership.

These machinations, the falsifications and accusations, the deceiving and influencing of Party members, were greatly facilitated by the fact that despite the many references to the June resolution, the Party members were not familiar with the true contents of the resolution, which in its complete form was available only to a narrow circle of Party functionaries. The majority of the Party members never had the chance to read the complete text.

The "left-wing" opponent within the Party leadership made certain that the June resolution did not become widely known. Instead of the full text, the Party organizations received directives on the resolution, in which the essential ideological and political aspects had gotten lost, as well as passages dealing with the question of responsibility and the new objectives. Even these considerably watered-down "directives" reached the Party organization with a two-months' delay. No efforts were made for their implementation. In sharp contrast to this attitude, Mátyás Rákosi and the Party apparatus made certain that the March and April resolutions were received by the Party members twenty-four hours after they had been passed, and they were also made public through the press.

The principle that the Party must have no secrets before the people was completely overlooked in the case of the June resolution. Up to the very present its contents have remained a secret to the people and even to the Party membership. It is no coincidence that, of the many decisive resolutions of the Party, the June resolution is the least frequently quoted.

For a long time we referred to the June resolution as a historic document. On the other hand, from the minute of its conception, Rákosi, Gerö, Farkas, and others meant it to become a dead letter. It is the task of the Party leadership to make the June resolution known to the Party members, thereby consolidating the principal foundation of the building of socialism.

Chapter 6.   Role and Significance of the March and April Party Resolutions

Behind the March and April Central Committee resolutions we find the following compelling motives:

A. The Central Committee resolution of October, 1954, was a turning point in the further development and realization of the June resolution. A successful carrying out of the October resolution would have destroyed irrevocably the last chances for a return to the exaggerated pre–1953 "left-wing" sectarian policy; it would have caused those who were resisting the trend hostile to the people and harmful to the building of socialism to lose ground. This made it urgent and timely for the sectarian "left-wing" deviationists to go into action against the June policy.

B. Certain internal and external factors were moving in the same direction, and they facilitated the realization of a return to the pre–1953 policy: Rákosi's misleading report to the Soviet Union's Communist Party on the situation of the Party and the country; an incorrect evaluation of the international situation leading to increased tension; and as a result the increase of internal efforts stressing defense preparations, which, in turn, brought about a return to the exaggerated speed-up of heavy industry, especially war industry.

Since the pseudoradical "left-wing" deviationists were able to put forward their anti-Marxist political views in the March resolution, though it brought dire consequences to the Party and the country, the situation within the Party had cleared up. The political views and methods of the "left wing," kept secret until then, had become evident in all their nakedness with regard to the rules of the Party's inner life and the Party's policy with regard to practical or theoretical problems of Marxism-Leninism, especially to the interpretation of the June, 1953, Central Committee resolution. In connection with the March resolution the political persecution conducted against me for a long time had come into the open and, as it was revealed then, often paralyzed the work of the leadership. This was not my fault.

Objectively, the March, 1955, resolution by the Central Committee was a turnabout, a return to the former bad policy on the basis of a completely distorted evaluation of the real situation and an exaggerated presentation of actual mistakes, with the undeniable political aim of the "left-wing" leaders that by returning to the former policy they might be able to continue their harmful activities interrupted by the June resolution.

The March resolution was justified by the following argument:

The June, 1953, resolution of the Central Committee has been proved entirely correct. But beside the successful struggle for the realization of this correct resolution there have been mistakes and errors in the execution; what is more, the resolution has been distorted by certain individuals in an anti-Marxist, opportunist fashion, which led to a harmful rightist policy, to rightist deviation. As a result, disturbing phenomena manifested themselves in the economic and political life of our People's Democracy.

The above is an abbreviated evaluation of the situation that necessitated the March resolution: the political and economic causes that had a part in bringing about the resolution, and a review of past mistakes. Considering the resolution from this angle, it can be asserted that a great discrepancy exists between the premises and the inference drawn from them, which indicates that the political conclusions are unwarranted.

In addition to the inner contradictions of the March resolution, there are more serious theoretical and political discrepancies between the March resolution and its execution, as well as between the interpretation, explanation, and motivation of the resolution. Yet this is exactly what reveals the true nature and goal of the resolution. The views, theses, or "theories" that came to the surface in the course of the explanation and application of the March resolution give a better definition to the real contents of the resolution than the actual wording of the resolution itself. The sharp contrast and discrepancy between the two make it absolutely necessary to decide the question: What is valid, what is accepted as a guiding principle for the leaders and the membership of the Party—the March resolution in its own wording, or the commentaries written on the resolution in the Party press? Where does the Central Committee stand? On the basis of the principles laid down in the March resolution, or on the basis of principles discussed in the explanations? For the latter contain—because of gross exaggerations and falsifications—a whole series of anti-Marxist views and erroneous pseudoradical "leftist" theories on basic problems.

The April, 1955, Central Committee resolution had been based on the guiding principles of the March resolution. The April resolution has no separate theoretical motivation. In spite of this, the two resolutions diverge considerably in evaluation of the situation, classification of mistakes, and conclusions.

While the March resolution deals with mistakes and shortcomings, and distortions on why our economic and political life shows disturbing signs, the April resolution speaks about views that are in sharp contradiction to the over-all policy of our Party and says that these anti-Marxist, anti-Party views form a comprehensive system and have caused serious damage to our socialist building, etc. In the April resolution the mistakes, shortcomings, and distortions have become a "comprehensive system" of anti-Marxist, anti-Party views, and the disturbing phenomena have become "a serious damage" to socialist building. This change came about in five short weeks in which I had been completely inactive in Party and in state life; in other words, the alleged mistakes mentioned in the March resolution had not multiplied or become more serious.

All this can be explained by the fact that at the exposition of motives for the April resolution in a "report" to the Central

Committee, Rákosi divorced the evaluation and enumeration of mistakes not only from objective facts but also from the assertions of the March resolution, and mixed it into the slough of calumny and gossip debasing the Party for the sake of a condemnation more serious than that of March, and a political persecution of myself on this basis.

Today, an exact evaluation can be made of the economic, political, and social results of the March and April resolutions on the basis of the "achievements" of the past few months. In the light of objective facts and figures the situation brought about by them is shocking. The consequences are very grave both in the domestic situation and in foreign relations, and cannot be improved upon by intentional bias in quarterly or semi-annual statistical reports, just as the slogans advocating peaceful coexistence and reduction of international tension cannot erase the political and moral blemish caused to the reputation and international position of our fatherland by the internal events of the past six months.

Where would the country be today if we had been permitted to build socialism on the basis of the October, 1954, Central Committee resolution and in the spirit of the June policy! The October resolution gave a clearly defined theoretical basis to further progress on the right way chosen in June, and assured the support of our entire nation.

It is a task for the Party leadership to determine whether the March resolution and subsequent resolutions passed in this spirit, as well as the overwhelming part of applied Party and state rules, caused a serious breach of principles in Party policy, a new turn, a deviation from the right road where the masses do not follow the Party and the Party membership does not follow the leadership of the Party. The policy based on the March and April Central Committee resolutions evoked passivity and resistance in the Party members. It slowed down the tempo of Party work, depressed enthusiasm for productive labor, and undermined trust in the Party and state leadership.

It must be realized that such a policy is driving the people into the arms of reaction and the enemy, and is bringing the country to the brink of an unprecedented political and economic crisis. It is the task of the Central Committee to persist in keeping the Party united despite these difficulties, to keep together its honest, faithful, and solid forces for action in every walk of Party, state, and social life, and to give guiding principles able to mobilize the people and the country in the spirit of the resolutions passed in June at the Party Congress and in October by the Central Committee.

Chapter 7. Characteristic Features and Specific Traits of the New Course

The Third Congress of the Hungarian Workers' Party confirmed the thesis that the June resolution of the Central Committee had opened a new course in the building of socialism in Hungary. Summarizing the resolutions in five points, the essential character and specific traits of the New Course are defined and described on pages 31 to 33 of the congressional report of the Central Committee. However, the definition of the gist and specific traits of the New Course lacks a good theoretical foundation and is not complete or satisfactory.

A correct definition of the concept, essence, and character of the New Course is of great importance because the unclear definition of the essence of the New Course is responsible for certain views, according to which the New Course is tantamount to an anti-Marxist, rightist deviation. Such views and the charge of anti-Marxism are incorrect and completely unfounded. A study of Marxism-Leninism will reveal that the classics of scientific socialism alternately used the expressions of "course" (*étape*) and "period," meaning the same thing. The principle and concept of a "New Course" is, therefore, not in contradiction with the theory of Marxism-Leninism. Stalin divided the New Economic Policy (NEP) into two "courses" or "periods," emphasizing that strategic tasks did not change in the former or in the latter course.

For an exact Marxist-Leninist theoretical definition of the

New Course, needed to avoid misinterpretations or to refute them, and for amending the incomplete and inadequate statements concerning the New Course voiced at the Third Congress of the HWP,* it must be established that the New Course initiated by the June, 1953, resolution of the Central Committee did not set new strategic tasks for the Party. The former strategic task—laying the economic foundations of socialism and building socialism in Hungary—had been left untouched. Therefore, the policy of the New Course had been directed toward the solution of the old strategic task by changing and improving the former bad tactics. The New Course gives expression to this tactical change. Arguments on the terminology and charges of anti-Marxism are only forms in the fight against the important economic and political measures stipulated by the June resolution.

The main strategic task, the Party's strategy, is based on historic "turns" and embraces whole periods. Therefore during the period of transition from capitalism to socialism the strategy and its main goal remain unchanged. At the same time, however, there are definite changes within the given periods, which are best expressed by the word "course." Within the unchanged principal strategic direction, these changes are expressed in new tactics. Thus, in the *étapes* of development, *within* the strategy, there can be and definitely will be changes. Such a change, in Hungary, was the New Course, the new tactic.

One of the main characteristics of the transitional period is the struggle between capitalist and socialist elements. Within the transitional period, the economic and political goals of the New Course were determined by these same basic tasks. The economic policy of the New Course is, therefore, the proper application of the teachings of Marxism-Leninism to the specific Hungarian conditions, on the basis of specific traits in the transitional period and the objective needs of building socialism in the field of socialist transformation and development of the people's economy.

In the transitional period, during the struggle between socialist and capitalist elements, it is of utmost importance that:

A. The Party and the state rely in all their activities on a

* Hungarian Workers' Party (Communist Party).

scientific basis, and, first of all on a knowledge of the law of harmonizing the forces of production with a proper ratio between the various types of production;

B. The Party's economic policy must be so directed as to increase the forces of production and to develop the people's economy in a proportionate and planned way. Increase of the forces of production and a planned, proportionate developing of agriculture in the field of building socialism will insure the realization of the basic law of socialism (raising the standard of living), and the realization of uninterrupted, augmented secondary production on the basis of the most modern technical achievements;

C. The Party's economic policy must be founded on the principles of proletarian internationalism and the pursuit of a lasting peace, peaceful coexistence, and economic competition of different systems. Furthermore, trade agreements between the two systems (communist and capitalist) must serve the improvement of international division of labor as well as the expanding of the socialist world market;

D. The Party's economic policy must take into account the requirements of national and international security based on the Leninist principles of peaceful coexistence, which makes disarmament and reduction of war expenditures possible and also makes it possible that the latest achievements of science and technology be employed for the purpose of peaceful construction and improvement of well-being and of the standard of living;

E. The Party's economic policy must take into account that in the world as well as in the People's Democracies within the socialist bloc, many socio-economic formations or sectors, or the remnants of these, exist side by side during the transitory period;

F. The NEP policy must be carried out unconditionally, as it means the establishment of increasingly closer relations in the exchange of goods between the city and the village, between socialist industry and the system of small holdings producing for the market, facilitating the switch to a socialist system of agricultural farms producing on a large scale.

These basic requirements and specific traits of the transi-

tional period's economic policy were either nonexistent in
Hungary or were realized only in part—partly because our economic policy lacked a scientific basis in Marxist-Leninist analysis, and also because, as a consequence, we simply copied the
Soviet methods applied at a much later stage in the building of
socialism, thus skipping whole stages of development. That is
the reason why Hungary needed a New Course in the building
of socialism—to make it possible that basic principles and requirements of transitional period could fully assert themselves,
leaving room for characteristic and specific traits arising from
concrete conditions, and at the same time assuring the most
effective ways, forms, and methods of developing socialism. But
for the very same reason the New Course cannot be simply
"abolished" or "suspended," because such action would deprive
the country of the possibility of a successful and easy way of
building socialism, and one requiring the least possible sacrifices from the population.

One of the main tasks of the New Course in Hungary was to
make it possible that basic principles of general validity and
normal development of the transitional period, which previously had been completely suppressed or just partly realized,
could fully assert themselves.

Another task was giving the green light to specific ways and
forms arising from Hungarian conditions in the building of the
people's economy on a socialist basis, in order to create conditions for basic principles of universal validity as well as for the
concrete and wide application of new ways and forms created by
specific conditions during the period of transition. It had to
guarantee democratism in the country and the Party; far-reaching activities and creative initiative of the masses; observance
of regulations by Party organization in the Party and of human
rights and duties and citizens' rights in state life as stipulated
by the Constitution; and it had to advance the activities of leading organs to the platform of legality.

It was a serious shortcoming of the New Course that in many
important fields it brought about only half-solutions. The economic policy of the New Course showed serious shortcomings
because of the resistance of the Party and state organs, especially
in the field of economy, and also because objective economic

laws were not always correctly applied as a result of not having
been scientifically analyzed, and because specific Hungarian
conditions were not clearly defined. The main error was not
that we established the New Course in Hungary for building
socialism, but rather the fact that we did not follow this course
consistently and fully. This, on the other hand, makes us draw
the logical conclusion that the New Course must not be liquidated but rather should be fully realized, eliminating its shortcomings and paying great attention to those specific tasks that
are necessitated by specific conditions in Hungary. Lenin laid
special emphasis on the latter problem, as I have demonstrated
in Chapter 1 of my present work by several quotations from his
works.

These teachings of Lenin were, unfortunately, all but forgotten in Hungary. One of the most important ideological tasks
awaiting Hungarian Communists is to revive these teachings
and apply them to the specific Hungarian conditions.

One must also point out the specific conditions that have exerted considerable influence upon the role played by the New
Course in Hungary in the transitional period:

A. International socialist division of labor and mutual economic help make efforts at economic autarchy unnecessary.
These efforts have put a great burden on the country and
pushed the building of socialism off the proper road, which is
determined by objective economic laws and which assures the
execution of the basic law of socialism;

B. The change to the New Course came after four and a half
years of the First Five-Year Plan of our people's economy, on
the basis of achievements and experience gained in the past. At
the same time the New Course had to eliminate mistakes which
had caused grave difficulties and had previously jeopardized, or
in certain fields frustrated, the attainments of the Party's main
political goal and several economic-political goals;

C. Proper evaluation and consideration of the existing level
of agricultural production, the condition of the forces of production, and the different levels of the ratios of production,
were badly needed for the socialist transformation of agriculture;

D. Our economic and natural resources had to be taken into

account to a much greater extent than in the past (raw material basis, density of population, etc.);

E. More attention must be paid to gradualism, and greater elasticity must be shown in politics, more patience and consideration should be shown to the intelligentsia, the small bourgeoisie, and the peasants, who carry considerable weight in our society.

Economic and political developments in the summer of 1953 necessitated the initiation of the New Course:

A. In the economic field we were faced with a completely hopeless situation. Main target figures in the economic plan were greatly exaggerated and impossible to meet. We had enforced the fulfillment of heavy industrial plans to a much too great extent. The rate and proportions of developing heavy industry were much higher than in countries that had more favorable conditions, and we had exceeded all the other People's Democracies in developing our heavy industry. Industry began to show a steady shortage of materials. The quality of products was deteriorating rapidly. Export difficulties became everyday phenomena, and foreign debts were rising steeply. Development of agricultural production had come to a standstill, and there was a danger of it going downhill altogether. The area of uncultivated land increased. The standard of living was deteriorating, and a further decrease became a certainty. The economic basis for the worker-peasant alliance had been shaken. Increasing dissatisfaction could be observed in the ranks of the workers' class. The keeping and consolidation of political power as the principal task facing the Party showed up in its full extent.

B. Politically, we had skipped several stages of development through which the Soviet Union had passed.

C. Faced with these specific conditions of our development, the Party should have done everything in its power to discuss the motives of its day-by-day policy with the membership, to teach the members how to form independent political opinions, to develop in the Party the practice of criticism coming from below, to realize the principle of collective leadership in all Party organs, and to apply consistently the Leninist principles of democratic centralism. Instead, the method of convincing by arguments was replaced by giving instructions. Criticisms and objections on the basis of principles or justified concern were branded more often than not as the voice of the enemy or at least as a petty bourgeois lack of judgment.

Economic difficulties piling up under such circumstances had to lead to the deterioration of the living standard, and consequently to a blow to confidence, to increasing mistrust, to the exaggeration of difficulties and the belittling of achievements.

All this actually happened in the spring of 1953 and made it necessary that a turn be taken with the introduction of the New Course.

The government program for carrying out the June resolution was received with tremendous enthusiasm. The same enthusiastic reception was given by the Party members and the working people to resolutions on the restoration of socialist legality, the enforcement of the principle of collective leadership, the extension of democratism, the greater assertion of criticism and self-criticism against dogmatism and schematism; on the struggle to be fought in the ideological and cultural fields; on a national cooperation resting on a wider basis; on the People's Front and the greater power given to local councils. All these resolutions were correct and necessary. Their correctness was proved by the unfolding political activity of the masses, by the flourishing of Party life, by the consolidation of the link between the Party and the masses, by the sudden invigoration of criticism and self-criticism, by the consolidation of the worker-peasant alliance, and by the greater trust of the nonproletarian masses in the state of the workers' class.

The freeing of the spirit of self-criticism and criticism brought about the inevitable consequence that the Party membership and the working masses themselves began to criticize the leadership. To a Communist, this should not have been a surprise: our Party has continuously emphasized that it was not afraid of frank criticism or self-criticism and was not worried that the enemy would try to take advantage of this. It was a mistake, however, that the Party did not give appropriate guidance to the extensive work of enlightenment and thus left the field open to counterpropaganda.

Chapter 8.   The Objective Economic Law
of Socialist Development

I have expressed my views on the objective economic laws of socialist development, their functions and enforcement, as well as their peculiarities under specific Hungarian circumstances during the transition period in a lecture given at the Hungarian Academy of Science on May 26, 1953, entitled "Economic Problems in the People's Democratic Countries During the Transition from Capitalism to Socialism" and in several works, most of which have appeared in print. My views on the basic principles of scientific socialism, expressed in these works, have never been challenged from a factual and objective point of view, and no actual errors were pointed out by scientific analysis.

Since the June resolution of the Central Committee, grave mistakes have been made, either unwittingly or deliberately, in the evaluation of the New Course's policy of "right-wing deviation" and connected errors in the political, economic, and cultural fields, errors that make the development of ideological activities and the scientific consideration of several decisive questions justified. This must be emphasized by the Party leadership all the more because the March and subsequent resolutions are not sufficiently supported by Marxist tenets.

In theoretical consideration of the objective law we are confronted by two types of criticism. Both of them consider the problems from an erroneous basic concept, and their advocates, who are not competent to explain the principal foundation of

Party resolutions, pass "judgment." Most of the time authors of such articles only display their theoretical confusion in these matters, so much so that by now it is impossible to tell what aspects of Party leadership they subscribe to and what they object to, or who is qualified to express the Party's point of view and who is not, or what is Marxism and what is deviation.

Wrong criticism is based on two mistakes:

A. The wrong evaluation of the transition period. The erroneous view is that the objective economic laws of socialism can and must be fully enforced in Hungary on the assumption that production forces and production conditions are such that this is possible. The mistake is to call for an economic policy that could be realized only if the objective economic laws of socialism were fully in force. In other words a sharp contradiction is created between the functioning of objective laws and the actual situation, specifically between theory and practice.

B. The misleading presentation of the problem, where statements are quoted out of context, where correct views, whole articles, and statements are ignored or correct statements become twisted, etc.

These practices, inconsistent with the Party line and Party morals, are not aimed at the elaboration and support of correct Marxist tenets, but seek to justify the attitude of individual Party leaders at any cost and to add prestige to their decisions, even if this means the falsification of Marxism itself.

Employing these methods, so contrary to the Party line, several articles have appeared concerning the functioning of objective laws, charging that my views were mistaken, that they were a distortion, or that they represented anti-Marxist right-wing deviation.

Dealing with the basic economic laws of socialism, Istvan Foldes, completely disregarding the scientific objectivity necessary in analyzing and clarifying theoretical questions or in criticizing opposing, possibly erroneous views, declared (in "Basic Economic Laws of Socialism and Party Policy," *Szabad Nep*, 1955) that "the October 20, 1954, article by Imre Nagy and his speech to the People's Front Congress were examples of demagogic interpretation of the basic law . . . from the narrow-minded point of view of the consumer." Then he tried to prove his point with a few lines of quotations, obviously picked out with the intent of falsification. Finally he stated that "this unpardonable separation of the goal and the means, the false interpretation of the basic law, created the illusions that without special efforts, irrespective of achievements in the improvement and perfection of production, the living standards of the workers can be raised." At another point of his article he added another, even more boorish lie to his "scientific" analysis, claiming that according to representatives of right-wing views (he does not say who, but obviously he refers to me) an increased enforcement of the basic laws may be achieved through the neglect of industrial, particularly heavy industrial production and by the support of the small farmers.

Foldes lied shamelessly:

A. He is trying to prove my alleged right-wing, anti-Marxist deviation, displayed in the all-important matter of the basic economic law of socialism, on the basis of my October 20 article and my opening address to the statutory meeting of the People's Front Congress. The purpose of my October 20 article was not the clarification of theoretic questions nor the analysis of the statutory development of socialism. Moreover, it dealt only with a few questions of our economic policy, questions that had arisen at the October meeting of the Central Committee. Consequently it cannot be regarded as a comprehensive analysis of the theoretical and practical problems of our economic policy in which all factors were to be considered and the principal questions reviewed. The purpose of the article was the same as that of the October Central Committee meeting: to readjust the ratios within the people's economy that had become unbalanced; to hasten and complete the reorganization of industrial production in accordance with the Central Committee's June resolution and the Third Congress resolution in the interest of creating circumstances favorable for a balanced, planned, development; and to eliminate opposition which became increasingly violent, whether expressed openly or indirectly, against the Party and the state, and which endangered the realization of correct Party and government resolutions.

B. If Foldes had really wanted to analyze anti-Marxist distortion and right-wing deviation in this field from the scientific

Marxist point of view, he could have referred to my innumerable articles, speeches, lectures, and studies, which have appeared in print and were therefore known to the public, and to Foldes too. In these he could have found ample material to prove the opposite of what he set out to prove in his article. It would be too lengthy to quote the pertinent material here. I only wish to refer to some of my speeches of the last two years, which would convince anyone of the falseness of Foldes' accusations. One of these speeches was made at the Hungarian Academy of Science on May 26, 1953, and also appeared in booklet form. The second speech was also delivered at the Hungarian Academy of Science on June 14, 1954, and dealt with the tasks facing Hungarian science. The third one, containing ample material on the subject raised by Foldes, was given to MAVAG in October, 1954. This should be sufficient (although there is more if required) to prove that I have not separated the two aspects of the basic economic laws of socialism, namely the aspect of the aim (raising the living standard) from the aspect of the means (development of production means on the basis of expanded production). I certainly did not keep repeating this in a parrotlike fashion, but whenever I was called upon to take a stand or to express my views, I did so. Up to May, 1954, the Foldes-type "theoreticians" never even thought of exposing these allegedly grave and dangerous deviations. But now they, too, join the ranks of the slanderers with their hastily drummed-up "theories."

C. If the aim of Foldes had not been falsification, in which case writing his article would have been pointless, he could have found material answering his question even in my October 20 article: "The road toward overcoming our temporary economic difficulties, and, beyond that, the road to building socialism, does not call for the lowering of the working people's living standards . . . it calls for increased and expanded production and the reorganization of industry." Or: "An economic policy that does not aim at the stepping up of production and the development of means of production, at satisfying of the growing needs of the working people, would be in opposition to the main Party line." Again: "If we do not seek the solution in the direction of developing means of production the situation will further deteriorate. . . . The curtailing and cutting down of the production forces is not part of socialist building." These few quotes alone prove beyond doubt that even in my October article I expressed the view that the development of the means of production and stepped-up production, including industry, heavy industry, and in fact our whole people's economy, was the primary goal. This in turn proves that I did not separate the two aspects of goal and means from each other; that I did not interpret the basic law from the narrow-minded point of view of the consumer; and that I did not represent the view that improved enforcement of the basic law may be achieved through neglect of industrial production, merely by the supporting of small farms—just as I did not try to create the illusion that the living standard of the working people can be raised without increased production. Every single statement made by Foldes is a slanderous falsification.

Another article that appeared in the June 12, 1955, issue of *Szabad Nep* also deals with my alleged rightist deviation in the matter of the laws of proportionately planned economic development. Although the article was published without naming its authors, I learned that they were Lakos and Szabo. The title was "Regrouping the Forces of Our People's Economy." The authors charged me with the following rightist mistakes:

A. In my June, 1953, speech I said that "we must modify the direction of development in our People's Democracy." They claim that this is in opposition to the June resolution of the Party and the stand taken by the Congress, according to which "industrialization will continue to be the principal objective of the Party line." The authors committed a crude mistake when they compared the principal Party line with the line of development of the People's Democracy. First of all, it must be established that the Party's main line is not industrialization, not the building of socialism which during the whole transition period is the strategic task of the Party. Further, the people's economy includes industry, together with the heavy industry branch. Thus, development of the people's economy includes also the development of industry. Consequently, if we modify the direction of development of our people's economy, which is what I was talking about, it means nothing else but that:

—a. ratios within our people's economy must be changed, which in itself means a change in the direction of development of our people's economy, inasmuch as greater emphasis must be placed on the development of agriculture;

—b. in the interest of proportionate, planned development, the course of industrial development must be modified, in order to readjust unbalanced production rates within industry through regrouping. Changing the course of development in our people's economy and, within this modification, of industrial development, is not in contradiction to the policy of socialist industrialization, which is the main objective of the Party. On the contrary, without such modification, without changing the incorrect course of development in our people's economy—i.e., if we continued progressing in the old direction—the building of socialism would come to a dead end. I must clearly state, in the face of the wrong argumentation and false conclusions of the authors, that the modification of the course of development of our people's economy does not at all mean the giving up of socialist industrialization. It merely means guiding it into the only correct direction as outlined by objective economic law. Instead of giving this interpretation to the modification of the course, the authors confuse the issues and play with words. At the same time they are also afraid of the "change of course" because they embrace the wrong interpretation of the June Central Committee resolution and the government program, completely underestimating their significance. According to them, only the excesses in the economic policy were to be eliminated, everything else could have gone on unchanged. But the Party resolutions decree that "the June Central Committee resolution basically modified the Party's line," that "the June resolution meant a turning point in the Party's policy," etc. The October, 1953, Central Committee resolution stated that "the June plenary meeting of the Central Committee determined the political and economic course of the transition from capitalism to socialism, applied to specific Hungarian conditions." The authors of the article falsify previous Party resolutions, using slanderous statements, in an effort to provide additional proof of my alleged right-wing deviation.

—c. It is no coincidence that the authors of the article, like

Foldes, seem to find proof of my right-wing deviation in my October 20 article and my opening speech to the People's Front Congress. In connection with the theoretical falsifications of Foldes, I analyzed the task and purpose of my October article and the speech to the People's Front Congress. In connection with the Lakos-Szabo article I must add to my statements that they shamelessly falsify my October article when they write: "Comrade Imre Nagy formulated his views even more sharply in his *Szabad Nep* article of October, 1954, when he calls the idea that heavy industrial production must constantly increase absolutely wrong and intolerable." In the article quoted I wrote the following: "The expanded Five-Year Plan determined the excessive tempo of industrialization on the basis of the completely wrong and intolerable concept that heavy industrial expansion may not decrease from one year to the other, neither in absolute capacity nor in percental output, but must increase constantly." What do I consider wrong and intolerable? The concept that the growth of heavy industry must be greater year after year, that is to say if, for instance, the growth of heavy industry was 10 per cent last year, then it must be greater this year, even greater the year after, and so on, because one year's growth cannot be smaller than that of the previous year. Thus it must not happen that if the growth was 10 per cent last year, it should be only 8 or 9 per cent this year. But this is absurd. The man who makes such a statement, and does this with reference to Marxist economic principles, is a common charlatan and has no place in the field of economic science. I still hold this view, as it was formulated in my October 20 article. This is in no contradiction to, on the contrary it is in complete accord with, Marxist teachings on the relationship between the first and second classes and the primacy of the development of the first class.

The Lakos-Szabo team have a good sense of humor. With fake indignation they write: "We are *confronted with a complete disregard* for heavy industry [underscored by the authors] in his speech to the Patriotic People's Front Congress . . ." Here it is the grave charge, the dangerous right-wing deviation: At the opening session of the Patriotic People's Front Congress I completely disregarded the question of heavy industry. As if the People's Front Congress had been called only to discuss the principal and practical tasks of the development of heavy industry! By the same token they could challenge me for not stating my stand on the primary importance of the development of heavy industry at the Third Party Congress, either in my opening speech, or in the presentation on state administration, or in the discourse on the duties of councils, or in the course of my speech to young voters at the meeting organized by the Communist Youth League, etc. It would have involved less effort for the authors if, instead of making up all these lies, they had searched out my works, in which they would have found the correct answers to all their charges.

—d. I do not consider it worth while to deal with the utterly absurd charges made in connection with regrouping of economic efforts, for instance the charge that I considered the regrouping as a sort of panacea, etc. However, there are two matters I must mention. One of them is the statement in the Lakos-Szabo article: "it is not a matter . . . of returning to the pre–1953 situation. This is completely out of the question. We do not want to commit and shall not again commit the same mistakes that were revealed by the June resolution of the Central Committee." I completely agree with this. But in direct contradiction to this statement are the ones I mentioned before. The whole "theoretical" concept propounded by the authors proves that they have returned to the wrong views of the pre-June period. They criticize my stand not from the point of view of the June resolution, but from a point of view based on the erroneous old political line, or at least they made a concession in that direction. This is supported by their statement that the process of regrouping has actually been successfully completed. When was it completed? Certainly not by early 1955! The 1955 yearly plan still called for big efforts in the field of regrouping. The claim that it has been completed means that efforts toward the implementation of the June resolution should be abandoned, and that one should indulge in a sense of accomplishment, pretending that mistakes have been righted, and then quietly continue the course of the pre-June period. Thus, despite all their protestations, Lakos and Szabo must have noticed that they reverted to the old line, but even if they did not notice it, the fact remains unchanged. At the same time they accuse me of having distorted the June resolutions.

B. The second matter I must mention is the following: Lakos-Szabo write in their article that "Comrade Imre Nagy . . . using the excuse of regrouping, wanted to stop the construction of the coke and ore preparing works at Sztalinvaros, the ore refinery of Rudabanya, the cement works at Labatlan, and the aluminum factory at Ajka, despite the fact that these works are based on the utilization of our domestic raw material resources and their operations would improve the material basis of our whole industry, and they are therefore of tremendous importance to our further progress." Each statement is a shameless lie. It is the most elementary requirement that those who make such charges should be able to prove them. As long as they are not able to prove their charges, I consider these blatant lies and their perpetrators common character assassins. I do not know whether they were forced into this despicable role or whether they assumed it voluntarily (in the final analysis that makes no actual difference). The fact is that by doing so they are trying to help the "left-wing" deviationists, who have a guilty conscience because of the criminal neglect of industry based on domestic raw materials. The authors of the article try to help them by charging me with their crimes. An old and dirty trick.

But they want more than that. It is not only a matter of embarrassing me. Using cheap demagogy, they are trying to deceive the public, creating the impressions that the June policy is directed against industrial progress and that it would involve the deliberate obstruction of development in the most promising branches of heavy industry by neglecting the utilization of the economic and natural resources of the country. This charge is justified against the Rákosi-Gerö leadership, which not only before 1953, but even during the New Course, followed a policy of such aims, steering our whole people's economy, particularly our industry and agriculture, toward a course of reduced production.

The authors of the article say I wanted to "stop the construction" of the above-mentioned works. However, they do not say why I failed in my endeavor, or who were the vigilantes who stopped me. This is in sharp contradiction to the oft-repeated charges that I was able to commit every mistake, caused all the trouble, and was able to realize all my vile intentions, despite the efforts of the Party and the government. Were they able to stop me in this one respect? Lakos and Szabo are confused in the maze of their own lies.

Chapter 9.   Socialist Expanded Secondary Production

Marx stated that social production and total output are divided into two categories. At the same time he pointed to the interdependence between the two categories and the necessity of a proper ratio between them.

On the subject of expanded secondary production, Marx pointed to the changes that occur in the process of accumulation. Accumulation is the only source of expanded secondary production. Accumulation, on the other hand, is possible only if that part of the net income which will satisfy the demands for production means and power shows up in its basic form.

Expanding secondary production, as contrasted with simple secondary production, presupposes that the whole net profit of society is not poured into the consumer stock. Part of the income is used for the expansion of the basic production, that is to say, for productive consumption.

Lenin pointed out the definite connection between technical progress, organic growth of capital, and socialist expanded secondary production. At the same time, according to Marxist classicists, technical progress, the organic growth of capital, require primacy for the production of production means. Consequently socialist expanded secondary production is generally based on increased output of production means, in harmony with the requirements of the basic economic law of socialism and the laws of the planned, systematic development of the people's economy. In other words the process of socialist expanded secondary production is dependent upon the maximum satisfaction of the constantly growing material and cultural demands of the whole society.

Thus it is obviously true that the Marxist-Leninist precept on the primacy of production means output, and applies to the socialist system too. However, this undoubtedly correct and general principle must be related to the basic economic laws of the given social order and the method of production: in the capitalist system with the economic laws of the pursuit of maximal capital gains, in the socialist system with the economic law of satisfying the material and cultural requirements of the society. However, we must not overlook the difference and the connection between the aim as set up in the basic law and the means serving the accomplishment of this aim. Since the aim can be accomplished only through the methods determined by the basic law, it follows that the means must be given primacy. This primacy, however, means that, under the socialist system, the improvement and development of production, based on the most progressive technical methods, does not become one-sided and does not lose sight of its ultimate goal—the best possible satisfaction of material and cultural needs.

In a socialist society, when determining the tempo of economic development and the ratio between the various economic branches, the proportion between production and consumption and between consumption and stockpiling must be in harmony with the requirements of the basic economic law of socialism, guaranteeing a gradual advance of society. In the planned management of the socialist people's economy, a basic requirement is a direct proportion between the two categories of social production—between the production of consumer goods and the output of means of production. Progress and development of society depend upon the correct solution of this problem.

This basic and general Marxist-Leninist precept is valid also in the transition period from capitalism to socialism. However, the complicated circumstances of the society and the people's economy must be taken into consideration at a time when, although in differing degree and manner, the laws of both capitalism and socialism have an influence. Furthermore, the peculiarities and the economic, political and cultural standards of the country in question must also be taken into account.

Development in a socialist society is not spontaneous; development loses its cyclical character (as in capitalism), and there are no crises. This means that in a socialist system there are no class differences and, at the same time, the conflict between production, consumption, and stockpiling is eliminated. Socialist expanding secondary production is characterized by a general prosperity, which extends to every branch of social production. However, even in a socialist society, this can be accomplished only if the objective economic laws are observed. The stepped-up growth of the first category, that of the production of the means of production and, within this, the very heart of heavy industry, i.e., the manufacture of machines, is directly connected with the laws of planned systematic development. To disregard this means that the development of the first category, primarily that of heavy industry, is placed under other economic laws, and this leads to the violation of the scientific ratios necessary to the smooth operation of secondary production. It means the introduction of voluntary adjustments into the policy of economics, which is incompatible with Marxist-Leninist tenets and leads to a break with the basic laws of socialism.

A disproportion between the first and second categories arises if the products of the second category are not sufficient to cover the needs of the population, that is to say if the second category develops more slowly than objectively possible and necessary, resulting in a lowering of living standards. This is what happened in our country between 1950 and 1953, due to the excessive development of the first category, and the June resolution and government measures were aimed at changing this situation. This was the basic purpose and theoretical justification of the economic policy introduced in June.

In periods of industrialization, and generally in times when the people's economy must adopt a new technique, development of the first category must exceed that of the second category, but only to a degree that does not upset the economic ratios necessary for expanded secondary production, which will assure the supply of the quantity of consumer goods required under the basic law of socialism for the constant raising of living standards. The proportion and tempo of heavy industrial development must not exceed this framework. If this is disregarded, the development of heavy industry will lessen the possibility of raising living standards, which leads to serious violation of the basic law.

Under socialist conditions it is inadmissible that the absolute and relative growth of social total output be based almost exclusively on the production of production means while growth of consumer goods production is at a standstill or moves at an extremely slow pace. In other words it is inadmissible that a numerically growing population should be forced to satisfy its needs at an unchanged or even declining level, as happened in this country between 1949 and 1953. It is a recognized fact that despite the immense growth of production living standards dropped between 1949 and 1953. To narrow down the concept of production to the producing of production means, serving the output of production means, is nothing but the vulgarization or even falsification of Marxist-Leninist tenets.

The primacy of the production of production means cannot be "independent" of consumption. This is demonstrated by the fact that we have raised heavy and machine-industry production to five to seven times the prewar level without correspondingly raising the living standards of the workers, and without utilizing this tremendously increased production for the welfare of the workers. Such self-contained production does not and cannot have a place in a socialist society, because such a production method is incompatible with Marxist-Leninist doctrine and the economic laws of socialism. If in this respect anyone "deviated" from Marxist-Leninist tenets, it was not I but those who, although constantly referring to and quoting from Lenin, actually seek to cover up their anti-Marxist views by revising the Leninist stand. These "left-wing" elements want to take up where they left off in 1953, and as recent developments indicate, they actually do so. This is also indicated by the division of expenditures under the current 1955 budget. Of the 9 billion forints earmarked for industrial investments, only 780 million forints, a mere 8.7 per cent, is allotted to the consumer goods industries, while 3.6 billion forints go to heavy industry. In 1954, 3.6 billion forints went to agriculture, while in 1955 the amount is only 2.3 billion forints, only two-thirds of last year's. And of this, only approximately 400 million forints will go to the individually working peasants who farm nearly 70 percent of the agricultural land of the country and produce the great majority of agricultural produce. The interpretation of "primacy" in this manner is wrong, because it is bound to lead to a lowering of living standards and involves the vulgarization of Lenin's teachings. Thus in the case of proper interpretation of the Lenin tenets there is no "right-wing" deviation. On the contrary, the vulgarization of Lenin's teachings is a "left-wing" deviation.

The production of production means, the primacy of heavy industrial development as a socialist economic law, cannot be placed above the other economic laws, and its implementation is not independent of time and space. Heavy industrial development must be carried out with full consideration of the specific characteristics of the individual socialist countries and in harmony with the economic development of other countries within the socialist camp, not disregarding the peaceful coexistence of the two systems, of the capitalist and socialist world markets, and the relationships of international division of labor—in other words all the internal and external factors of socialist buildings.

The primacy of heavy industrial development as an economic law of socialism does not exclude the possibility that during a certain transition period, when the economic ratios required by expanded reproduction became unbalanced for some reason, leading to the violation of the basic law, the growth of the second category is quickened. Moreover, if from the point of view of the basic law this becomes necessary, then the production of the second category is increased more rapidly than that of the first category. Consequently there may be transition periods when the increased development of the second category becomes the prerequisite of the further development of heavy industry. This was the situation in the summer of 1953, and this was the basis of the economic policy of the New Course. Therefore the more extensive development of the second category as compared with that of the first category, at a certain period of time, does not mean a right-wing deviation, but the application of Marxist-Leninist teachings under given circumstances, when the objective economic law, primarily the basic law, make this necessary.

The question is merely whether such a situation existed in our country in the summer of 1953. According to the June Central Committee resolution, it did. Marxist-Leninist teachings are not limited to the essentially correct views of giving primacy to the first category and demanding for it a more rapid growth than that of the second category, but establish the fact that under the socialist basic law the tempo of the second category's development may be similar, even greater than that of heavy industry during the period necessary to correct the disrupted balance of the economic ratios. Those who fail to recognize this, branding such a course right-wing deviation, are falsifying Marxist-Leninist teachings and leveling unfounded accusations. The same mistake is committed by those who claimed that the increased pace of second category production during the twenty months beginning June, 1953, theoretically absolutely correct and justified and necessitated by practical requirements, indicated an underestimation of the importance of heavy industrial development, in violation of the principal interests of the nation. This statement, which only seeks to justify and defend the excessive heavy industrial development pursued during the first three years of the First Five-Year Plan, is essentially an attack on the June resolution of the Central Committee.

The question must be raised: What was the decisive, principal task of the economic policy during the New Course after the June, 1953, period? Was it guaranteeing the primacy of heavy industrial production, excessively pursued up to June, 1953, or was it the correction of the grave discrepancies caused by the very emphasis on the excessive development of heavy industry, which had inflicted such serious damage on the whole people's economy and on the working masses by the modification of development rates between the first and second categories and by a cut in heavy industrial development? The Party resolutions unanimously endorsed the second view. This correct attitude is labeled by the March resolution of the Central Committee and the many articles dealing with the subject as opportunist right-wing deviation.

The March, 1955, Central Committee resolution states:

> Recently there has been a growing tendency to right-wing, opportunist deviation from the correct Party line in matters concerning socialist industrialization.
>
> The right-wing, anti-Marxist deviation in this field is demonstrated in the following manner: there have been efforts toward the frustration of socialist industrialization, and views have been expressed denying the necessity of the constant development of heavy industry. Should the right-wing, opportunist policy, opposing the main Party line, become victorious, our country would ultimately be pushed into the ranks of the backward nations.

Although the charge is not leveled against me personally—and I do not take it personally—I consider it necessary to express my views in order to avoid misunderstandings.

I have never held or propounded views denying the necessity of the constant development of heavy industry, unless it is claimed that the government measures taken in the spirit of the June resolution concerning the cut of heavy industrial investments and a certain slowing down of heavy industrial development, plus the regrouping of production and in the course of this the modification of the ratio between the first and second categories, can be construed as a denial on my part of the necessity of constant heavy industrial development.

For a year and a half resolutions of Party leadership charged that we continued the excessive development of heavy industry instead of cutting it down, and that the tasks outlined by the June resolution of the Central Committee were not carried out vigorously enough in the fields of investments, industrial regrouping, and the further cutback of heavy industrial ratio.

The government activities, concurring with the Party resolutions, were not in contrast to the necessity of the constant development of heavy industry. But they were in contrast to the excessive development of heavy industry of the period preceding the June resolution, and also in contrast to aspirations and views advocating the development of heavy industry in the old manner, disregarding the objective economic laws, and above all the requirements of the basic law of socialism, which were violated by the industrial development policy of the pre-June period. These aspects must be considered when seeking to determine what is the Marxist-Leninist point of view and what is right-wing deviation under the given circumstances. After years of excessive development of heavy industry its slowing down and the stepping up of consumer goods production cannot be called right-wing deviation.

The June resolution called for far-reaching measures for the slowing down of excessive heavy industrial development, which involved the elimination of several large-scale investments and the reorganization of heavy industrial production. A review of the Central Committee's June resolution and the tasks outlined by it show that we have done far less than was required by the resolution in the field of cutting down excessive heavy industrial development and the reorganization of production. This was stated by the October, 1953, Central Committee resolution, the Third Party Congress, and again by the October, 1954, Central Committee resolution. The incorrect opinion, which we encounter in so many articles, studies and even Party resolution, and which labels the slowing down of heavy industrial development as a right-wing deviation, is due to a great extent to the fact that the Party membership, the masses, and the scientific institutions are even now unfamiliar with the full text of the June, 1953, Central Committee resolution, which exposes the mistakes and outlines the new tasks. The June resolution reached the public through government statements, and since the Party was silent, the sharp turn that we had to take was given from the very beginning a double interpretation, which contributed to the impression that there were contradictions between Party and government policies. At present this is sharply expressed in the views that the June resolution was distorted in the course of its implementation by the government, meaning by Imre Nagy, without, however, defining the character of the distortion but keeping it in very general terms. Charges are clad in meaningless clichés, such as "right-wing opportunist policy" and "opposing the Party line" without an exact definition of its nature. Such "general" accusations are not born out of coincidence. The fact is that these accusations cannot be substantiated with theoretically solid arguments, because they are not founded on truth. This is all the more so because the subjects in question have not been analyzed scientifically and especially not with regard to their application to specific Hungarian conditions. This is the source of the practice, so alien to the Marxist spirit, of not drawing theoretical conclusions on the basis of scientific analysis, but to fit preconceived statements. Those engaged in such practices make a mockery of Marxist-Leninist teachings, at the same time claiming the right of hailing their most absurd views as the only correct Marxist interpretation. And as the only (self-styled) rightful interpreters of Marxism, they reject and brand as right-wing deviation any opinion or view that does not concur with their own.

In their theoretical considerations they also violate basic scientific methods. Speaking of the speedier development of the first category, they violate the Marxist-Leninist principle of the historic approach. When invoking the example of the Soviet Union or referring to Lenin's works, they disregard the changes that arose in historic development and level of economic standards. Their arguments in support of the necessity of stepped-up development of heavy industry in the present are based on conditions that prevailed in the Soviet Union some thirty to forty years ago or can be found in the works of Lenin.

The view, arising from ignorance or superficial considerations, identifying the first category with heavy industry is the source of grave mistakes. Although heavy industry is the main producer of production means, such an identification distracts attention from the role of heavy industry in the field of consumer demands and obscures the fact that Category I means not only heavy industrial but also agricultural and light industrial products.

Foreign trade is an important factor in Hungary in the determination of the proper proportion between the first and second categories. Only in a completely self-sufficient country can the law of proportionate development assert itself without foreign trade. Since the law of proportionate development requires not just any proportions but those outlined by the basic law, they can be created without foreign trade only under exceptional circumstances in a very large country, possessing varied natural resources and versatile climate and soil conditions.

Stepped-up industrialization increased the demand for imports, not only in raw materials but also in goods required for heavy industrial investments. The construction of huge plants demanded the importation of large quantities of machines, instruments, etc. In 1953 the goods imported for investment purposes amounted to 25 per cent of total imports. These circumstances resulted in the fact that, although our foreign trade increased considerably, certain discrepancies arose in the composition of our exports and imports.

The drop in agricultural production affected our foreign trade all the more seriously because our industry was not always able to keep up with export requirements. This was primarily due to the fact that we did not pay enough attention to technological improvements. The poor quality of our industrial goods was often a brake on their export possibilities.

An increase of our industrial, particularly heavy industrial, exports and the finding of the proper types of goods are all the more important because the further growth of our heavy industrial production necessitates the import of heavy industrial raw materials in greater quantities.

It is worth while to deal with the question of how the Soviet comrades acted and criticized, and what statements they made and what advice they gave concerning the statements of the June Central Committee resolution on the development of heavy industry, the relationship between Categories I and II, and on mistakes of the past and tasks of the future.

In June, 1953 in Moscow, during a conversation preceding the Central Committee meeting, Comrade Mikoyan made the following statements concerning our economic planning and industrialization policy:

The matter of economic planning shows a certain adventurous spirit, particularly the excessive development of your own iron smelting industry. Hungary has no iron ore, nor coke. All this must be imported. No one in Hungary has figured out yet exactly the price of a ton of iron ore and steel in Hungary. Hungary is building foundries for which no one has yet promised to supply the ore. In 1952, for instance, there was a shortage of 700,000 tons of coke. There is also extravagance in the field of certain investments.

Early in 1954, at a Moscow conference, Comrade Kaganovich made the following statement concerning our economic policy:

Earlier mistakes in the economic policy have not yet been completely corrected. The proportion between the heavy and light industries is almost the same as in the past. You wanted to build socialism, on which we have been working for thirty-five years, too rapidly. The situation is entirely different in Russia than it is in Hungary, and you do not want to face this fact. The situation must be changed more profoundly.

Resolutions of the Twelfth Congress of the Russian Communist (Bolshevik) Party on industrialization, the relationship between industry and agriculture, industrial stockpiling, and expanded reproduction state the following:

Under the general economic construction of our country the rebirth of nationalized industry will necessarily depend to a great extent on the development of agriculture, because before industry can take a big step forward a necessary rotating fund must be created in agriculture, through an agricultural surplus in excess of the village requirements. However, it is equally important that nationalized industry should not stay behind agriculture, in which case a sizable privately owned industry would develop, which at the end would swallow up nationalized industry.

An industry can be successful only if it yields more than it consumes. An industry that is maintained at the cost of the budget, that is to say at the cost of agriculture, could not form a solid and permanent basis for proletarian dictatorship. The production of surplus values in nationalized industry is the key issue in the fate of Soviet power, i.e., in the fate of proletarian dictatorship.

Expanded reproduction by nationalized industry, which is unthinkable without a state accumulation of value surplus, is the prerequisite for our agricultural development in the socialist direction instead of in the capitalist direction.

For many years I myself have expressed my views in these matters. Now I limit myself to the most important statements:

Consequently the reconstruction of industry and agriculture must progress in parallel fashion, supplementing each other. If we neglected either one or the other, or supported one at the cost of the other, we would thereby undermine the economic foundation of the Hungarian democracy.

It is beyond doubt that we can talk of the development of production in both essential branches of our national economy when more than the used-up production forces is produced, and not a simple reproduction process is followed, in which case we could only speak of stagnation. But only if surplus production forces (capital, machinery, etc.) are produced (by the method of expanded secondary production) and poured back into production result in progress can we talk of progress.

The above will convince every objective judge that in matters of expanded reproduction, the relationship and proportion between Categories I and II, primacy of production of production means and the development of heavy industry, I have taken the correct Marxist-Leninist stand. Consequently all charges of right-wing deviation and distortion of the Party line are completely unfounded.

We will reach the same conclusion if we compare my views with the statements and advice given by the Soviet comrades. It may be found that they are in complete accord. If in the course of the implementation of these principles there was any distortion at all, it could only mean that, due to the resistance put up by the Party apparatus and leading economic agencies, we were unable to realize these principles fully, as a result of which the country suffered considerable damage.

The "distortion" as interpreted by recent Party resolutions and the press refers to an excessive cutback of heavy industrial development. In other words, in cutting back and regrouping we have allegedly exceeded the limit set by the requirements of a proportionate planned development and guaranteeing the people's economic necessities of an expanded socialist reproduction. Quite the contrary is the case. We did not do that, because of the resistance because we could not even reach the limits set by the requirements of the objective economic laws.

With the March resolution the danger arose that the further development of Hungarian industry will be determined without changing the existing proportions, and with disregard of the serious lesson derived from the industrialization policy of the pre-June period, in other words it will be continued where it was left off in June. A great many facts already support this statement.

Now let us take a look at the problem of expanded reproduction in the peasant farms. The March resolution states:

Bourgeois theories, long ago destroyed by Marxist tenets, have been revived and even printed in certain technical magazines, according to which the simple commodity-producing peasant farms in the People's Democracy are characterized by the method of expanded secondary production. Based on this and other false concepts, there were some who challenged the commanding necessity of the socialist reorganization of agriculture and set out to destroy the kolkhoz movement. . . .

The incorrect views concerning the expanded secondary production system of the small peasant farms not only serve the slowing down of the socialist reorganization of agriculture, but also disrupt the friendly relations between the kolkhoz members and the independently working peasants.

There is no need to deal with correct or incorrect views of others, but I consider it necessary to make my own position clear, even though the charges are not leveled directly against me. Since generalizations may be interpreted in any way desired, I wish to avoid the possibility that my silence on this matter be construed as a desire to avoid the issue. It is not difficult to give an answer because I have made my position clear on various occasions. Of these I quote:

On the disintegrating small farms, accumulation, if any, is much smaller than it used to be on the large holdings, and a single poor year is sufficient to reduce to nothing the accumulations of several years. We can hardly speak of expanded secondary production in the case of small peasant farms, which form the basis of our present agricultural production. It cannot be said that there is absolutely no expanded secondary production because this would mean overlooking the fact that some agricultural sectors do show good progress. Yet this type of expanded secondary production is of a very low level, and aside from a certain progress of production forces is mainly based on more labor, particularly in the case of new farmers.

Can we allow our agriculture to remain at this stage? No.

Therefore it is imperative that in our reconstruction plan we strive to provide the decisive factors of development, the possibilities for expanded secondary production and capital accumulation. For this purpose we must place great emphasis on those economic "levers" that will aid us in our efforts to induce agriculture to take that course.

The stand taken by the Politburo is reflected by the following statement, made in May, 1954:

In connection with agricultural development, or rather the mobilization of the reserves present in the independently operated small and middle-sized peasant farms, the question was raised whether the middle-sized peasant farms, but particularly the small farms, were capable of expanded reproduction.

The Politburo believes that during the present stage of development in the Hungarian People's Democracy, middle-sized and even small peasant farms are capable of expanded secondary production within certain limitations, because the extensive support granted by the socialist state, the elimination of the capitalistic exploitation of old times, as well as the guarantee of a certain market for farmers' produce, provide the necessary favorable conditions.

During the pre–1953 years the Party's agrarian policy came into conflict with Marxist-Leninist teachings, which emphasize that a cooperation between the kolkhozes and individually farming peasants is necessary and that they must not be pitted against each other. Lenin spoke repeatedly and with great emphasis about assistance to be granted to individually working farmers, about how to help increase the yield of small and middle-sized farms and about the methods by which machine stations can assist the peasants with machines and other means. In our country exactly the opposite happened, due to the extreme "left-wing" agrarian policy. In 1949 the machine stations performed 51 per cent of all mechanical work for the independently farming peasants (calculated on the basis of regular acres) but in 1952, when the number of tractors was nearly three times the 1949 figure, only 1.3 per cent of mechanized work was done on independent farms.

Under these circumstances the produce yield of peasant farms could not increase, the soil became depleted because, due to the uncertainty, peasants did not fertilize it and it is small wonder that under such conditions the peasants not only failed to apply expanded secondary production methods but had very limited possibilities even for simple production. However, the reasons for this must not be sought in the independent peasant farms, or in their production methods, or even in their shortcomings, but must be attributed to the wrong agricultural policy of the government. The "left-wing" deviationists conclude, on the basis of their own faulty policy, that peasant farms are incapable of expanded secondary production, even within limitations. Indeed, they go so far as to replace the political economic concept of expanded secondary production with the meaningless expression "production reserve," which is nothing else but the vulgarization of Marxist-Leninist tenets, a "scientific cowardice."

The question must be approached in the following manner: Will the People's Democracy truly support the small peasant farms, in which case there is a possibility for them to expand production within a certain limitation, or will this support be given in mere words, as is the practice of "left-wing" extremists, while in reality they curtail small peasant farm production, thus eliminating all chance for expanded secondary production? The first course is in accordance with Leninist policy, the latter is in direct contradiction, from a theoretical as well as a practical point of view, to Marxist-Leninist teachings.

Marx states in the first volume of his *Capital* that "in the most varied social and economic formations not only simple secondary production takes place, but also expanded secondary production, even though to different extents. Increasingly more is produced and more consumed, consequently more products must be converted to production means."

In this instance Marx referred also to the independently farming peasants, and if we consider that at present at least 70 per cent of the total agricultural output is supplied by the independently working peasants, it becomes quite clear that Marx, though fully conscious of the limited possibilities of expanded secondary production within the peasant farming system, did not deny its possibilities.

The March, 1955, resolution speaks, either by mistake or deliberately, but in any case in a misleading manner, of "simple goods-producing peasant farms," and states that expanded secondary production is not characteristic of these. But who ever did say that expanded secondary production was characteristic of the simple goods-producing peasant farms? Such a statement could not be considered anything but extremely stupid.

Chapter 10. Productivity of Labor and Reduction of Production Cost

In a social society the part of the national income used for accumulation is of decisive importance for the development of the people's economy. There are two ways to increase the national income: one is the increase of labor used for production, the other is greater productivity. The rapid progress of the latter is accomplished mainly by better technical methods, which is part of the law of planned, proportionate development and the increase of Category I output, with due consideration to the requirements of the basic law of socialism. This means that the ratios and relationship between Categories I and II of social production have a decisive bearing on the shaping of labor productivity. Marxist classics have come to the scientifically supported conclusion that the increase of labor productivity may be assured most effectively through a more rapid development of Category I, although it is not the only factor to be considered.

Marxist-Leninist theories place great emphasis on labor productivity in the process of secondary production. Lenin said:

> The new technique of large-scale production, introduced by socialist industry, greatly promotes socialist development also in the field of agricultural labor productivity. For labor productivity is the most important, decisive factor in the success of the new social order. Capitalism created a type of productivity that was unknown under the feudal system. Capitalism can be and shall be permanently vanquished by the introduction of a higher level of productivity of socialist labor.

The March, 1955, Central Committee resolution refers in two instances to right-wing views in the matter of labor productivity. In one instance it deals with the issue in general terms:

Concerning socialist industrialization, right-wing views are evidenced not only by the fact that their advocates reject the primacy of heavy industrial development, but also by their tendency to belittle the role and significance of increased production and productivity and that of reduced production cost. This is dangerous demagogy and deception of the people.

As we see, here again appears the already refuted charge of denying the primary importance of heavy industrial development. And based on this unfounded statement comes the charge of "belittling the significance of greater productivity and reduced production cost." In the other instance the charge is leveled against me personally:

Disregarding this basic tenet of Leninist teachings, Comrade Imre Nagy committed the mistake of overlooking this most important issue in the matter of socialist victory, namely the necessity of systematic increase of productivity without which the country is unable to create a strong and flourishing industry, and without which all promises of higher living standards for the workers become unfounded and empty and result in the deception of the people.

These statements would be correct if they were based on truth. To prove how unjust the criticism is I wish to quote a few passages from my speeches in which I dealt with the theoretical and practical sides of the issue. On June 14, 1954, in a speech given at the Hungarian Academy of Science, I said the following about labor productivity:

The Marxist science of economics has the great and important task of analyzing the matter of productivity of social labor and its everyday, practical application in the building of socialism. Vulgarization and generalization must be countered with scientific analysis of the question. Without this the cut of production cost and our efforts toward profitable production, the central issues of our economic policy, can achieve only a half-success.

Marxist-Leninist classics attributed extreme importance to the matter of social labor productivity. According to Lenin this is the most important issue for the victory of the new social order.

And Stalin says:

Why can, must, and will the socialist economy defeat the capitalist system? Because it can introduce higher working standards and can result in higher labor productivity than the capitalist system. Because it is able to give more goods to society, thereby making it wealthier than the capitalist economic system.

I continued to say in my speech at the Academy:

Consequently the increase of labor productivity is an indispensable factor in the building of socialist society. This is the only way toward economic development and a higher living standard for the population. This proves that among the conditions necessary for the building of socialism, the constant increase of productivity of social labor is an objective economic law, which together with the law of proportionate, planned development of the people's economy must be enforced in the interest of socialist victory. It is based on incessant technical development, better technological training of the workers, improvement of production administration, etc.

Continuing to express my views on labor productivity, I said:

Attention must be directed also to the establishment of scientific methods of evaluation, which at present are limited to industry alone. Scientific research must be extended to every important branch of our people's economy, including the field of agriculture, in which the question of productivity is of prominent importance in connection with the development of socialist, cooperative farms, requiring scientific evaluation methods.

I think the above excerpts from my speech at the Hungarian Academy of Science prove beyond doubt that my attitude toward the matter of labor productivity was in absolute harmony with the Marxist-Leninist spirit, and dealt with this subject more profoundly and in greater detail than by any one of my accusers.

I also dealt with the matter in my speech to the Hungarian State Railways (MAVAG) in November, 1954:

> In our industrial production greater attention must be paid to thrift, productivity, lower production cost, and economy in the use of raw materials; we must strive to achieve these through modernization of production procedures and technological improvement. . . .
>
> Further great efforts must be made by our industry, leaders, and workers toward a systematic increase of productivity. The necessary increase in productivity may be achieved by the elimination of lax labor discipline, by good labor administration, and by assuring the technological requirements. For this is the soul and the essential factor in the proper functioning of our huge industry.
>
> The mere approval and official sanctioning of resolutions do not solve the problem. These must go hand in hand with the raising of labor productivity. The June policy, which by now is accepted and supported by the whole nation, demands the constant increasing of labor productivity in industry, agriculture, and every field engaged in productive work.

This was my opinion on productivity then and it is still the same. Whenever I saw fit I expressed it and did everything in my power in the interest of the practical application of these principles.

However, I pointed out and emphasized the great importance of accumulation and labor productivity and their decisive effect on increased production, not only during recent years, during the period following the June resolution, but I have spoken of these on several occasions even in previous years. I took up the matter in detail in the course of a conference held in the Home of Party Instructors:

> Labor productivity is . . . a decisive factor because in the final analysis, social progress, the transition from a lower to a higher social order, from capitalism to socialism and the ultimate victory of socialism—as was pointed out by Lenin—depend upon labor productivity. . . . We have a great potential in this field. Looking at the technical facilities at our disposal, it becomes evident that neither kolkhozes nor machine stations nor state farms make

complete use of the existing mechanized facilities. . . . Are there great possibilities and reserves here? Yes . . . closely connected with this matter is the question of accumulation. In the socialist sector, expanded secondary production is still very limited, consequently accumulation is also at a rather low level. Yet without a constantly progressing expanded secondary production system, kolkhoz production cannot advance at a higher rate. The fact that there are possibilities and considerable hidden potentialities indicates that production can be, and in fact must be, increased with the application of all means at our disposal.

The above excerpts show that I raised the question and pointed to the importance of labor productivity and accumulation, not only in general terms and with reference to industry, but also in the field of agriculture, connecting the issue with the development of large-scale socialist kolkhoz production.

I could continue quoting passages from my articles and speeches, but I believe the above will suffice and prove that:

A. Concerning accumulation, labor productivity, and reduced production cost, I represented the correct Marxist ideology. I continue to do so, and my attitude can be branded as anti-Marxist or right-wing deviationist only by those who deliberately overlook or falsify the facts. Furthermore I must point out that my views, expressed in the above quoted articles and speeches, were never challenged, criticized, or censured.

B. The quotations furnish factual evidence that the charge that I have overlooked this all-important Marxist-Leninist tenet is totally unfounded.

C. The quotations also prove that I dwelt on these important matters not by mouthing empty clichés but that I went into their very core, always emphasizing my own attitude and the tremendous significance of their application in industry.

D. I raised the issue more often and in greater detail than any other member of the Politburo, including Mátyás Rákosi and Gerö. In this connection it is not without interest to determine not only who spoke, and how often, about labor productivity and reduced production cost, but also what was said and whether it was only a matter of speaking or whether efforts were made toward the practical implementation of the principles.

In January, 1954, in my six-months' report on government activities to Parliament, I said the following:

> The previous extreme rate of industrialization did not make possible the provision of the technical requirements of production. Under the 1954 plan we are giving industry a certain breathing spell in order to enable it to make up for previous deficiencies in maintenance and to carry out the necessary work of repair and renovation. It is a mistake that managers, key technical personnel of our plants, even the ministries fail to attribute sufficient importance to these questions at a time when they are gradually growing into the key issues in our industrial production, as for instance in our electric power industry. Mistakes of several years must be corrected, and the necessary conditions must be provided for this. Heads of ministries must assure completion of this important task through stricter measures and increased control.

It is an indisputable fact that technical progress, economic superiority over the capitalist countries, finally labor productivity are of decisive importance for the countries of the socialist camp. This fact lends special significance to the consistent application of the Leninist principle concerning the primacy of the production of production means. Yet technical progress must not be limited to Category I alone; it must take place also within Category II. For labor productivity is an important factor also in the production branches of Category II (light industry, agriculture, etc.).

If, however, the two categories did not develop in this manner, but if the second category stayed far behind the level of the first category, then it becomes imperative that the rate of development of Category II exceed, temporarily for one, two, or a few years, the development rate of Category I. Otherwise a sharp discrepancy is inevitable between production and consumption. Under the socialist system the development of Category II must not fall behind Category I to such an extent that Category I shows the highest possible rate of progress, while there is a virtual stagnation within Category II (as was experienced in Hungary between the years 1949 and 1952). Agricultural production in Hungary is approximately at its prewar level. At the same time industrial production shows a 3 to 3.5 times increase, and within this heavy industrial output is at 5 times, and machine industry production at 7 times the 1938 level, while light industrial production is merely 2.3 times higher than that of the prewar period. A large percentage of even this is credited to the period from 1948 to 1951. The rate of light industrial increase is maximally 4 per cent per year, while the yearly rate of increase in the production of capital goods (machine industry) is 17 to 18 per cent. Moreover, between 1949 and 1952 the average yearly increase in the productions of capital goods was 29.1 per cent, while production of consumer goods increased a mere 7.5 per cent.

I concede that Party and state leadership, including myself, did not pay sufficient attention to this important question, which should have received greater consideration and more strenuous efforts. Briefly, it should have been made the central issue of our economic policy. But even so the blame should not be placed on me but on those who paid much less attention to it than I did, or none at all. It should be placed on those who, when the question arose, reacted with empty slogans, and who are now putting on airs as my accusers. For he who has looked into the matter to any degree at all and possesses only a trace of sincerity must know that the charges against me are unfounded accusations. The charge must be brought against those who are responsible for the backward level of labor productivity and for the damaging results to the country, those who for years neglected the technical improvement of our industry, who developed our industry along extreme lines as a result of which the newly constructed plants were forced to apply essentially the same technological methods as before and were therefore, even on the basis of their original plans, not more productive than the old installations. Charges must be brought against these men. They are responsible for the lack of improvement in labor productivity and for the resulting damage, men whose negligence was responsible for the fact that the basic pattern of our investments remained unchanged.

In my January, 1954, parliamentary report I said the following:

Beyond providing a material basis for future objectives, the most important factor in our investment policy, a factor that has an immediate bearing on the further development of our industry, in fact on our whole people's economy, is the task of reorganizing and modernizing the two basic industries, our coal mining and electric power industries. Development of these two decisive industries has not kept pace with the general rate of industrialization, and although demand for their products is constantly increasing, their technical development has been neglected. . . .

Charges must be brought against those—and the extent of their responsibility must be established—who are trying to increase labor productivity even today, not through technical improvement but primarily by administrative methods. Such a course is unpardonable under the conditions of socialist building, and it only introduces capitalist methods in labor productivity and production cost cuts. Leading Party circles are familiar with Mátyás Rákosi's views, which he has repeatedly expressed since June, 1953, and has tried to incorporate in our economic policy, according to which an artificial unemployment had to be created in our industry, which he claimed was the most effective method to improve labor discipline and to increase productivity. Such a view is incompatible with any socialist economic policy, and it is in sharp contrast to the basic Marxist-Leninist principles. It is an attempt to re-establish capitalist methods, and it had to be and still must be flatly rejected. My accusers themselves give indication of the fact that I am right and that their charges are unfounded when they put the blame on me for the unsatisfactory development of labor productivity. They blame me for neglecting the technical development of our industry, which is the direct cause of the absence of increased labor productivity and reduced production cost. Yet they use an entirely different tone when they seek to explain and justify the readjustment of norms. Then they proclaim that during the last eighteen months important measures have been taken in the matter of technical progress. On May 23, 1955, in an article entitled "Timely Comments on Work Norms," *Szabad Nep* writes among other things:

Technological norms are changing primarily because the technical standards of our industry are constantly improving. . . .

During the last three years a technical improvement, even though not to a satisfactory degree, has taken place in the iron industry, despite the dangerous right-wing views that minimized the role of heavy industry. During this time more than two billion forints have been invested in the machine industry . . . a considerable share of investments was used to acquire new machines. As a result work is easier and faster . . . and has been further facilitated by the introduction of modern production methods. . . . During the three years not only has technique improved, not only has technology been modernized, not only has the administration of plants improved, but the technical knowledge of the workers has increased greatly.

There it is: so many proper measures have been taken, even according to *Szabad Nep,* where it is a matter of justifying the adjustment of norms and not the mistakes of Imre Nagy. That is how "right-wing" deviation and its criticism along the "Party line" look in the newspaper of the Party.

Chapter 11. Problems of Socialist Industrialization

The March resolution of the Central Committee on harmful rightist views pointed out that these views manifested themselves, first of all, in a distortion of the correct policy of socialist industrialization. The resolution stated further that the June, 1953, resolution of our Party, the resolution of the Third Party Congress, and other important Party resolutions put it on record unequivocally that socialist industrialization is the most important means of building socialism, and that primary importance must be placed upon the production of capital goods. Following the Central Commitee's March resolution, articles in the Party press, in papers, and in periodicals, employing every means of unscrupulous falsification and taking advantage of the resolution's general assertions, tried to prove the correctness of the resolution disregarding the rudiments of objective and Partylike criticism that form the basis of Communist morality.

Editorials in *Szabad Nep* and *Tarsadalmi Szemle,* as well as numerous articles by various authors printed in the Party press, outdid one another in concocting fabrications and slander. In many cases they revealed in their zealotry that "criticism" of the right-wing deviation was aimed at smuggling back and justifying the erroneous, exaggerated, mistaken, pre-June, 1953, policy of industrialization condemned in the June resolution, which has been valid since then and even has constituted the basis of the Party's guiding principles.

Of the many articles published since March, we shall deal here only with the latest, written by Gyorgy Csatar and printed in the July 31, 1955, issue of *Szabad Nep* under the title "Possibilities for Developing Heavy Industry and Right-wing Ideas." Csatar wrote, *inter alia:*

> Representatives of rightist ideas repudiated, first of all, the necessity for socialist industrialization in our fatherland. Certain individuals made open statements to this effect. Others gave theoretical recognition to the necessity of socialist industrialization, i.e., speeded up development of industry and the primary importance of developing heavy industry, but declared that because of specific local conditions socialist industrialization could not be carried out in our fatherland.

It is not clear from the above quotation who are the "certain individuals" and who are the "others," and to which category I belong. One thing is certain from Csatar's article: in whichever group he included me, in his opinion I was essentially against industrialization.

In order to expose and destroy such irresponsible slander, let us go over my more important declarations, speeches, and writings, in which I stated clearly my views on the main problem of socialist industrialization and its importance from the point of view of other branches of the people's industry.

In my inaugural address in May, 1953, at the Hungarian Academy of Science, "On Politico-economic Problems of the Transition from Capitalism to Socialism," I stated:

> The efforts of People's Democracies in the field of industrialization, and the success achieved with the unselfish support given by the Soviet Union in every way, fully vindicate the Leninist-Stalinist theory of socialist industrialization.
>
> Development of socialist industry increases the forces of production in tremendous degree in every branch of the people's economy, and also in agriculture. Socialist industrialization creates opportunities for the development of agrarian techniques—mainly by the establishment of machine stations—and this forms the financial-technical basis of agricultural large-scale farms. The theory of socialist industrialization was worked out by Lenin and Stalin. Lenin wrote on the decisive role of socialist industry in the

socialist reorganization of agriculture, as follows: "The city must give far-reaching technical and social support to the backward and disunited village, so that this support creates the material basis for a great increase in the productivity of agricultural work, and stimulates, with the force of good example, the small farmers to change, in their own interest, to large-scale, collective, mechanized farming."

Continuing my address, I emphasized:

All this makes it evident that without the leading role of industry, a socialist transformation of the people's economy, the creation of large-scale farming and collective agriculture, and, as an ultimate goal, the creation of a socialist socio-economic system is not possible. That is why five-year plans aimed at industrializing the people's economies have such a paramount, decisive role in the transitory period.

In this same speech I stressed the importance of industry in the people's economy:

In that profound economic metamorphosis in the course of which Hungary turned from a capitalist country into a People's Democracy, building socialism, industrialization—by developing industry and putting it on a socialist basis—had a decisive role in creating favorable conditions for the development of agricultural forces of production and for the change from individual to collective farming.

Those who claim that I was against socialist industrialization or that I denied its importance are but common slanderers. The exact opposite is true: I advocated the necessity of socialist industrialization and supported it a long time before the liberation, in articles published in the monthly *Uj Hang* [*New Voice*] of Moscow, and especially after the liberation, from the very beginning.

For the first three issues of 1940 of *Uj Hang,* I had written a lengthy study entitled "Industrialization and the Agrarian Problem," published as a serial in three installments. In the third part, bearing the title "A Few Characteristics of Hungarian Imperialism," I enlarged on the development of prewar industry, its connections with domestic and foreign markets, and the sharpening discrepancies. I wrote the following sentences in the concluding part:

> The elimination of internal contradictions of monopolistic capitalism through an imperialistic war is the *last word* of reaction in the "solution" of the inner conflicts of capitalism. Historic development has given the clue to the working people, to democracy. Hungary reborn as a People's Democracy will lay down a wide basis, by destroying the system of large estates and by democratizing the landed estates with a radical land reform, for the sake of the development of a domestic market, for industrialization and an economic boom. Thus, the people's Hungary will enter a period of peaceful development and will be a solid pillar of understanding between peoples.

My position taken in the matter of socialist industrialization is not new, nor is it an unsubstantiated and useless view. It is a firm standpoint, theoretically resting on the ground of Marxism-Leninism and rooted in Hungarian conditions, which I have consistently represented during the ten years following the liberation, keeping in mind the phases of the development of the people's economy and looking at the problems from the perspective of socialist construction. My oral or written statements at various times and on different occasions are the proof.

I have devoted my time to the question of socialist industrialization not only from a general, theoretical point of view, but also from the angle of practical tasks, always in keeping with the spirit of Marxism-Leninism, doing this just as extensively and just as well as those who now fabricate charges against me. In January, 1954, in the General Assembly, in my report on the government's work during the past six months, I said as follows:

> Our industrial production, as is shown from the plan figures for 1954, is faced by great tasks: to assure a supply of goods for the population's consumption by increased manufacture of consumer goods; to meet industrial demands for the development of agricultural production and for assuring important materials necessary to solve all these tasks successfully; to fulfill completely,

in time, and on a good qualitative level, the export plan for industry, especially that for the machine industry. But we are looking forward to these tasks calmly because our excellent workers' class, which has successfully passed so many tests of strength during recent years, will with its unselfish, enthusiastic labors and high technical skill be able to find the best possible way to deal with all tasks of building socialism in the field of industry. . . . The growth of the socialist labor competition movement, which has been invaluable for past successes in fulfilling production plans, is giving us tremendous support in coping with the tasks. All this, coupled with the support of the workers' initiative unfolding in ever increasing proportions, will bring about a successful solution of production tasks stipulated by the plan.

I believe it can be ascertained beyond doubt from the above how unfounded are the charges that I forgot about the problems of raising production and that all my promises concerning raising the living standard of workers were unfounded, empty, and aimed at misleading the workers. All this only proves that the inferences drawn from an unfounded charge also will be wrong.

In the same speech I pointed out the extraordinary tasks that have to be coped with in the field of industrial production:

In the field of fulfilling the plans of industrial production the country expects great results, not only from miners, foundry workers, and iron workers, but also from the workers in the light and building industries. The realization of our program is dependent, first of all, on their good work. Outstanding in the field of industrial production are those extraordinary tasks which have to be solved in coal mining, iron foundry and electric power production. The work which will be done in the immediate future will have a decisive influence in this field.

In a speech I made at the MAVAG factory, in November, 1954, I spoke on the problems of investments, the level of technical work, the problems of the technical intelligentsia and the skilled laborers:

I have reserved a few general problems of industry for the end of my speech. First of all we have to exploit our existing industrial basis in a more profitable way. Prescribed investments must be used, first of all, for modernizing our plants and for raising our technical level. A part of investments not used up fully must be gradually utilized. Plants that are not up to the demands and scope of our economic policy must be transformed and utilized in some other field.

In the production, organization, and management of our industry, wide-range use of technical sciences must be enforced to a greater extent. Special care and respect must be paid to the technical intelligentsia and the staff of skilled workers who are the greatest assets of Hungarian industry and the gold standard of socialist industrialization. For this reason we must prepare a man-power balance sheet to determine the right direction of our industrial policy, sizing up the situation of skilled and semiskilled workers, apprentices, the technical intelligentsia, and man-power replacement, as well as migration of man power. Great emphasis must be placed on organizational problems of industrial production and industrial management, in which fields our entire people's economy must be guided by universal principles.

I have repeatedly stated my viewpoint on the decisive importance of socialist *industrialization* and the development of *industrial production* for the increase of *agricultural production* and the socialist transformation of agriculture. I spoke about some socio-economic problems of the transformation in my inaugural address to the Academy of Science on May 26, 1953:

We find innumerable rules in Lenin's works telling us that without a well-developed socialist industry agriculture cannot have socialist, cooperative large-scale farms. Only a highly developed socialist heavy industry can provide the new technical basis for socialist reorganization of agriculture, for mechanization of every branch of production—including animal husbandry—and further, in the interest of this goal, the building of a network of machine stations embracing the entire agricultural land. Socialist industry is the most effective factor in the People's Democracies during the transition from capitalism to socialism, for developing the forces of production, for the transformation of property relations and means of production, and for adjusting these in

harmony. It is beyond doubt that socialist industry has considerable effect in this direction.

At an October, 1953, conference of outstanding agricultural
experts, I said, *inter alia:*

> I find it necessary to call your attention to some specific phe-
> nomena in the present stage of development. In recent years
> agriculture has been left behind because of the enforced rapid
> development of industry. Thus we violated the law of propor-
> tionate development. We must make up for this now. In the field
> of industry we shall not enforce a continued rapid rise of pro-
> duction, but rather try to win a respite of one or two years. In
> other words, we shall want time to consolidate achievements, to
> correct mistakes, to schedule new tasks, and to prepare for further
> development.

It can be ascertained from what I have related here, but also
from my work done during the past twenty months in the field
of socialist industrialization, that neither I nor the government
of the Hungarian People's Republic under my leadership, nor
its economic policy, have ever given up the idea of continuing
socialist industrialization. On the contrary, it has been regarded
from the very beginning as the principal means for building
socialism. The June policy pointed out that within industry
individual branches of the people's economy have to be re-
grouped, and that in the course of socialist industrialization
consideration must be given to the fact that we are not building
socialism alone, as the Soviet Union had to do it at one time
for a long period; further that, with respect to industrialization,
we must take into account our existing possibilities, the load
that the country can support, and the international division of
labor.

The ratio between the Soviet Union's industrial and agricultural production was, in 1929, approximately 1.6 to 1 in favor
of industrial production. The socialist sector in industry was
then about 99 per cent, and about 5 per cent in agriculture (i.e.,
99 per cent of industry, but only 5 per cent of agriculture, were
socialized). In Hungary the ratio of industrial and agricultural
production in 1954 was 5 to 1. At the same time, industry was

almost completely socialized, agriculture 30 per cent socialized. It is natural that such a ratio sharpened the already existing contradiction between industry and agriculture, due to the principle of increased secondary production. But in eliminating this discrepancy, it is not a good method to distort proportions to an even greater extent through "ultra-industrialization," or to be hasty about the socialist transformation of agriculture that is doubtlessly necessary. Rather we must try to bring the proportions of the people's economy into balance by increasing agricultural production. There is no justification for the fact that our total agricultural production is still vacillating near the prewar level, reaching from 85 to 105 per cent of that figure, depending, first of all, on the weather. While the Soviet Union in 1929, despite a small socialist sector of agriculture, considerably exceeded the prewar (1913) level of agriculture production, Hungary in spite of a socialist sector of almost 30 per cent, and with individual peasant farms owning modern means of production, manages in the best of cases a production level of 1938, which we should have exceeded long ago. The main fault lies not with the peasant farms but with the poor economic policy that has kept our agricultural production on a low level. All this shows that the "leftist" zealots have not analyzed the specific conditions of our country or those of the Soviet Union. Instead, they replaced the views of Lenin and Stalin with quotations that could not breed anything else but dogmatism.

The June policy laid down as a rule that industrialization must be parallel to the development and socialist transformation of agriculture, and also to the continuous improvement of the standard of living of the masses. Vigorous development of agriculture and increased production of consumer goods must be regarded, also for the future, as very important factors of the economic policy of party and government. This leads, on the other hand, to the realization that the development of heavy industry must serve the technical needs of agriculture and of light industry to a much greater extent in the future than in the past.

The flagrant violation of the law of planned proportionate development manifests itself in the sharpening discrepancy between production and consumption. The ratio of industrial to agricultural production is, at present, approximately 4.5 to 1. The ratio between "A" and "B" sectors of our industry in 1953 was 63 to 37. Industry accounted for about 70 per cent of national income. The population's individual consumption basis shrank to 58 per cent of the national income, in comparison to a previous figure of 75 to 80 per cent. The policy of socialist industrialization, the enforced primacy of the production of capital goods, prevalent in Hungary between 1950 and 1953 and shown by figures and facts, did not bring about a continued improvement of the workers' well-being, as stipulated by the basic principle of socialism, but resulted in its deterioration. The "leftist" zealots caused thus exceptionally grave political harm to the Party, to the country, and to the international workers' movement.

When Subdivision A/1 of Category I diverges sharply from Subdivision A/2 of Category I and also from the development of Category II, as it happened in Hungary, there is but one solution: slow down, as a temporary measure, the development rate of Subdivision A/1 of Category I and channel the accumulation from there to Subdivision A/2 of Category I, that is, to Category II. This is the gist of the economic policy we had tried to carry out in the New Course, which was very far from denying the primacy of producing means of production, as the "leftist" zealots have asserted. This policy meant simply that our industry would temporarily produce more means of production for manufacturing consumer goods than was the pre–1953 practice, when our industry produced mainly such means of production as served the manufacture of other capital goods.

The classic tenets of Marxism did not conceal the difficulties arising in the course of building socialism or the difficulties in the process of industrialization. They have established a connection between the shortage of goods and the fast tempo of producing means of production. In connection with this question, Stalin said:

> The fact that we are developing the production of capital goods at a faster rate than light industry—this fact in itself means that in the coming years we shall have with us the elements of a goods shortage.

The correct general principle that abundance of goods can be achieved only through the primacy given to the manufacture of the means of production, which has to be emphasized, becomes untenable if we do not add that an exaggerated speed-up of production of capital assets will cause a shortage of commodities. Stalin remarked in connection with this problem that all those who want to solve this by "ultra-industrialization" are fools and ignorant persons. In Hungary, on the other hand, the "leftist" zealots refuse to admit that an unjustified high speed of industrialization will lead to a temporary shortage of goods, as had been proved true in the years between 1950 and 1953, partly because of the primacy given to the manufacture of the means of production; partly because of the retarded development of agriculture; partly because of the slow development of light industry; and partly because there was too much export (and also for other reasons). It is unavoidable that the balance of goods supply and consumption becomes upset to a certain extent during the years of high-speed socialist industrialization. Those who do not take these realities into account, or keep silent about them, are misleading the workers of the country.

Development of industry, therefore, is an integral part of the June policy. Rather, it can be achieved only by applying the basic principles laid down in June.

At the Fifteenth Conference of the Soviet Communist Party, in November, 1926, Stalin stated in connection with deviations within the Party:

> It is the Party's point of departure that in its policy and especially in its economic policy, industry cannot be made independent of agriculture; that the development of these two basic economic fields must follow the line of reciprocal connection, of unification within the socialist people's economy. The socialist method of the country's industrialization is a consequence of this, making it imperative that we *continuously improve* that material situation of the working masses, and thus also the material situation of the overwhelming part of the peasantry, which is the main basis of the development of industrialization.

I wish to remark here that between 1950 and 1953 the "leftist" zealots, exaggerating the rate of industrial development seriously, damaged the material situation of the working peasantry as well as that of the workers' class, forgetting about Stalin's directives with regard to industrialization.

In Hungary, therefore, the "leftist" pseudoradicals followed the same procedure as the opposition in the Soviet Union in those days: they pushed industrialization to the detriment of the majority of the peasants and the living standard of the workers' class, and resorted to methods of industrialization that disrupted the alliance between industry and peasant farms and undermined the financial situation of the poor and middle-level peasants. In this manner they have actually attacked industrialization at its foundations. This can be proved without shadow of doubt by data on the situation between 1950 and 1952.

Stalin paid scrupulous attention to the right proportions and rate of industrial and agricultural development. He mentioned that the Soviet or the Party could easily double the sums appropriated for developing agriculture or industry. But while in the first case nothing would be left for industry, as a consequence of which industrial development would lag far behind that of agriculture, in the latter case the development of industry would be of an extremely high rate, "which [he said] we could not keep up because of the great lack in free capital, and which would most certainly make us go bankrupt, not to mention that we would not have sufficient reserves for credit loans to give to agriculture."

Therefore a serious consideration and correct allotment of the sources of power is of great importance to avoid creating disproportion in the people's economy.

We are dealing here with a basic question of the building of socialism, to quote Stalin:

> Our industry will be able to fulfill its role of leading economic transformation only if it does not break away from agriculture, from the rate of our stockpiling, and from the sources of power and reserve at our disposal. In the army, the officers' corps that detaches itself from its troops and loses contact with them is not an officers' corps. Similarly, an industry that detaches itself from the body of the people's economy and loses contact with it cannot be a leading factor in the people's economy.

It seems that the pseudoradicals had forgotten this between 1950 and 1953, and refused to remember it as late as 1955.

Certain articles, and even the March Central Committee resolution, contain repeated references to the twisting and distortion of the correct policy of socialist industrialization.

Such unfounded charges are needed by certain people and also have been smuggled into the Central Committee resolution of March, because no one can, for the time being, come out openly against the June resolution. At least the appearance must be kept up in words that they constitute the guiding principles of the Party's policy. The only way to deal with the June resolution and, through it, with me, is by the repeated and emphatic assertion of the charge of "distortion." Whatever they do not like in the June resolution is branded "distortion" so that they can turn back to the pre-June bad industrialization policy.

The ill-conceived charge of "distortion" is being put on my shoulders by them for the very transparent purpose of making themselves appear the staunch avant-garde, the defenders of the June resolution. They are the very same people against whom the June resolutions made very grave charges; who covertly or openly—but incessantly—fought against the June resolution from the time of its birth until its inglorious demise in March; who in the Party and in the state machinery organized and directed the resistance to the realization of the June policy (this is supported by Central Committee resolutions and other important decisions); and against whom I and other comrades faithful to the June resolution had to fight day in, day out with great energy under very difficult circumstances. In addition to all this, Party and government activities in the period between the March resolution and now, economic and political sanctions made under the pretext of fighting rightist deviations, and the situation created by those in the Party and the country, make it clear as daylight that I was right when I pointed out in my memorandum to the March meeting of the Central Committee that behind the crude and unfounded charge against me and my viewpoint there was actually hidden an attack against the June resolution from the "leftist" zealots who have gained the upper hand in the leadership of the Party. This maneuver was greatly facilitated by the fact that the June resolution has been kept a secret from the Party membership until today. Thus they read into it whatever suits their purpose, and no one has a chance to know, or even to find out, who really distorts the resolution.

Such base calumnies were started in connection with socialist industrialization too, as if I had tried to block the development of heavy industry built on the basis of domestic raw materials. This brazen lie serves the "leftist" pseudoradicals to counter the justified criticism of the pre-June industrialization policy—a criticism that met with wide approval in the broadest masses of workers, who knew it to be true from their own experience and who fully agreed with me.

This charge came to the surface on several occasions, the last time in the July 30, 1955, issue of *Szabad Nep*, in the previously mentioned Csatar article. The rightists, wrote Csatar "argue that our country does not yet have the raw materials necessary for developing heavy industry. They have cried out that we are a 'poor country' and Hungary's economic resources can assure only the development of agriculture, of light and food industries. Let us develop only agriculture, light and food industries—they said —and let us obtain the necessary heavy industrial products by exporting, first of all, agricultural products." I never came across such ideas, and I believe no one else did: they were born out of Csatar's overheated imagination. Why does he not quote the source of the above assertion, why does he not name those who have advocated these views? The answer is very simple: it is much easier to tell lies and make charges in this irresponsible fashion.

Csatar cannot pass up the occasion—how could he?—to turn his general charges against me with a transparent idiotic sleight of hand by patching them up with another lie, more vile than the first one. Csatar—speaking of me by name—delivers himself of the following fabrication:

As is known [?], at the personal intervention of comrade Imre Nagy [!] construction work at the Rudabanya ore plant has been stopped. The Hungarian ore is especially suited for smelting. Building up this ore plant in Rudabanya, we shall be able to meet more than 40 per cent of our iron ore demand from domestic sources.

As regards Csatar's assertions, I wish to point out that:

A. His statement that construction work on the Rudabanya ore plant was stopped at my personal intervention is a shameless lie;

B. My alleged activities in this matter are unknown to me. If he has inside knowledge of a similar nature he should make it public;

C. Until the time when he can prove his allegation I shall regard him as a common calumniator, and I shall ask for the due legal procedure customary in such cases.

I have defined the question of a basis of industrial primary products as an important factor in the development of our people's economy. In my January, 1954, address to Parliament on the semiyearly activity of the government, I said:

> Our investments, in addition to purchasing the necessary materials, must be used also for a purpose that has bearing on our whole industry, on the development of the entire people's economy: i.e. the improvement and modernization of coal mining and the electric power industry. The development of these two industrial branches of paramount importance has not kept pace with the over-all rate of industrialization. The demands have steadily increased, nevertheless, and technical development of production has lagged behind.
>
> Irregularities in power supply can be accounted for to a great extent because of the above-mentioned reason. Besides serious damage to the people's economy, power shortage considerably affects the workers of certain branches of industry. We shall make tremendous efforts to bring about a well-balanced situation in this field as soon as possible.

Those who assert that in the course of carrying out the June resolution I neglected opportunities to develop our heavy industry built on domestic primary materials ary lying and cheating.

However, I also paid great attention to the research work aimed at a scientific evaluation and exploitation of our country's natural resources and sources of raw materials, and I called the attention of competent authorities to this grandiose task. Why did I do this? Because I was against developing heavy industry based on a supply of domestic primary materials? I, of all people, who have repeatedly and emphatically stressed the importance of exploiting domestic resources for industrial development.

In a lecture at the Hungarian Academy of Science, on June 14, 1954, I said the following:

> Science has gradually failed to fulfill its leading role in many fields and, as a consequence, the development of production, or in many instances our entire policy of industrialization, has been without a scientific basis, has drifted away from it, and has lost the foresight, purposefulness and methodical order that can be assured only if science lays the groundwork for industrialization. Mistakes made in the course of developing industry have their roots in this basic shortcoming. It is unquestionable that neglect of a scientific survey and of scientific plans to use our domestic raw materials, the material basis of our people's economy, had much to do with exaggerated industrialization and especially with the overhasty development of heavy industry. The right proportions, rate, and direction of our industrialization must be determined on a scientific basis, which makes it necessary that the Academy of Science give more consideration to those fields of scientific research—such as the scientific survey of our country's natural resources and sources of raw material—that play the decisive role in determining the rate and direction of developing the individual branches of the people's economy.

I have made the survey and discovery of our natural resources and raw materials a concrete task, in order that we may be able to broaden the domestic primary material basis of our socialist industrialization. This would assure the necessary tempo and proportions of development and prevent setbacks caused by neglect of our raw material resources—as in the past.

Guiding principles of a long-range plan for the Party and the government in the field of socialist industrialization should have been developed in a program of work. The idea was accepted by the October, 1954, meeting of the Central Committee, and the Political Committee put me in charge of working out the details of this program at the head of a committee appointed to direct this work. Preparatory work would have enabled us to start with the actual work as early as December of

1954. I had prepared the outlines of my introductory speech. The Political Committee prevented me from delivering the speech because of the stand taken by Rákosi and Gerö, notwithstanding my repeated and urgent requests to make the speech.

The planned work would have advanced the policy of socialist industrialization with a giant step in the spirit of the June resolution, on the basis of resolutions brought by the Third Congress and the Central Committee in October, and from the point of view of a creative application of Marxism-Leninism. The blocking of the realization of this plan was an important manifestation of resistance. In the outline of my introductory speech I stated my viewpoint on various theoretical and practical questions of socialist industrialization, which is the best refutation of charges against my alleged rightist deviation. This outline is still in the drawer of my desk, and should the Central Committee deem it necessary I could make it available to them at any moment. Besides, in December, 1954, copies of the outline of this speech were sent to several members of the Political Committee, the Central Committee, and the Council of Ministers.

Chapter 12.   The Socialist Reorganization of Agriculture

The Central Committee's resolution of March, 1955, stated that "exceptionally great damage was caused by those right-wing views, alien to Marxism-Leninism, that have affected the principal questions of our Party's policies regarding the peasantry." The resolution then points out that certain Party members incorrectly interpret the problem of the worker-peasant alliance. In their work in the villages they do not rely on the poorer peasants and they forget about the leading role of the working class and the aims of the worker-peasant alliance. They also forget about the building of socialism and the fight against exploitation.

"Such views," states the March resolution, "are largely to blame for the fact that last year the cooperative movement did not grow in numbers but actually decreased somewhat, despite the fact that in most of the cooperatives the members live better than individually farming peasants with medium holdings." With regard to bourgeois ideas concerning the expansion of "small-scale peasant farms," the resolution states that "certain individuals began to deny the absolute need of socialist reorganization and on these grounds sought to thwart the cooperative movement." The Central Committee's March resolution, in the section dealing with the socialist reorganization of agriculture, likewise only contain general accusations (without so much as attempting to show concretely the facts) on the basis of which it arrives at such grave charges, and without naming those whom it accuses of these transgressions.

Before considering the charges with which they seek to prove right-wing deviation, I must first take note of the persons who wrote such "commentaries" in the columns of the Party press on the subject of the Central Committee's March resolution and subsequently on the subject of its resolution dealing with agriculture.

Szabad Nep's June 10, 1955, editorial, entitled, "In the Interest of a Flourishing Agriculture," among other things states the following:

> The Central Committee's March and April resolutions have unmasked the right-wing anti-people [sic] views and have made it plain to all that our party and government stand united, and unequivocally, for the socialist reorganization of agriculture. . . . No thought was given either to the facts or to the interests of our people by those who created conflicts between the two interdependent tasks, and who meanwhile made speeches about the fostering of agricultural production at the very time that they obstructed the healthful development of agriculture, delayed the socialist reorganization of agriculture, and thus impeded the building of socialism.

The two interdependent tasks in question are the expansion of agricultural production and the socialist reorganization of agriculture.

Andras Hegedus, in his speech at the Central Committee's June 7, 1955, session, declared that one of the gravest consequences of right-wing deviation was that "the worker-peasant alliance had been weakened and that uncertainty had arisen among the members of the cooperatives—which in 1953 and 1954 led to many resignations and to the disbanding of many cooperatives."

Andras Hegedus above all else finds it necessary to fight the harmful right-wing views purportedly represented by me, views according to which "the small and medium peasant holdings in their own fashion also develop towards socialism and, under the conditions prevailing in a People's Democracy, are capable en masse, and year by year, of expanding their production systematically." This is a falsification. I never said any such thing.

From such fabrications he forged the accusation that proponents of these views "set themselves against the Congress' resolution, apparently seeking postponement of the socialist reorganization of agriculture, but actually with the intention of pigeonholing it for good." Of me, Andras Hegedus states that in my opinion the small and medium peasant farms automatically develop toward socialism within the framework of small-scale production. He might at least try to prove his statements with facts or arguments. Here, however, Andras Hegedus fails to deliver.

In *Szabad Nep*'s June 12, 1955 issue, Ernö Gerö wrote an editorial entitled "On the Way to Progress" wherein, on the basis of various assumptions, he strives to give the accusations a semblance of probability. In the above-mentioned article, Gerö states that "Imre Nagy and the right-wing deviationists in general start from the premise that we *either* build socialism in the villages—and in this case agricultural production and the yield per acre cannot be increased—*or* increase agricultural production and the yield per acre, but then socialism cannot be built in the villages. And even though not openly, [these "right-wingers"] have reached the conclusion, in fact, that we must give up the idea of building socialism in agriculture." Then Gerö tries to sketch the harmful consequences that the right-wing deviationists' aims *would have had if* they could have been realized. "Thereby," writes Ernö Gerö, "they not only would have brought the building of socialism in agriculture to a standstill in our land, but would also have bankrupted agricultural production. A victory by right-wing opportunism ultimately would have disrupted the worker-peasant alliance and undermined the power of the working class."

These utterances comprise the charges fabricated against me in the matter of the socialist reorganization of agriculture. All other writings or speeches, so frequent in recent months, are merely doltish echoings of these libels.

The Central Committee's resolution of June, 1953, analyzed concretely and in detail the grave and injurious errors committed by the Party leadership before June, 1953, in the field of the socialist reorganization of agriculture and production, describing also the catastrophic economic and political consequences produced by these well-known errors.

Summing up the grievous errors committed before June, 1953, in the field of agriculture, the Central Committee's June, 1953, resolution stated the following:

> The exaggerated tempo of socialization in agriculture was an error aggravated by the fact that within the Party Comrade Imre Nagy opposed this policy, but instead of adopting these views the Party leadership improperly called them "opportunist" and subjected Comrade Nagy to Party discipline.

The Central Committee's resolution of March, 1955, ascertained that the June resolution continues in effect without change and that, combined with the resolutions of the Third Congress, it comprises the basic principles of the March resolution. Mátyás Rákosi in his speech supporting the April resolution—which to this day I have been unable to obtain—stated in connection with the 1948–1949 debate on the agrarian question that at that time I already had represented the stand of right-wing opportunism. This statement lacks all foundation. It reflects Rákosi's persistent endeavor to brand as right-wing deviation the justified Marxist criticism of the harmful pre–1953 agrarian policy; he seeks to justify the old errors retroactively, and thereby to facilitate the continuance in 1955 of the errors committed in 1948 and 1949. The facts already have pretty much unmasked this endeavor. All the more surprising is the fact that members of the Central Committee, the great majority of whom must be familiar with the resolution of June, 1953, do not notice, or at least gloss over, Rákosi's assertions which flout the validity of the June resolution and invalidate its criticism of the agricultural policy, along with its conclusions and goals, which he would like to commend to oblivion.

To my knowledge there is no Party decision that would have voided one or another portion of the resolution of June, 1953. On the other hand there are Party resolutions that have confirmed it again and again. This the Central Committee must know, and Mátyás Rákosi must know it, too. Anyone who openly or covertly denies this opposes the June resolution.

In October, 1953, the Party Committee ascertained the following with regard to the situation of the cooperatives:

The reassurance of independently working peasants was fostered by the decision of our Party and government this year to allow resignations from cooperatives on the part of those members who, for any reason, wanted to resign; in fact they also made it possible for those cooperatives to disband, if the majority of the membership decides to do so. Many comrades did not understand that a cooperative does not grow weaker but stronger when members leave who are not at home there, and who retard rather than advance the cooperative's affairs. On the other hand, independently working peasants have realized that we take seriously the principle of free choice, and that there is no danger that those unconvinced of the superiority of cooperative production may in future be forced into the cooperatives. There is no doubt that, upon the resignation from the cooperatives of dissatisfied or unsuitable members, the cooperatives will be far stronger and far more united.

In my January, 1954, report to Parliament on the government's activities during the previous six months, I said:

The government has taken far-reaching steps to assure the economic and organizational stability of our cooperatives, the bettering of the members' welfare. Despite initial difficulties, our cooperatives have shown that the socialist transformation of the Hungarian village has grown firm roots. Last fall the test was passed with flying colors. It became manifest that most of our cooperatives are healthy and capable of development. They provide a stable and sure foundation for the socialist reorganization of our agriculture, the expansion of production, and the increase of material well-being. In the development of agricultural production, in the assurance of ample crops, the cooperatives have a pre-eminent role. Relying on the advantage of large-scale operation and potent government aid, by increasing the yield they must surpass independent farming and forge ahead into the lead. The economic and technical conditions for this exist. The results depend on leadership, organization, work discipline, and the quality of the work accomplished.

As Party Committee members know, since 1953 Mátyás Rákosi on countless occasions has tried to revise the June resolution, giving now the Beria case, now international tension, and at other times my alleged errors and excesses, or still other reasons. In this connection Comrade Khrushchev clearly stated:

> In June, 1953, we correctly passed judgment on the Hungarian Party's leadership, and that judgment is still entirely correct today. They can't hide behind Beria as Rákosi is trying to do. We were there, too, when these errors were ascertained, every one of us! We were right, and what we decided then is also right today. This should have been acted on already!

Mátyás Rákosi knows about all this but keeps silent before the Party, and tries to void extremely important sections of the June resolution or to reverse their import. Yet it is as if it were exactly against such endeavors that the Soviet Communist Party at its Fifteenth Party Conference established the principle below:

> The Fifteenth Party Conference . . . most emphatically condemns the opposition's attempts to use the defense of the interests of industrialization as a pretext to change this policy with regard to the peasants and thereby strike an irreparable blow at cooperation between town and village.

If anyone tries to regard the peasantry merely as a tax base, thinking by excessive taxes and selling prices to squeeze more material wealth from the peasantry, this necessarily must lead to the stifling of the rural productive forces and to a decrease in agricultural production. It would produce the risk of destroying the alliance between the working class and the peasantry, and would thus endanger socialist construction. The pseudoradical "left-wingers" among us follow the same improper policy pursued in times past by the opposition in the Soviet Union.

I stand unalterably on the basic principle of the June resolution, and, in the knowledge of being right, maintain my stand as expressed and implemented in 1949, a stand validated by the resolution of June, 1953, by the development of economic life, and now also by the Party's agrarian policy as expressed in the agricultural resolution of this June, which has turned a new page.

In contrast to those who accuse without proof, it is most proper, most Partylike, most convincing to counter the charges raised against me with simple facts. The sectarian "left-wing" deviationists, among them Ernö Gerö, as quoted from his article, keep talking of all the evil that *would have resulted if* right-wing opportunism had triumphed. In contrast to the assumptions brought against me, the grave errors of the "left-wing" deviationists are documented by facts that the Central Committee's resolution of June, 1953, acknowledged. The "left-wing" deviationists, primarily Rákosi and Gerö, in the years 1949 to 1953 brought the socialist reorganization of agriculture to a dead end, bankrupted agricultural production, destroyed the worker-peasant alliance, undermined the power of the People's Democracy, trampled upon the rule of law, debased the people's living standards, established a rift between the masses and the Party and government—in other words, swept the country toward catastrophe. These are not assumptions as to what damage the Rákosi-Gerö leadership might have caused if . . . No! these are facts, which all became evident by June, 1953, facts that the June resolution analyzed in detail, statistically and palpably.

Now the "left-wing" deviationists pretend that by "unmasking" right-wing deviation, they prevented us from undermining the People's Democracy along with all socialist construction. They speak as if right-wing deviation should have been resisted and as if it were their great merit to have done so. Thus by baseless charges and falsifications, the resistance that prevented the implementation of the June resolution and ultimately defeated it and saved the Party and country from serious consequences are now extolled as Communist virtue redounding to the glory of certain leaders. Thus do they re-evaluate and praise the resistance that stigmatized many Party decisions; thus—proclaiming the implementation of the June resolution and anti-Marxist right-wing deviation—do they motivate the justification of resistance. Thus, from one day to the next, anti-Party and antipeople "left-wing" deviationists become champions of Marxism-Leninism. Such about-faces are nothing new in their case. Astounding, however, is the fact that they should have been able by deception, to insure Central Committee approval for such un-Partylike activities.

To counter the charges and libels, let us look at the facts. What was and what is my stand, what views did I and do I profess on the question of the socialist reorganization of agriculture? Before well-intentioned, objective, Party-spirited judges, there would be no need to prove the validity of my views. Among Central Committee members, including Party Committee members, no one concerned himself so much, so intensively, from a theoretic and practical standpoint, with the development of socialist cooperative, large-scale agriculture, with the problems of its organization and operation, as I did, ahead of all others, beginning as early as 1946. In my daily classes at the University of Agriculture and the University of Economic Sciences, I dealt for years with this question from a theoretic and practical standpoint. One portion of my lectures also appeared in book form under the title *Agrarian Political Studies,* and this was used as a textbook. My lectures met with no objection, whether from a political, theoretical, or practical standpoint. Yet these lectures exhaustively discussed all important points dealing with the agrarian question and the socialist reorganization of agriculture. I don't intend to quote from these lectures, which are at the disposal of the Central Committee. Anyone who wants to check on the charges may do so in my lectures. Nor do I wish to touch on those brochures that I wrote on the socialist agriculture of the Soviet Union at various times, and whose content never provoked any sort of criticism from either the Party or other organs.

Now, in connection with the weightier charges leveled against me, let us see what views I professed and do profess, so that we may establish that I was confronted with baseless charges, falsifications, and libels, rather than with a well-founded judgment.

In my September 30, 1946, report to the Third Congress of the Hungarian Communist Party, I dealt among other things with the question of increasing agricultural production, mechanization, and cooperatives. I said:

From the standpoint of the economic strengthening and development of the People's Democratic system, the transformation of agriculture can only be said to be effective if the agrarian organization of small peasants supplements and surpasses the production of the abolished large landholding system. The small and medium-sized peasant holdings that are built up mainly through cooperative family labor cannot independently achieve such an expanded production. But they are able to do so by joining forces. Mechanization also aids in this direction by fostering the concentration of small holdings in cooperatives.

I believe this to be a clear Marxist-Leninist stand on the cooperative question at a time when in our land no one yet outlined theoretically the perspective of agrarian development or the socialist reorganization of agriculture.

Even at the first national cooperative conference held by the Hungarian Communist Party, on June 29, 1947, I dealt extensively with the tasks of the cooperative movement. I pointed to the main task of the Party's economic policy by saying that "henceforth the cooperative movement must play a far greater and more important role than heretofore in all areas of our economic policy." I stated that the main road to the socialist transformation of agriculture is via the cooperatives, and I related this to the question of state power: "There can be no People's Democracy without a cooperative movement, just as the cooperative movement can only develop and realize its great goals completely in a People's Democracy." At the same time I rejected the perspective that capitalist cooperatives bring to agriculture, mentioning Denmark as an example. It is characteristic how Mátyás Rákosi spoke of this same question about a year later, in the spring of 1948. I proved by the Danish example how Denmark's working peasants were ruined after the establishment of capitalist cooperatives, and rejected this method. "We have no need of a cooperative movement," I said, "that cannot assure us of those advantages for the small peasants that are needed for their improvement." In contrast to this, Mátyás Rákosi even a year later argued, "We must not allow the thought of cooperatives—which will be just as important a weapon to achieve the improvements of the Hungarian peasants as that of peasants in other lands, such as, for example, Denmark—to fall into bad repute and scare off the farmers." I believe it is not difficult to decide which view is the proper Marxist view and which represents the "perspective" of capitalist cooperatives.

About the economic significance of the cooperatives I also wrote as follows in 1947:

> The task now is that the two main productive branches of our economy, industry and agriculture, should develop uniformly in one direction from capitalism toward socialism, and that the speed and level of such progress gradually be equalized. In the transitional phase represented by the People's Democracy this is the main task the cooperatives are destined to solve in the field of agriculture.

In my speech before the activist session of the Agrarian Political Committee held May 19, 1948, I said among other things:

> This means that the development of agriculture proceeds most unevenly. Proportionally, the greatest development of productive forces is made possible by the cooperative system. This enables agriculture to rise to the level of industry, and this assures the unity of our economy. That is how living standards rise, that is how culture advances, and only thus do we progress toward socialism.

Then I wrote as follows on some economic problems:

> In such fashion the socialist reorganization of agriculture, the transition from small-scale peasant farming to a well-developed cooperative large-scale agricultural system, not only gives great impetus to the development of agriculture's productive forces, but by putting the whole people's economy on a uniform socialist basis, speeds its over-all development.

About the role of the cooperatives in connection with the need for a parallel development of industry and agriculture as a condition for socialist construction, I wrote in my article entitled "Stabilization, Reconstruction, Agriculture":

The cooperative is the lever with which agricultural production can be lifted from today's backwardness and be made not only to supplement the advantages of large holdings but even greatly to surpass them.

Via the cooperatives, agriculture can be led along the road of a democratic economic development, thus facilitating the parallel progress of industry and agriculture and doing away with the conflicts between the two branches of production. Thus, in the field of reconstruction, one of the main tasks which differs from industrial reconstruction is the broader and proportionately greater expansion of the network of cooperatives.

We should not forget that I wrote this in 1947.

About the connection between industrialization and the transition to large-scale socialist production I wrote in this same article:

> This development not only means that the expansion of the domestic market opens a field for increased industrial production, but also that agricultural production itself similarly proceeds in the direction of "industrialization." By this we mean that just as once in industry, so now in our agriculture, freed of feudal shackles, there is similarly a possibility of moving from primitive hand labor to production based on mechanization, to intensive large-scale production. This, however, is possible only through the development of the cooperative movement, through mechanization, more intensive labor, varied types of farming, and gaining by-products from the crops.

I also often and intensively dealt with the internal organizational questions of the cooperative enterprise, obviously not because I wanted to undermine the cooperative economy, as the libels say, but to aid its development. After the Fourth National Cooperative Conference I said:

> The cooperative is that form of enterprise that offers limitless possibilities of economic development. Our factory workers, with great effort and splendid achievements, are creating the technical conditions for the members of our cooperatives to utilize these possibilities in ever greater measure. The farm cooperatives can thus produce amply and profitably, and become sources of prosperity. . . .

The farm cooperative is a form of productive enterprise wherein members of the cooperative are not only its workers but at the same time its fully accredited owners. The close cooperation of management and members, the participation of all members in production as well as in management, is a force that all chairmen of cooperatives should rely on. The broad development of cooperative democracy is the guarantee of good management and an indispensable condition for implementing the agricultural resolution in the cooperative economy. . . . The other source of strength lies in the size of the plant—in the fact that skilled workers, mechanization, and the achievements of agronomic science can be broadly employed, making the same amount of aid far more potent in the cooperatives than on private farms.

Common labor and good work organization represent a huge source of strength. There is no need to prove, for example, that two hundred men in a coordinated effort are capable of far more accomplishment than the same number of men working one by one. Common labor is far more fruitful; which is a decisive factor in cooperative production. Our farm cooperative system provides all this. With good management these factors can give a great boost to the economy.

Already in my July 4, 1953, speech in Parliament dealing with the government program, in the course of presenting the plan to slow down the cooperative movement with regard to numbers, I stressed the principle of free choice, pointing out that "at the same time the government will continue to lend far-reaching support to the farm cooperatives, contributing through loans and investments to their economic development and to the welfare of the members, because it is convinced that this is the most practical way to improve the life of the peasantry."

Nor did I neglect to alert those organs for the support of the farm cooperatives—primarily the local councils—that day by day must deal practically with the problems of the cooperatives:

Along with the general development of cooperative farming, our local councils should give keen attention to the socialist reorganization of agriculture. The economic and organizational strengthening and development of our cooperatives is a key task in the work of the councils.

On the local councils especially devolves the important role of helping the farm cooperatives increase their income and helping them against the enemy's disruptive aims. We must stress the need for defending cooperative property and for strengthening work discipline. With due regard for the independence of farm cooperatives, the executive committee of the district council must give increased and more expert aid in preparing and coordinating financial, budgetary, and production plans. The local council members much maintain constant and lively contact with the cooperatives and feel responsibility for the work of the latter. Special attention of every kind is to be given the weaker cooperative; let increased concern for the latter be an important task of our district councils.

In my speech of September 29, 1953, at Kecskemet I clearly stated my stand in support of the farm cooperatives:

Rightly the question arises of whether it is sensible to leave the farm cooperatives when the mistakes and troubles that occasioned dissatisfaction are being radically remedied by the government. Should men think of leaving precisely when—after much struggle —we finally have won out over the troubles? It goes against common sense to think of doing such a thing. Would they begin anew the old bitter life, which they already once left because it was hard and devoid of promise? Should they face uncertainty and the difficulties of a fresh start? This is neither wise nor profitable, comrades! Before taking a final step, it is worth thinking it through—and reconsidering.

Comrades, the waverers and prospective resignees are no less wrong when they blame the cooperative system for the faults and troubles, the low share in crops and profits. The fault lies not here but in bad management. Bad management unquestionably ruins the cooperative. However, bad management—and this shouldn't be forgotten by those wanting to leave—ruins the economically far weaker private peasant holdings even more quickly. So let members of bad cooperatives blame not the cooperative but themselves for bad management. Those who leave in order to farm their own land, even if they work much harder, won't make out as well as in the cooperative, where the same amount of work is far more effective and profitable than on private peasant holdings by virtue of the advantages of large-scale production. All this is well worth thinking over before anyone decides to leave.

It is also worth considering that in private enterprise each resignee takes on the struggles of individual existence. One should also remember that withdrawal ends the privileges and concessions due members of the cooperatives, and at the same time entails responsibility by the member to turn back his proportionate share—which is certainly just and fair, but burdensome too. I can assure those who, despite all these considerations, leave the cooperatives that they will soon regret it. Perceiving the effect of the government's measures to foster cooperative enterprise and a better and richer life, they will ask to be taken back into the cooperative. Such persons, comrades, look on the cooperative as a certain man once long ago regarded the railway. At first he wouldn't consider riding under any conditions; he preferred to walk. But then, when the train had left him behind, he regretted his decision. These men will also regret being left behind by the cooperative.

Withdrawal, as it is known, is regulated by the decree of the Minister of Agriculture. All resignees must heed its provisions carefully. Infractions, comrades, will clash with the law and will result in punishment.

At the Bacsmegye Cooperative Conference in September, 1953, I said:

In connection with withdrawal, acts committed against cooperative property will be more gravely regarded. Cooperative property is no free-for-all but stands under the law's protection. The government program has created and assures production and the security of property in agriculture. Indubitably this means, in the first place, the security of cooperative property. The law will strike with full severity against anyone who raises a hand against it, and the law will be enforced effectively by our organizations of law and public order.

At the same time I emphasized further that the government would care increasingly for the farm cooperatives because "both government and Party are unalterably of the opinion that cooperative farming is the sole viable and effective road to increasing agricultural production and improving the lot of the peasantry." This opinion of mine can scarcely be regarded as an attempt to undermine the cooperative movement, as the charges against me now proclaim.

I could go on endlessly with quotations and references that clearly and convincingly prove that in the matter of socialist reorganization in agriculture I stand on the basis of Marxism-Leninism, and that my view is no right-wing deviation. But such evidence also proves that the charges against me are baseless common libels. All this, incidentally, shows that there are sharp conflicts between the pseudoradical excesses of "left-wing" views and my views regarding the socialist reorganization of agriculture.

Rákosi, Gerö, Hegedus, Matolcsi, or others, when accusing me, at least might have taken the trouble to quote the objectionable parts of my speeches or writings. Instead, they make general statements and falsify my views. For example, I never held the view that small and medium-sized peasant holdings automatically develop in the direction of socialism within the limits of small-scale production, as Andras Hegedus charged. On this question I wrote as follows:

> By contrast with the rapid expansion of heavy industry, agriculture lags more and more. We cannot count on the possibility of catalytic development, i.e., that nationalized industry will automatically carry agriculture along with it. There is a basic difference between the two: one is a socialist economic type or at least is surely developing in that direction, the other is a diversified small-scale economic type which from day to day breathes capitalism. It is the task of the cooperative movement to close the rift apparent at the present developmental phase of the People's Democracy; to create the conditions for the development of agriculture's productive forces; to put production on the basis of expanded crop rotation and stockpiling; and, by bringing into being the main conditions for the cohesive unity of our people's economy, to guide agriculture to the road leading toward socialism.

I think it is clear that this substantially differs from what Andras Hegedus stated.

Hegedus likewise knowingly prevaricates when he writes that, as a result of the spread of right-wing views, "uncertainty arose among members of cooperatives and led to many withdrawals and to the disbanding of many cooperatives in 1953 and 1954." Here Hegedus tries to pin the responsibility for this as well on the right-wingers, meaning Imre Nagy. Andras Hegedus simply acts as if he didn't know what he knows just as well as I do. For the June resolution plainly states that the farm cooperatives must be allowed to disband if they wish to do so, and explains why. Therefore this is no right-wing view but part of the June resolution, which comprises the basis of the guiding principles contained in the Central Committee's March resolution. It should also be noted that the above directive with reference to the cooperatives did not get into the Central Committee's resolution by accident but was proposed by the Soviet comrades. Mátyás Rákosi on several occasions tried to shift the responsibility to Beria, with a view to compromising both the June resolution and those who carried out its provisions. For this he has frequently sought Istvan Dobi's backing—whether successfully or not I do not know. However, the fact is that when we expressed some anxiety concerning the question of the farm cooperatives at the June, 1953, Moscow conference, Comrade Molotov (and not Beria) reassured us as follows: "The farm cooperatives must not be disbanded by fiat, but, should they choose to disband voluntarily, they shouldn't be hindered. No harm will come of it." Thus, and for this reason, did the June resolution provide for the free disbandment of cooperatives which the "left-wingers" now seek to call right-wing deviation so as to forge a weapon against me. But the facts remain facts despite all falsification.

The conclusions of the Central Committee's June resolution dealing with farm cooperatives and the advice of the Soviet comrades proved correct and were direct consequences of the brutal and widespread violation of the principle of free choice for the sake of exaggerated collectivization by intimidation and financial pressure (taxes, crop requisitions, etc.), and by the application of punishments and other lawless procedures, in the course of which dissatisfaction in the villages flared high, and hundreds upon hundreds of unviable farm cooperatives came into existence wherein the forcibly recruited members simply did not work.

Moreover, the Central Committee's June, 1953, resolution and the Soviet comrades' advice also proved correct in another respect. In the period between 1949 and June, 1953, owing to excessive industrialization and to the excessive development of heavy industry which sapped the country's material resources to an extraordinary degree, the leaders not only neglected agriculture in general—in consequence of which production fell—but neglected the financial, organizational, and political strengthening of the young, weak cooperatives battling against initial difficulties; factors which by the summer of 1953 had plunged the whole cooperative movement into crisis and potential catastrophe—in consequence of the views and policies of those "left-wingers" who then, as now, like to describe themselves as champions of the cooperative movement.

We must also deal with Ernö Gerö's extreme "left-wing" agrarian views, before they bring about even greater chaos in the ranks of the Party and grievously damage our people's economy. The economic policies represented and directed by Ernö Gerö once did bring us to the brink of catastrophe in the summer of 1953, and according to the conclusions of the Central Committee's session of June, 1953, were irresponsibly reckless policies. Then his anti-Party and antipeople views were revealed by unlimited forced industrialization, resulting in an overexpanded heavy industry that lacked the necessary conditions for development. Now, as he declared in his June 12, 1955, *Szabad Nep* article, "On the Way Up," he wants to put into operation the same conception in our agrarian development. In those days, as we know, Ernö Gerö excused the forced speed-up of industrialization in the raised Five-Year Plan by saying, among other things, that without this the socialist reorganization of agriculture could not be realized, on the other hand, he excused the forced speed-up of farm collectivization by saying that without it socialist industrialization could not be realized. He linked both aims to the prospect of a significant rise in living standards. In the course of the Five-Year Plan he didn't take into account the fact that for long years to come excessive industrialization would deprive our producers and consumers of the resources of the people's economy, while, on the other hand, the increase in the number of workers and the increased need to import raw materials require a significant increase in food production, even in the event of only a minimal increase in living standards. It became evident that agricultural production could not be increased simultaneously with forced collectivization. The speeding of the socialist reorganization of agriculture presupposes a great increase in agriculture's productive forces, which would devolve primarily on heavy industry and the building industries. Inasmuch as heavy industry, under the First Five-Year Plan, primarily produced for itself—as a result of the improper trend of forced industrialization—the quantitative increase of industrial goods produced for agriculture lagged far behind the needs, in fact fell off in many areas. Yet, concurrently, the accelerated collectivization of agriculture demanded significant food reserves to insure proper supply of the working class and city dwellers in general; but we have not had such reserves since 1951, precisely because of the grave financial sacrifices demanded by forced industrialization.

One of the most important lessons of the First Five-Year Plan was that the resources of our people's economy cannot assure the simultaneous realization of two goals so huge as forced socialist industrialization and the forced collectivization of agriculture.

It seems Gerö either forgot this or, worse still, in the face of all experience, now is repeating the past mistakes that severely damaged our people's economy.

Gerö now goes so far that, after the increased forced industrial development of the Five-Year Plan—which without the June resolution and the subsequent New Course would have imperiled the existence of the People's Democracy—he proceeds to announce his plan for intensified collectivization. In the years 1949 through 1952 it was proved that the raising of agricultural production and living standards is an empty phrase when coupled with extreme industrialization and the emergency development of heavy industry. Party and state documents as well as statistical data show that agricultural production, and with it the living standards of the workers, have greatly declined. Now Ernö Gerö, simultaneously with a crash program for heavy industry, would have the Party and state plan not only to increase agricultural production significantly, but also to realize the plan for intensified collectivization. In the course of the First Five-Year Plan the country could not bear the double load of extreme industrialization and the increase of agricultural production; so at this point we can still less realize the triple program of extreme industrialization, forced collectivization, and the increase of agricultural production without a drastic decline in the living standards of the workers.

In the question of collectivization, Ernö Gerö goes beyond the resolution of the Third Party Congress when in the above-mentioned article he declares that conditions for collectivization are better in Hungary than formerly in the Soviet Union, since we enjoy more and better-developed technical facilities. By this he essentially says, if they could achieve mass collectivization in the Soviet Union under less favorable conditions, why could we not realize it under better conditions? In other words, Gerö in this article goes beyond the Third Congress and the March resolution of the Central Committee by proclaiming what amounts to mass collectivization. This would be a matter for careful thought, even if technical facilities were the sole condition essential to collectivization. On the basis of Marxist-Leninist teachings, however, we know that it is only one condition among many. The teachings of the classic Marxists are well known, especially as regards the problem of leading the peasants of countries such as ours toward collectivization. Anyone who claims that technical facilities are the sole condition for collectivization opposes Marxist-Leninist teachings, or, in other words, proclaims collectivization by force.

In our case the simultaneous realization of the two goals of increased collectivization and increased agricultural production is even less feasible. For this there are precedents and facts that Gerö simply ignores, not daring to face them because that would reveal his sectarian anti-Marxist views. This is why he doesn't write one word about either the special conditions in our country (conditions which, incidentally, apply to all countries where capitalism and private property have deep roots among the peasantry), or the differences between our situation and that of the Soviet Union that slow down and hinder collectivization, matters Lenin discussed so extensively and intensively. Unconcerned with all this, Ernö Gerö reaches the anti-Marxist sectarian conclusion that the transition from private farming to socialist cooperative farming may be even swifter than it was in the Soviet Union. Gerö, and with him Rákosi and others, has fallen into the error most dangerous to revolutionaries—that of mistaking their own fancies for reality. Another and no lesser fault of theirs is the attempt to solve with revolutionary rules the most crucial and complex question of the transition —socialism's most decisive economic problem—instead of taking the course of gradual development via progressive reforms in the economic field; and this, amid the conditions of socialist construction, involves the grave violation of the objective laws regarding progress.

I do not know to what extent the Party leadership espouses the guiding principles and practical goals enunciated by Gerö in connection with the socialist reorganization of agriculture in the Party press and in other articles. For it is evident that not only is there an essential difference between the June, 1953, resolution and that of March, and the Party's agricultural resolution with regard to the collectivization of agriculture, but there are also differences between these resolutions and the articles on that portion of the resolutions which pertains to the socialist reorganization of agriculture, as in the case of Gerö's article. These articles increased the already notable chaos in the theoretical and practical field. The Party resolutions do not clarify the proper Marxist-Leninist standpoint in the question of collectivization as it relates to the special conditions prevailing in Hungary. This uncertainty becomes more apparent if in certain important areas we compare the guiding principles and practical aims of the March resolution, and this year's June resolution for developing agriculture, with the theoretical and practical aims of the Polish United Workers Party. The August 3 and August 4, 1955, issues of the Polish Party organ *Trybuna Ludu,* in discussing the Polish Central Committee's agricultural resolution, state among other things that they wish to foster an increase in the production of independent farmers. They also wish to increase the use of machinery on independent holdings and, with the help of modern techniques, will increase the yield per acre on independent farms. *Trybuna Ludu* points out that the Central Committee has also decided to create a central type of cooperative, and stresses that the fears, doubts, and prejudices of the independent farmers must be gradually dispersed. According to the program of the Polish Party's Central Committee, during the period of the next Five-Year Plan in Polish agriculture the independent peasant farms will be in the majority. According to the Central Committee's decision a dynamic fight will be waged against all those who distort the policy of isolating and restricting the kulaks. These excesses before all else find expression in the practice of treating peasants with medium holdings as kulaks, undermining the productive capacity of kulak farms, and seeking to liquidate them.

Speaking of due processes of law, the Polish Central Committee assures the independently working peasants that their personal property will be protected under the constitution of the Polish People's Democracy. "The working peasant is entitled to demand," writes *Trybuna Ludu*, "that the state justly establish the amount of his crop obligations, and that his requests and complaints receive thorough, humane consideration." The Polish Party regarded all these measures as essential because it is convinced that without increasing the production of independent farmers there can be no general rise in agricultural production.

Concurrently with these measures, the resolution of the Polish Party's Central Committee has decided to establish viable cooperatives, and on this basis has combined the bolstering of agricultural production with the promotion of the cooperative movement. Thus, on the basis of progressive development, collectivization can be reconciled with increased production. We too could achieve this by establishing our farm policies on the theoretical basis of the June policy, the policy of the New Course. Now the agricultural resolution of the Polish Party's Central Committee in essence parallels our June policy as the basis for solving agriculture's two essential goals: increased production and a fostering of the farm cooperative movement.

Why, then, should Marxist-Leninist policy, as carried out in the Polish People's Democracy, be regarded in the Hungarian People's Democracy as opportunist, anti-Marxist, harmful right-wing deviation? Or could it be said that the Poles also have strayed onto this dangerous path?

For here in Hungary the Central Committee's March and April resolutions, and the flood of articles that arose in their wake, characterized as harmful, anti-Marxist, opportunist, right-wing deviation, and as an anti-Party and antipeople attitude, all that the Polish Party's Central Committee approved in its resolution. Should anyone here try to espouse these same views, as I have done, I think he too would meet with my fate as foreshadowed by the Central Committee's March and April resolution.

It is also apparent, from the resolution of the Polish Party's Central Committee, that it is not an anti-Marxist right-wing deviation nor an anti-Party and antipeople attitude if one does not envisage the collectivization of the majority of the peasant holdings in the Second Five-Year Plan; that it is not a right-wing deviation if one holds that, in the promotion of cooperatives, gradual progress and the introduction of an intermediate type of cooperative and a more moderate tempo are feasible; that it is not right-wing deviation or an anti-Marxist stand if, in the interest of bolstering the production of independent farms, one should desire to assure the use of machinery for them; just as we do not sin against the Marxist-Leninist theory of crop rotation and the Marxist view on the possibility of expanded crop rotation on independent peasant holdings when we aim to increase the productive forces on peasant farms and step up the yield per acre; that the increased productivity and acreage yield of peasant holdings does not contradict but supplements the gradual transition to collective large-scale farming. We must also establish that it is not opportunism, not a harmful right-wing deviation or anti-Party and antipeople policy, to direct the main fire against those who distort the policy of restricting and isolating the kulaks, against those who undermine the productive capacity of kulak farms and seek their liquidation. The Polish Party's Central Committee acts in the spirit of Marxism-Leninism when, in place of obligatory sales to the state, it increases the wider application of contractual sales of the peasants' surplus grain.

Here in Hungary the opposite of all this happens. What for

the Polish Party is a guiding principle and a practical aim with regard to the activity of Party and state, we find in our circles to be an anti-Party, in fact an antipeople, stand that must be prosecuted and calls for the gravest Party discipline and stigma. Justly, the question arises as to which stand is right. Is it, or is it not, the Marxist-Leninist stand? A clarification of this as a matter of principle, in the true Party spirit, is a task that cannot be side-stepped, that must not be "settled" peremptorily with the throttling of all criticism.

Chapter 13. The Question of Independent Peasant Farms

In the March resolution and in the writings that appeared thereafter it became customary to generalize the charges, and even if they didn't specifically say so, these charges implied right-wing deviation; and by right-wing deviation the accusers meant primarily me. It is therefore also necessary for me to touch on cases where the charges are directed against me without mentioning me by name. The March resolution asserts the following:

> The working peasants are hoodwinked by those who claim that through independent farming the mass of peasants with small or medium holdings can attain a high degree of prosperity, and that an agriculture consisting of many hundreds of thousands of independent peasant farmers can become flourishing and exemplary without the formation of cooperatives.

Just as in the case of other charges, the resolution does not bother to state who said this and when. I certainly never held or promulgated any such views. So far as I am concerned both premises are false. By way of demonstrating this and clarifying my position, I should like to quote a few characteristic passages from which my views on this question may be judged. A much more thorough knowledge of my views can be gained by those who take the trouble to read my published speeches and writings, provided they have access also to those that were arbitrarily removed from circulation.

In the light of a few quotations let us see what I said then, and still say now, about these two main questions:

A. What possibilities are there for the promotion of productive forces on independent peasant farms? What about the question of expanded crop rotation?

B. Is it with or without the promotion of cooperatives that agriculture can be made to prosper and to progress toward socialism?

Let us see what I wrote with regard to these questions.

A. What possibilities for the development of productive forces do small holdings and cooperatives afford?

> On peasant holdings the outlook for technical development is limited. No matter how much capital or what type of machines are used by the small farmer, this can develop production only to a limited extent. A large-scale use of technical facilities is not possible or even economical, and does not result in a proportionate increase of production. This is not true of the cooperatives. They afford almost limitless possibilities for the use of mechanical and scientific advances. The productivity of labor—low on independent peasant farms—is incomparably greater in cooperatives.

I said this in a speech at the activist session of the Agrarian Political Committee on May 19, 1948. It strikes me as a clear and proper stand, which shows no sign of right-wing deviation or any distortion of Marxism-Leninism.

But let us proceed. In this same speech I go on to say:

> We must also lead our agriculture in a direction that assures the concentration of capital and labor, creates reserves, and expands intensified production. Without these it is vain to speak of the peasantry's new form of life, culture, and prosperity. If we do not achieve the latter, all remains empty talk. Intensified crop rotation assures the material basis for the development of production, culture, and prosperity. So the road we must take is the road of cooperative development.

At the Bacsmegye Farm Cooperative Conference on September 29, 1953, I explained the reasons for this:

Today, too, an acre is only an acre. We cannot perform miracles. We must assure our people of rising living standards and greater satisfaction. This, however, cannot be realized through peasant production on small holdings. For this cooperative production is needed, which through the voluntary association of many small peasant farms gives its members the possibility of large-scale production with all its advantages. Through cooperatives we gain more land. He who cannot make out on a plot of a few acres finds almost limitless possibilities as a member of a cooperative: he becomes part owner of a great agricultural plant. On small holdings each farmer struggles by himself. In the cooperative many families can surmount all difficulties through the strength of large-scale operations. The independent farmer assumes responsibility for all the risks of production. A cow dies and he feels it for a long time. A bad harvest can ruin him. Essentially this is why independent small peasant farms, despite the government's far-reaching help, support, and liberal concessions, inescapably lag behind the cooperatives in both production and profits. On small peasant farms there are strict limits to the development of production. The cooperative is that form of farming wherein agriculture finds limitless possibilities.

Our whole people's economy, the raising of the workers' living standards, and the peasantry's social, economic, and cultural progress demand the full and unequivocal support of cooperative production.

I believe this is a clear and frank statement, which most certainly did not aim at deceiving the working peasants, as the resolution libelously declares.

Not only did I expound the question in popular fashion, but also theoretically in pure Marxist-Leninist fashion. In my acceptance speech at the Hungarian Academy of Science on May 23, 1953, I said:

The advanced techniques created by socialist industry can be applied only to a limited extent on independent farms; the latter cannot keep step with technical advances. This shows that those productive forces that socialist industry has brought into being have already outgrown the framework of independent productive and property relationships, and these expanded productive forces demand new conditions of production—large-scale production.

In my opening address at the January, 1951, conference of the Agricultural Industrial Association of Sciences, I said:

The small-scale productive sector undoubtedly causes grave difficulty in connection with the work of our agricultural industry and obstructs our further advance. There are two conditions we must meet in order to surmount these obstacles. One is the socialist reorganization of agriculture, the transition to large-scale cooperative enterprise, which, with its planned production, high average yield, and quality products, will be the firm basis of our agricultural industry.

B. On the subject of the closely linked dual goal of production on independent peasant farms and the promotion of the cooperative movement, I quote the following from my speech at the Party activist meeting in Pest on July 11, 1953:

With regard to our independently working peasants, I mentioned a week ago in Parliament the far-reaching measures whereby we desire to aid agricultural production, the degree to which we wish to increase investments, and the help we mean to assure by way of agrotechnical tools, artificial fertilizer, seed, credits. We affirm this promise without change, and will keep it, too. Our independently working peasant will not have long to wait.

This, however, in no sense means that we will neglect cooperatives. On the contrary, we shall be concerned with them even more than heretofore. Our aim—and we shall attain it—is that our cooperatives shall be amply productive, profitable farms, the source of prosperity and a happy and carefree life for their members. The state has every means to assure this.

So we see that there was no question then, as there is no question today either, of separating the two connected tasks or of giving up the idea of cooperatives. At the same time I clearly established, true to the Marxist-Leninist principles laid down in the June resolution, that in the interest of the general, comprehensive, and swift acceleration of agricultural production, we would give extensive support to the small and medium-sized peasant holdings so as to insure their increased production.

Here in Hungary, only a few years after the land reform was

completed, the "left-wing" fanatics, in contradiction to Lenin, already were speaking of the limits to the development of agriculture's productive forces and were scoffing at the possibility that proper economic policies could raise the productive level of small-scale peasant farming to any significant degree. This explains why in Hungary the "left-wing" deviationists, despite a 30 per cent socialization of agriculture, have kept agricultural production at the prewar level, though it should exceed that by at least 25 to 30 per cent. With such policies we cannot ameliorate the situation of the workers, or strengthen the worker-peasant alliance and the dictatorship of the proletariat. "Any proletarian or representative of the proletariat," said Lenin, "who does not seek to achieve the improvement of the situation of the workers in this way would actually be the accomplice of the White Guardists and capitalists."

The improper policy that the "left-wing" deviationists pursue in the field of agricultural production essentially could produce similar consequences here too, whether this is intended or not.

From my January, 1954, speech before Parliament on the government's activities during the previous six months, I quote the following:

> The farming opportunities of the peasants with medium holdings, the government program, as well as the resolution dealing with the development of agriculture, afford great possibilities for increasing production. The peasants with medium holdings love to work, know how to farm, and if in the villages they work in exemplary fashion, espousing the cause of increased agricultural production with the good farmer's sense of responsibility, if they spur on the weaker and less successful farmers—with their advice and if need be with their economic resources—increasing production by supplementing the state's extensive help with their own contributions and their own investments, then indubitably we shall meet with success in realizing the aims of the resolution.
>
> Parallel to the promotion of large-scale farm cooperatives, an indispensable condition to the swift elimination of our agricultural backwardness is the development of the prosperity and increased production of the peasants with medium holdings. The government's successive measures aimed at helping agriculture

and assuring production have strengthened a will to produce on the part of peasants with medium holdings. That is how it should be. Let them expand their farms, supplement and renew their mechanical and other equipment, increase their livestock herds to the extent that members of their family can take care of them and that they themselves can tend to the tasks of the farm. In this no one restricts them; on the contrary, the state itself greatly aids their economic advancement.

Today, too, I maintain that this is the right course. Only malice can claim that these views represent anti-Marxist, opportunist right-wing deviation.

The agrarian policy that essentially denies the possibility of intensified crop rotation (even if in a limited way) on the farms of our more well-to-do small peasants, instead of doing everything to make the most of the opportunity, artificially fosters the conflicts between socialist industry and small, independent peasant farms. The main reason for this lies in the fact that the representatives of this policy, no matter how much they proclaim it, do not believe in the superiority of large-scale production. They fear the competition of small-scale production. However, this is so only because, while aiming to increase the number of cooperatives, they neglect to strengthen them economically and organizationally this scarcely leads to a convincing demonstration of the superiority of large-scale production.

The representatives of this mistaken agrarian policy fail to notice that we have exhausted the moral capital that the land reform meant to the peasantry from the standpoint of an alliance with the working class. As in the years previous to 1953, so now in consequence of the June, 1955, agricultural resolution, the working peasants' normal farming is made so difficult that there is scarcely any chance for even simple replanting, not to speak of intensified crop rotation. In days gone by this resulted in a mass exodus of the working peasant from the land, and the present policy likewise can lead to no other result.

Stalin said in June, 1928, that "those comrades are wrong who claim that the small peasant holdings have exhausted the possibilities of further development and that it therefore isn't worth aiding them any longer. This is quite incorrect. Independent peasant farming still enjoys plenty of possibilities for development. Only we must help it to utilize these possibilities."

Stalin said this when agricultural production already had reached and surpassed the pre–1913 level.

In the March resolution we read the following:

> In the face of Lenin's teachings there has been a resurgence of the long-disproved claim that not only the farm cooperatives but also the independent peasant farms are developing toward socialism "in their own way" and that the latter also build socialism.

This is what is expounded and used against me by Andras Hegedus, the man who bears primary responsibility for the parlous state of Hungarian agriculture and for its lack of progress, both as the former head of the Party's agricultural division and as the former Minister of Agriculture and Minister of State Enterprises. This is the man who, without any basis, pretends that I represented the view that small and medium peasant holdings automatically develop into socialism, and that small and medium peasant holdings, en masse and year by year, are capable of systematically intensified crop rotation.

It is worth observing what stand was adopted in the Soviet Union, whose experience we follow with particular attention. In the resolution relating thereto we read the following:

> The crudest mistake of the opposition is that it transfers, mechanically and *in toto,* the factors applicable to the development of peasant farms in the era of capitalism to the era of the dictatorship of the proletariat, and thus clings to the apron strings of bourgeois ideology. The opposition fails to see that the road of the villages toward progress is determined by the city's development, and that in our circumstances the rural capitalist elements are confronted not only by the agricultural worker and the peasant of small and moderate means, but simultaneously by the whole system of the dictatorship of the proletariat with its own potent key posts (primarily in socialized industry), with the cooperatives, and with other factors within a planned agriculture. The opposition thereby misconstrues many key premises of Marxism and Leninism with regard to large-scale and small-scale pro-

duction and with regard to the relationship between town and village, industry and agriculture; and it reverts to those bourgeois revisionist theories which proclaim the proletarian state's "Thermidorist" degeneration and aver that private capital and the kulak operating with limited capital will vanquish the dynamic forces of the socialist proletariat, the whole people's economy and the mechanized socialist industry, which is centralized to a degree unknown anywhere else. . . .

One of the main prerequisites for the Soviet Union's *development in a socialist direction* is to foster the rural productive forces and to increase the welfare of the great peasant masses. Only in this way can the socialist town sweep the village with it; at the time time, however, we must in all ways push the gradual transition of independent farms—which for a good while will represent the basis of our whole agriculture—toward the collective forms of agriculture.

The above observations are completely applicable to the methods and policies of our "left-wing" extremists.

My long-held, rightful Marxist-Leninist stand regarding intensified crop rotation on small and medium-sized peasant farms has been clearly revealed by the preceding quotations. Since Andras Hegedus directly accuses me of representing anti-Marxist views in this question too, let us add the following by way of supplementing the other extracts:

Under the circumstances prevailing in a People's Democracy, agriculture's productive forces develop least in the noncooperative sectors. Not that the democratic government opposes such development—for the constant raising of the workers' living standards demands the maximum development of agriculture's productive forces in the noncooperative sector too—but because without the advantages of cooperative association the simplified system of replanting, characteristic of production on small farms, inevitably blocks their progress.

The quotation below also deals with this question:

That means that hundreds of thousands of peasant farms and millons of farmers have no possibility for intensified crop rotation and accumulation, owing to the conditions of production and property relationships. As a result their development lags. In the capitalist agricultural system of large-scale production there is likewise a lower level of reinvestment and accumulation than in industry, and since a significant portion of the production of small peasant farms is on the basis of simple replanting, the general development of agriculture lags far behind industrial development. By virtue of proportionately greater capital accumulation the development of industry is accelerated; thus agriculture is left more and more behind.

The next few lines perhaps best summarize all that I have said on this question:

The economic basis of the people's democracy disintegrates if, alongside large-scale diversified industrial production and capital accumulation, agricultural production stalls at the level of today's primitive, extensive, small peasant farms.

I believe that the above quotations from my writings and speeches, which I could still expand considerably, convincingly prove that the charges of opportunism and anti-Marxist right-wing deviation leveled against me are baseless and that my accusers have not even taken the trouble to examine my views. It is hard to determine whether ignorance of Marxism or malice plays the greater role in this campaign of libel.

Characteristically, in the matters discussed in this chapter, my opponents question my Marxist-Leninist views when branding me a right-wing deviationist. I have amply and intensively dealt with these matters in the spirit of Marxist-Leninist teachings. I have always been ready, and am ready now, to debate the views of others. But which ones among the members of the Political Committee ever concerned themselves with these problems? What, where, and when did they write about them? Now those shout loudest about right-wing deviation who for years were mute on crucial questions and till now have done very little in the interest of clarifying and applying Marxism-Leninism to argriculture.

Yet after the first ill-fated attempt at collectivization they might have realized that, in the transition period, the crucial questions affecting the development and fate of independent peasant farms cannot and must not be "settled" on a superficial or dogmatic basis, and especially not on a demagogic basis.

On several occasions during the past ten years I have expressed my views in detail with regard to the question of independent peasant farms, both in a theoretical and a practical way. Among the more important of these utterances I refer to my opening address delivered on June 29, 1947, at the first national cooperative conference of the Hungarian Communist Party, and also to my speech of May 19, 1948, at the activist session of the Agrarian Political Committee and to my papers, "The Significance of the Cooperative in the Development of Agriculture" and "1948–49 Debate on Questions Relating to Peasants with Medium-Sized Holdings." In these speeches and writings I dealt intensively with the complex interrelated problems connected with the development of farm cooperatives and independent peasant holdings, and with the socialist reorganization of agriculture. The experiences and events of the past seven years have fully vindicated my stand and my views. For, just seven years ago, I outlined the developments to be expected. Looking back over this period, the facts already have proved the rightness of my stand.

In these days when in the face of all experience the old mistakes crop up again under conditions graver than in the past, I find it necessary to revitalize the key standpoints relating to the progress of independent peasant farms toward socialism. I wish to stress that the development toward socialism of our whole People's Democracy and of the people's economy, including agriculture, and the socialistic progress of small and medium-sized peasant farms under the conditions of proletarian dictatorship (People's Democracy) undoubtedly is not identical with the "grafting" of peasant farms onto socialism. The identification or confusion of one with the other is either ignorance or demagoguery. Regarding the development of small-scale peasant farms toward socialism, Stalin wrote as folows:

> Peasant farms are not capitalist farms. Peasant farms, for the most part, are a form of small-scale production. But what do we mean thereby? They constitute an economic type halfway be-

tween capitalism and socialism. They may develop toward capitalism, as in capitalist countries, or toward socialism, as in our country under the dictatorship of the proletariat.

It is evident that this is not a question of two different ways of building socialism, nor of small-scale farming being in itself a socialist type of economy, but of the mode of progress of differing agricultural sectors and of the transition of the independent sector into the cooperative sector. Under our prevailing circumstances, in accordance with proper Marxist-Leninist economic policy, the independent small and medium-sized peasant holdings can develop only toward socialism. But they become large-scale socialist enterprises—which in agriculture means the victory of socialism—only by coalescing into farm cooperatives. Of this I wrote as follows:

> The main road of agriculture—this is unquestionable—will be the road of cooperative association. But, until this becomes the sole road, progress will take other paths too. Basically there will be two roads to progress side by side: the cooperative and the noncooperative roads. In fact, for a fairly long stretch, cooperative development itself essentially will take two parallel roads along the way to the simplified and more advanced form of cooperative association. It would be wrong to think that only cooperative forms distinguish the two. The more advanced type, i.e. the farm cooperative, produces a proportionately greater development of the productive forces constituting the prerequisites for the creation of the concentration of material means and labor, without which a dynamic production increase, approaching the development of industry's level, is not possible. The simpler type of cooperative does not bring into being a significant concentration of material means and labor, and though through a certain broadening of productive forces, it nevertheless restricts them within narrow limits, thus providing a slower transition to socialism as compared with the higher type of cooperative which accelerates this transition and the raising of the level of production. We must therefore be prepared to find that the development of agriculture in the People's Democratic sector also will be very uneven. Besides the cooperative sector—in which, as we have seen above, there will be significant differences in principle—we must also reckon with a noncooperative sector which is not restricted

only to the kulaks but embraces other strata of the peasantry.

It would be wrong to regard the noncooperative agricultural sector simply as a *capitalist* sector. True, in this sector we find the capitalistic kulak farms, yet mostly there are the peasants with small and medium-sized holdings who with their own work maintain small-scale farms which by virtue of their dual nature are not capitalist enterprises. But even the noncooperative sector as a whole cannot be considered a capitalist sector because the conditions of its development have been decisively changed by the democratic transformation of our economy, with the nationalization of large-scale industry and the big banks, and the economic effect of this will be felt in the noncooperative sector as well. Thus the capitalistic tendencies evident even on small-scale farms will be restricted more and more in the course of development. The uneven development described above is clearly apparent—even if to a gradually diminishing degree—and will persist during a significant stage of development. But that does not mean the cooperative sector will advance toward socialism while the noncooperative sector retrogresses toward capitalism. It means that, with the exception of kulak-capitalist farming, the noncooperative sector also will take the road toward socialism and thus arrive at the decisive step: the transition from independent farming to cooperative farming. This circumstance automatically decided the question of whether—political considerations apart—we should, from an economic standpoint, strive for the greatest possible development of productive forces in the noncooperative sector too, and, if we did so, whether we would not thereby strengthen capitalistic tendencies in agriculture. We may ascertain, on the above basis, that we would not. Certain capitalistic perils undoubtedly exist, mainly in the event that our People's Democratic political power and economic development should suffer a sudden decline through internal or external forces.

The uneven development within agriculture undoubtedly is only a transitional phase; development leads toward equalization, and in this the cooperative movement will have a decisive role. Equalization will appear first in the cooperative sector—in the highest type of cooperatives, where the development of productive forces is based on the greatest concentration of material means and labor, making it possible to exploit all the advantages of large-scale production and all the advances of science and technology. For the time being such collective association is limited, to be sure, but its significance and effect are prodigious, because in startling fashion it increases the productive forces and conditions which assure a flourishing growth to those very farms that till now, on the basis of independent farming, were incapable even of simple replanting. Undoubtedly such collective association will significantly and swiftly raise the level of farming.

Simple collective association not based on the concentration of material means and labor (procurement, marketing and credit associations, etc.) unquestionably also encourages the development of productive forces, which in the more advanced stage of progress will provide the decisive masses of the peasantry with the basis for the transition from simple cooperative association to the highest type of cooperative.

With regard to the progress toward socialism of the socialist transformation of agriculture, I wrote as follows:

We should be aware that the noncooperative sector in agriculture—though it will also exist for a fairly long time—is a transitory phenomenon. For beyond any doubt, as between the two roads of development, the one that wins and becomes the sole and main road of development will be the one that achieves the most advanced form of production and thereby raises agriculture and the peasantry, both economically and in terms of everyday life, to a higher level. This will undoubtedly be the cooperative. The gradual transition of the noncooperative sector into the cooperative sector, and thus the creation of a uniform cooperative agriculture through the liquidation of the noncooperative sector, will be fostered first by those great material advantages that the cooperative alone can assure to the peasantry; secondly, by the planned economy and its effects, which, in the interest of stimulating production, encourages the small-scale producer to choose the road of cooperative association; and thirdly, by the elimination and liquidation of capitalism in other sectors of our economy, which will break the last links between agriculture and capitalism. Developments unquestionably are heading in this direction, and the prospects clearly indicate the victory of the cooperative way. At the present stage, however, we are still far from this and face a long journey before reaching our goal.

One must remember that I said all this nearly seven years ago, in December, 1948, before our economy had completely adopted Marxist terminology. The road I outlined is equally

proper and practical from an economic and political standpoint. That is why I still support it today and recommend it as
a Party program. I dare propose this all the more because it
was Lenin who established and worked out the theoretic bases
for such a peasant policy, and the policy adopted in the resolutions of the Bolshevik Party is such a policy. In the resolution
adopted at the Russian Communist (Bolshevik) Party's Twelfth
Congress on questions concerning the peasantry, farming economy, and collectivization we read the following:

> Our Party, at whatever point in its deliberations, must not for
> an instant forget or be unmindful of the really crucial significance
> of the peasant economy. To disregard this circumstance even to a
> minor degree would wreak countless dangers both in the eco-
> nomic and political field, for inevitably it would undermine or
> weaken the alliance of the proletariat and the peasantry, the
> peasantry's confidence in the proletariat; and that alliance and
> confidence, in this historic era of transition, is one of the main
> supports of the dictatorship of the proletariat, and to guard and
> strengthen it is the basic condition for the firmness of Soviet
> power. Consequently this is the Party's main task.
> We must be sure to recall the resolutions of the previous Party
> congresses, which rightly stressed that the peasantry can be con-
> vinced only by objective proof of the rightness of socialist meth-
> ods in agriculture, i.e., only if over the years we demonstrate to
> the peasantry in a practical manner the fact that collective farm-
> ing is economically more advantageous, more sensible, etc.

The resolutions of the Bolshevik Party's Fifteenth Congress,
which were forged in the battle against the extremist "left-
wing" Trotskyist opposition, asserted among other things:

> A very important premise of Lenin's, which serves as the basis
> for our whole economic orientation—namely the premise that
> proletarian industry must produce cheaper goods for the peasant
> than the capitalist order provided—has evidently been held in
> scorn by the opposition. In sharp contrast to Lenin, the opposi-
> tion has set up the thesis that more must be taken from the
> peasant than the old order took, that the policy of raising the
> already excessive prices should be continued, etc., etc. Only under
> the sharpest critical pressure could the opposition be forced to

give up this policy, which is the policy of breaking with the peasantry, the policy of plundering the working consumer. . . . In sharp opposition to Lenin, who warned against "ultraindustrialist" views; who stressed the need of marching shoulder to shoulder with the decisive masses of the peasantry; and who rejected such superficial phrases as "peasant obtuseness.". . . The Trotskyist opposition urges that we proceed without the decisive masses of the peasantry on a course that inescapably would bankrupt our Party's policies.

We must at all costs avoid this peril, which again threatens us. The only way to do so is to return to Lenin's teachings on the peasant question.

Chapter 14. Production, Standard of Living, and Economic Planning

In the spirit of the June resolution, the October, 1953, session of the Central Committee summarized the major tasks of economic policy as follows:

> In the future, the primary goal of our economic policy will be to raise constantly and considerably the standard of living of the people, especially that of the working class; to improve the social and cultural situation of the workers; and to continue at a slower pace the socialist policy of industrialization, which will remain the main line of our Party. In accordance with this, the pace of industrialization must be retarded, especially the pace in the development of heavy industry, and plans for economic development as well as relevant investments must be reviewed. On the other hand, investments in agriculture must be raised, and agricultural production and yield must be increased, including that of the independent peasants. The numerical increase of the producer cooperatives must be slowed down.

In the accusation directed at me, the March resolution of the Central Committee states the following: "To speak of raising the standard of living while ignoring the economic prerequisites thereto is nothing but cheap demagogy, misleading to the people." In an article entitled "The Work Program of the Working People," *Szabad Nep* of April 24, 1955, said, "The right-wing deviationists with their harmful policies . . . actually wanted to force on the party a policy of undermining the standard of living." This statement is a lie, the unavowed purpose of which is to erase from memory those antidemocratic regulations by which the standard of living of our working people had been intentionally and consistently lowered for years. The "left-wing" extremists did not give up their efforts in this direction during the time of the New Course either. Some of them attempted simply to thwart the regulations aimed at raising the workers' standard of living, while others took positive action to reduce the standard of living. Acting without the knowledge of the government, the Economic Policy Committee enacted a number of resolutions and took action on the basis of these resolutions—which it had no right to do in any case —and this action caused a great deterioration in the economic, social, and cultural status of persons living on wages and salaries, especially industrial workers. The Economic Policy Committee did not attempt to remedy the economic situation by increasing production; it sought to do so purely by economizing. However, it attempted to effect all economies at the expense of the worker. The ideological basis for this harmful, antiworker action was derived from Mátyás Rákosi's assertion that supposedly our workers live "extravagantly." The so -called economy regulations were proposed in this spirit. The regulations provide that the following savings must be achieved in 1955: 290 million forints in social insurance, 74 million forints in state-subsidized sports, 34 million forints at day homes and nurseries, 300 million forints by decreasing state subsidies to factory canteens, 40 million forints in the field of health foods, 300 million forints through the introduction of a new pension plan, and 100 million forints through the reduction of travel at discount rates. Only the blind could fail to see that the "left-wing" extremists were directing their attack primarily at the workers' standard of living, calling it "economy" necessitated by the workers' supposedly "extravagant" mode of living.

But they didn't forget the peasants either. Upon instruction from the committee, the Ministry of Finance prepared a proposal increasing the taxes of the peasants by 600 million forints and raising local taxes by 200 million forints. It was I who took a stand against this crude attack on the workers' standard of living launched under the pretext of "economy." As a result of my stand, many of the unjustified "economy" regulations were successfully prevented and the interests of the workers were protected. I brought up this question very pointedly at the October, 1954, session of the Central Committee; I outlined the situation and expressed my point of view, with which the Central Committee agreed entirely.

It is characteristic that the Economic Policy Committee did not make a single proposal for increasing production or for realigning industry, although it had been instructed to do so. Neither did it ever do any preparatory work that would have made possible the actual reduction of production costs. Yet, at that time, the work of the committee was under the direction of Ernö Gerö and Istvan Friss, the very people who accuse me of opportunism and right-wing deviation for neglecting the problem of reducing production costs, whereas it is a proved fact that I paid no less attention to these probems than they did. Gerö and Friss, whose duty it would have been, and who had been instructed to work out for the government proposals for measures to increase productivity and to reduce production costs, did not solve these problems—they did not even take them up.

In 1947 I had already emphasized the economic significance and the close connection between the people's standard of living on the one hand, and increased production and the development of the forces of production on the other. At that time, among other things, I wrote the following on this subject:

> The difficult economic situation of the country, the increase in the standard of living inherent in the democratic system, and social development in general compel us to produce more and to develop the forces of production. . . . If the economic plans are to promote development, they must not be confined to increasing the productive forces of agriculture, but must play a guiding role in all sectors of the economy in the fight against plutocracy.

At the October, 1954, session, where I took a stand against the resistance manifested to the implementation of the June policy, I emphasized, with the complete agreement of the Central Committee, that socialism cannot be built by narrowing the basis of production but only by broadening it; not by restricting or neglecting the material interest of the producer but by augmenting it; not by discouraging the buyers but by increasing the stock of merchandise. In any case, the members of the Central Committee are familiar with the speech I made at the October session; it is worth rereading that speech in connection with the charges brought against me, so that the members can convince themselves that these charges have no foundation.

The work of the Economic Policy Committee, which instead of being aimed at increasing production concerned itself with economy measures, shows that the members took the line of least resistance: economy regulations can be realized with simple administrative instructions and measures, whereas increasing production calls for broad measures and a great effort on the part of the workers as well as the entire economic apparatus.

In connection with the charges leveled against me in the March, 1955, resolution and the commentaries attached thereto, let us look at the facts, in my speeches that appeared in print and in my writings, that prove that the charges are baseless. As early as July 4, 1953, I emphasized in the government program:

> The welfare of the people and the constant raising of the standard of living of the workers and the population—which is the focal point of the government's activities—depends on the productive work of our people. The abundance of merchandise required for increasing prosperity can be assured only by increased production, overfulfillment of planned quotas, and enthusiastic, broad, socialist competition both in industry and agriculture.

In this same speech, I went into further detail about the close connection between production and the standard of living.

> The fulfillment of our industrial production plans is an indispensable prerequisite to all the regulations that the government desires to implement in its economic policy and in the field of

improving the standard of living. Without the unconditional fulfillment of industrial production plans, the development of agricultural production is impossible. The key to the successful realization of the government's goals is in the hands of the working class. This implies two kinds of obligation. It obliges the government, in working out regulations, to devote the greatest care to raising the standard of living of the workers and to satisfying their material, social, and cultural requirements to the greatest possible extent. The government assumes this obligation and will meet it. At the same time, it obliges the working class to ensure the punctual fulfillment of production plans by increasing work discipline; our industrial workers will have to assume this obligation and meet it. I am convinced that they will do so honorably and wholeheartedly.

But even after the government program of June, I did not forget about the relation of production to the standard of living, about the need for increasing productivity. Last fall, only a few months before such serious charges were made against me regarding these problems, I delivered a speech at the MAVAG. This speech also bears witness to the fact that I considered production the primary and decisive condition as far as raising the standard of living was concerned. They ignored this speech completely so that they would be able to maintain their baseless accusations. This speech is a sharp refutation to those contentions with which they slander me. One or two quotations from the MAVAG speech illustrate and prove plainly the correctness of my point of view.

We know that in our circumstances the consumers themselves are the producers. Whom can we call to account if there is a shortage of some product, if quality is poor or the price too high? Only ourselves. From this we must draw the final conclusion: we must produce more, better, and cheaper. This is primarily in the interest of the working class itself, and a factor influencing the improvement of real wages and the standard of living. Thus the fate of the workers' living standard is in their own hands, and the realignment of industrial production is essential to it.

In the same speech I declared that our main task in 1955 would be also to increase production:

We are preparing to solve still greater problems next year, because we must achieve better results in all fields of production in order to take another great step forward along the June way; to broaden the population's supply of food and industrial products; to improve our mode of living; to satisfy our cultural demands— in short, to make life better, more beautiful, and happier. Consequently next year's economic plan must lay the foundation for further improvement in the standard of living, and to do this, we must make sure that industrial and agricultural production will increase more than it did this year.

I am also blamed that in 1954 the standard of living rose by 15 per cent, although industrial production and productivity did not increase and production costs did not drop. This statement is true only when taken out of context. Why do the "left-wing" extremists fail to speak of the development of industrial production and productivity, of production costs and the rise in the standard of living between 1949 and 1954? Shouldn't there have been a rise in the standard of living corresponding to and resulting from the tremendous increase in production that occurred between 1949 and 1953? The rise in the standard of living that came about in 1954 as a result of the implementation of the June policy in the New Course was not a kind of advance payment, as the "left-wing" extremists try to make it appear, but simply a payment of the debts incurred by the "left wing" before 1953. These "left-wingers" promised a considerably greater rise in the living standard for 1950–1951, at which time they were speaking in terms of a 30 to 50 per cent rise, although they realized in the meantime that, due to their fantastic industrial plans, they would not be able to keep the promise. This was indeed cheap demagogy and a betrayal of the people.

What do the few quotations above, which I could supplement from countless other speeches of mine, prove? Do they perhaps prove the correctness of the March resolution, which maintains that I merely spoke of raising the standard of living and made no attempt to establish the prerequisites for this by increasing production? On the contrary, they prove that the charges of the March resolution have no basis; that they won't hold water;

that they falsify my point of view by suppressing it; and that they therefore deceive the Party and the people.

But let us look further. Agricultural production is an important factor with regard to raising the standard of living. Did I disregard this or make light of it? Did I want to raise the standard of living without increasing agricultural production, as the slanderers claim I did? In my speech at the MAVAG, I dealt with this problem as follows:

> The key question in the development of the economy is the rapid promotion of agricultural production. The work that began as the result of the Party and government resolutions of last year has already shown results. This program must be developed further on the basis of last year's experiences; better conditions must be established so that it can be implemented successfully and more rapidly. The work is in progress and will soon be ready, and this will give agricultural production a new and tremendous boost.

In discussing this same question at the Fourth National Conference of Producer Cooperatives, I said among other things:

> It is the job of today's national conference to promote the successful implementation of the Party and government resolution on agricultural development by backing said resolution with the great strength, organization, and purposefulness represented by cooperative farming. . . . Despite the prevailing shortcomings, we have great hopes for cooperative farming. . . . The Party and the government will provide extensive aid in the form of money and machinery to every producer cooperative; it is simply necessary to make use of the possibilities. We know, of course, that machines without technicians are of no value; but in the hands of the right people, they can achieve miracles. So in the final analysis, it is up to the members of the producer cooperatives themselves to achieve outstanding results and to prove the superiority of large-scale cooperative farming.

I made a maximum increase in production and a consequent constant rise in the standard of living the main objective and the most important basic prerequisite of the basic rule of socialism, even in the field of economic planning. I emphasized this particularly in my speech before the national assembly on January 23, 1954, when I reported on the government's activities for the preceding half-year:

> Economic planning, in its broader aspects, had to determine the outline and details of the government's economic policy activities for 1954. The mistakes of the past had to be eliminated; plans had to be made on a more secure basis and more realistically, because we cannot afford to repeat the mistakes of the past. With scientific foresight that will prevent any upsets in the national economy, we must plan those far-reaching changes that are necessary to correct the mistakes of the past.

In this same speech I stated that one of our major tasks was to bring the further development of production forces into harmony with a rise in the standard of living; furthermore, that we must develop the proper proportions for production, consumption, and stockpiling. On this subject, I spoke as follows:

> The main task is to take increasing care of the material and cultural needs of the population, based on a realistic survey of the nation's resources, the population's capabilities, and the performance capacity of certain fields. Man himself, with his varied needs, stands at the center of our efforts to produce material goods. Consequently the fundamental law of socialism must prevail before all else in our planning. The new aspect here is that we will bring into harmony the further development of production forces with the further increase of the standard of living. The mission of our economic planning is to develop the proper ratios between production, consumption, and accumulation. We must accomplish this task in our 1954 plan. In evolving the plan, it was important to determine the proper rate of development for each branch of the economy.

In the light of these statements the charges leveled against me in the March resolution, with regard to my stand on production, look pretty bad indeed. One must ask who it actually was who committed cheap demagogy, misleading the people? On the basis of what I said, it is evident that it certainly was not I.

Chapter 15.   The Question of National Indebtedness to Foreign Countries

At the November, 1955, meeting of the Central Committee and in the resolution adopted by the Committee, Mátyás Rákosi held me responsible for the national indebtedness to foreign countries, especially capitalist countries, which had increased greatly in 1953 and 1954 and became still greater in 1955. As has been unanimously established by any number of party and government resolutions, our foreign indebtedness was due mainly to the erroneous economic policies of the First Five-Year Plan. One of the serious consequences of too rapid industrialization, undertaken without regard for national resources, was that it developed industries for which primary materials were lacking in Hungary, and neglected or even restricted those industries that were based on Hungarian resources and primary materials. Consequently industrial development required more and more imported basic and raw materials, which we acquired on less and less favorable terms. In other words, we were supposed to balance imports with more and more exports. But while the price of raw materials on the capitalist world market quickly consumed our reserves of gold and foreign exchange, our exports could not keep pace with our imports because our production costs were higher than world market prices. We were able to make these transactions only by supplementing them with national income derived from other branches of the economy; this supplement amounted to 12 billion forints per year. The pace and trends of our industrial development during the First Five-Year Plan were thus the direct cause of our foreign indebtedness and the indirect cause of our increasing difficulties, and, in the final analysis, they were responsible for the impoverishment of the country.

Let us look at the problem more specifically. It is well known that the pace set for our industrialization during the First Five-Year Plan was disproportionately high, not only in so far as our own capabilities were concerned but also as compared to the other People's Democracies; and this despite the fact that of all People's Democracies our country had the least in the way of industrial raw materials. For example, industrial development amounted to 158 per cent in Poland from 1949 to 1955, to 98 per cent in Czechoslovakia during the same period, to 92.3 per cent in the German Democratic Republic from 1950 to 1955, to 144 per cent in Rumania from 1951 to 1955, to 120 per cent in Bulgaria from 1949 to 1955, and to 210 per cent in Hungary from 1949 to 1953. This rate of development in Hungary caused an unusually great and ever increasing gap between the supply of raw materials available for planned industrial development and the demand for basic and raw materials. This was the major source of foreign indebtedness. But this also accounts for the fact that the role of foreign trade in our country increased suddenly and dangerously during those years. Life itself exposed and crushed this dangerous anti-Marxist theory of superindustrialization. It also proved that all our economic problems could not be solved by rapid industrialization alone without leading to increased foreign indebtedness. During this period, agricultural production declined; the promised 50 per cent rise in the standard of living failed to materialize; the necessary balance of trade was not established. The concurrent decline in agricultural production made it impossible for this branch of the economy to meet both domestic requirements and the ever increasing export commitments. This was one of the causes of the ever growing lag in the fulfillment of export plans. Taken together with industry's growing demand for basic and raw materials, which led to constant overfulfillment of import plans, it could lead only to a rapid increase in foreign indebtedness. As the quantity of domestically produced and imported raw materials grew, its degree of utilization decreased. Less and less of the basic materials produced were of usable quality. For example, as the amount of coal produced increased, the amount of breakage and waste increased even more rapidly. Consequently the shortage of basic materials was not reduced but actually increased by forced production, and this shortage had to be covered more and more through imports.

Another serious trouble was that industry, and especially heavy industry, was not developed on the basis of scientific analysis, with due regard for economy and practicality. At the time when it was decided to build the great industrial establishments, a complete lack of information prevailed as to their cost or the amount of imported material that would be required to establish and maintain them. This applied also to practically all the figures connected with the industrial development plan. All this became evident only after the great industrial establishments had already been put into operation. By then it was too late to do anything but import the necessary basic and raw materials, unless we wanted to close down the establishments. Thus the precepts of economy fell by the wayside.

Serious errors developed in the internal ratio of industrial production between 1949 and 1952 also. For one thing, the new producing units were developed in the wrong direction; at the same time, the existing factories were required with increasing frequency to turn out products unsuited to their capabilities. Consequently the demand for the materials of heavy industry, which was producing export goods largely from imported materials, grew disproportionately, and this demand could be and was met solely through still further imports. In establishing the internal ratio of industrial development and its ratio to other branches, no one took into consideration how greatly industrial development, as a whole and by branch, effects the activeness or passiveness of the foreign trade balance. Between 1949 and 1954, according to statistical data, the foreign trade balance for industrial import and export goods was constantly passive and deteriorated from year to year.

How the volume of industrial production "suitable for satisfying social needs" developed in the course of the First Five-Year Plan merits review. Statistics show that at the end of the

First Five-Year Plan producing capacity was twice as great as in 1949 and three times as great as in 1938. At the same time the volume of industrial production "suitable for satisfying social needs" had increased by only 35 to 40 per cent as compared to 1949. This proves that, due to improper development and poor economy, industry was consuming a large part of its own output. In other words, it was industrial development for its own sake. The sacrifices that the workers made for the development of industry, and especially heavy industry, brought no returns. Since industry could export only a relatively small volume of its own product, it was far from capable of meeting its own import requirements, and this applied in still greater degree to heavy industry.

The First Five-Year Plan made no basic changes in the technical backwardness of our industry; while great investments were being made in increasing production capacity, almost nothing was being done to perfect production and improve technology. Even a good many of the new establishments are no exceptions to this. For example, the new Inota power plant is less modern and less economical than the Ajka power plant, which is twenty years older; the Gyor power plant requires 7,200 calories to produce one kilowatt hour of energy, whereas most of the factories need only 5,000 for the same amount of energy. The power plant at Sztalinvaros operates at a boiler pressure of forty atmospheres. Such boiler pressure is now obsolete. Even our more modern power plants are designed to operate on lignite, which greatly increases production costs. All these facts show that, despite the fact that our industrial basis was greatly expanded during the First Five-Year Plan, the difference between the technological standards maintained in our country and in industrially progressive countries increased. To put it plainly, progressive techniques elsewhere left us further and further behind. It is a well-known fact that most of our textile machinery is over fifty years old; our transportation industry machinery is over forty years old; and most of our machine tool equipment is more than fifteen or twenty years old. The measuring equipment and other instruments of the factories are deficient. We have relatively better production equipment only in the pharmaceutical and the telecommunication industries.

The increase of industrial production for its own sake, combined with the neglect of technical standards, inevitably allowed almost no increase in productivity during the First Five-Year Plan. Although the results calculated on the basis of incorrect value indices show a significant growth, the facts and the existing difficulties plainly contradict such data. The augmented Five-Year Plan called for a 92 per cent increase in productivity, which was supposed to bring about 75 per cent of the required increase in production. According to the statistics, achievements fell far short of the goal. Furthermore, if we view total industrial output in the light of the increase in the quantity "suitable for satisfying social needs," which amounted to between 35 and 40 per cent during the First Five-Year Plan, then it becomes evident that productivity in industry increased hardly at all after 1949, because production in excess of 35 to 40 per cent was achieved at the cost of a 40 per cent increase in man power. The stagnation of productivity was due not primarily to a deterioration in the worker's attitude toward his work, but to the faulty economic policy described above, with its over-acceleration and the erroneous goals of unsound industrial development.

Rise in productivity was retarded also by the emphasis on those branches of industry, such as metallurgy, coal mining, the machine industry, etc., where productivity is lower than average in any case. Furthermore, the gradual decrease in the standard of living that occurred during the First Five-Year Plan inevitably resulted in a drop in productivity, while the failure to develop technology made a general increase in productivity impossible. These circumstances explain why our production costs are higher than those of the world market in both the capitalist and the socialist markets. This, of course, has been a great drawback as far as the export of our industrial products is concerned, and has all but put a stop to their salability. Due to the price differential and the deterioration in the quality of our export products, we have lost a major part of our previously dependable foreign markets. At the same time, the acquisition of new markets has been made especially difficult—partly for the reasons outlined above and partly because of the inflexibility and ineptitude of our foreign trade organs.

Export plan fulfillment, which lagged increasingly year by year because of the unfavorable development of production factors, was seriously affected also by the disadvantageous foreign market situation, all of which together led inevitably to a growth in foreign indebtedness.

It must be pointed out that, although the economic cooperation and mutual assistance between the socialist countries brought significant results, the activity of CEMA from the point of view of industrial production and development was exceptionally limited during the period of the First Five-Year Plan. This also contributed to the rise of inequities in work distribution among the friendly countries. Despite the fact that agreements were made with some of the democratic countries with a view to assigning work in a way that would promote economic production and work distribution, parallel manufacturing, especially in the field of machine industry, had an increasingly detrimental effect on our export opportunities and consequently on our foreign trade balance. Parallel manufacturing affected not only trade among the friendly countries themselves but led to an unhealthy competition among them in the capitalist markets as well. The exaggerated trend toward autarky, which manifested itself in the machine industry in the other friendly countries too, was most apparent also in the fields of precision instruments and telecommunications. This was a serious blow to our most developed and most favorably producing export industries. Parallel manufacturing and the exaggerated trend toward autarky within the socialist camp not only reduced our opportunities to export within the camp, but also deprived us of chances of importing basic and raw materials. Consequently our foreign trade was shifted more and more toward the capitalist world and increased our indebtedness in this direction.

The foreign trade situation was further aggravated during the second half of 1954, when trade conferences with the Soviet Union and the other friendly countries revealed that in 1955 we would get from them only 50 per cent of what we received in 1954 in the way of essential products and raw materials; the remainder would have to be obtained from the capitalist countries. This also meant that, to compensate for the sudden jump in the need to import from capitalists, we would have to augment our exports to them drastically. But neither our industry nor our foreign trade was prepared for this.

The Council of Ministers, acting on the resolution of the Political Committee, established the volume of foreign trade imports and exports for 1955 in such a way as to release one billion forints more in assets to the socialist camp. Furthermore, it ordained that in 1955 our indebtedness to capitalist countries was not to increase, and we made it our goal to limit the import of material to the quantity set in the 1954 barter agreement (calculated without credit). We planned that the Soviet Union would supply more material and credit than it had supplied in 1954, and would accept more machinery in exchange. However, the outcome of the conferences, concluded in January, 1955, was that the Soviet Union was willing to guarantee us only 50 per cent of the 1954 import volume and only 36 per cent of the items on our want list for 1955. Our export possibilities developed in approximately the same way. At the same time the democratic countries, especially Rumania and Poland, also desired to reduce their export of materials to us as compared to 1954. They were willing to let us have important raw materials only in exchange for goods obtainable exclusively from capitalist countries, or agricultural products that we had not stockpiled and would also have had to purchase from capitalist countries.

Thus the situation that developed between November, 1954, and January, 1955, posed unusually great difficulties for our entire economy. It seriously affected our supply of material and again made it necessary to realign production. The effect of this on foreign trade was to further depress the trade and foreign payment scale to such an extent that only a tremendous increase in credit could remedy it. However, there was no practical possibility of accomplishing this on the world market. Furthermore such a solution ran counter to the government resolutions on this subject. It became apparent that the only way in which we could have provided material for industry, without drastically reducing our production plans and realigning the production of industries requiring large quantities of imported material, would have been by getting from capitalist countries the several billion forints' worth of raw materials and goods that the socialist camp would no longer supply. Even so, some of the import materials, such as metallurgical basic materials, would have been hard to obtain from the West even had foreign exchange been available to us for the purpose.

In general, the increase in our foreign debt, especially our debt to capitalist countries, can be traced back to the foregoing causes. As a result of the harmful economic policy of the First Five-Year Plan, the New Course inherited a heavy burden in this field also. The effects of this were especially noticeable in 1954 and were far from disappearing. They could not have disappeared; on the contrary, owing to the reasons already outlined, they continued to exert a harmful influence. The serious consequences of an erroneous and harmful economic policy that has been pursued for years cannot be eliminated in eighteen months, especially when the government's new corrective economic policy is resisted to a great extent. Not only internal, but much more powerful external forces and factors exerted a harmful influence, especially in the field of foreign trade agreements; this made it all but impossible to overcome the difficulties. Since it is a state secret, I will give no figures and be brief, but it must be pointed out that a considerable part of our foreign debt derives from expenditures and investments for security and defense, which place a heavy load on our foreign trade balance. The June, 1953, resolution pointed out that there were excesses in this field also.

The already difficult position of our foreign trade was further aggravated by an accumulation of unpaid debts in virtually all of the capitalist countries. Payments falling due on expensive short-term foreign credits constantly used up our foreign exchange income, making it impossible to use the exchange to purchase essential import products. Despite the fact that in the given international situation it would have been possible for us to convert our capitalist debts and concentrate them in just a few places, thereby reducing our payment balance, and despite the fact that on several occasions I specifically instructed the leaders of the Ministry of Foreign Trade to do this, our debts were not liquidated. This was primarily because the Political

Committee, at the recommendation of Mátyás Rákosi, took the attitude that such a solution would be dangerous and should be resorted to only later and then with extreme caution. In the meantime, other People's Democracies successfully solved similar problems in this way, and lightened their financial obligations in this way.

The unusual slowness and inflexibility of our foreign trade organs added to the difficulties of locating and winning new markets, of financing our exports, and of issuing letters of credit. Our foreign trade was unable to see the opportunities offered us by the semicolonial countries, the Near and Middle East, and South America. The mistaken foreign trade view—which is not entirely attributable to our difficulties—that a deal could be closed only upon immediate payment of exchange added to the problems. It was possible to alter this harmful inflexibility to some extent, but it is still prevalent even today.

In broad outline, these are the causes of our foreign indebtedness. I cannot be held responsible for it, because in the first place it was due to the mistaken economic policy of the First Five-Year Plan, for which, before June, 1953, in the period of individual leadership, Mátyás Rákosi was responsible—Rákosi, who was both the First Secretary of the Party and the Premier. In the second place, our economic policy, including our foreign trade, was directed by the Party, and every new foreign credit action had to be carried out on the basis of Party resolutions. And finally, I cannot be held accountable because, within the Council of Ministers, foreign trade was not under my direction but under the supervision and direction of Ernö Gerö, First Deputy Premier. As far as actual responsibility is concerned, it must be asserted that all important foreign trade resolutions—such as those concerning trade and pay agreements, credits, export-import plans, foreign exchange management, and long-term contracts and their terms—were made on the basis of the decision of, and in entire agreement with, the Political Committee. After the questions had been debated, the decisions were pronounced by First Party Secretary Mátyás Rákosi, who presided over the meetings of the Political Committee. In not a single instance did the Political Committee's decision concerning any question related to foreign trade run counter to, or fail to agree with, the opinion of Mátyás Rákosi. So, if certain persons want to blame any one person, they can and must blame Mátyás Rákosi, who as Party First Secretary and leader of the Party directed economic policy as he directed all aspects of the implementation of the Party's leading role. Furthermore, since Rákosi considered foreign trade his special field, he kept it under his immediate direction.

I, as former Premier and member of the Political Committee, share in the collective responsibility that falls upon the Party and the leading government organs for having been unable to overcome the serious consequences of the harmful economic policy practiced by the Party and the government under the direction of Mátyás Rákosi during the First Five-Year Plan. The foreign indebtedness of the country as regards both socialist and capitalist countries is nothing more than an accumulated and unliquidated debt from the First Five-Year Plan. This debt proves plainly the correctness of the contention that the persons in charge of economic policy prior to the New Course failed to take into account the nation's capabilities, and that they set up goals that exceeded the country's economic strength.

Chapter 16. The Role and Significance of the NEP

The March, 1955, resolution of the Central Committee did not deal with the question of the NEP,* its role and its significance, and not even with those problems in this field that the Party and the government had to resolve. Thus the March resolution of the Central Committee did not commit the Party to the NEP policy, although it pointed out that the June resolution of the Central Committee, which opened up a new phase in the application of the NEP, was still in effect without change and constituted the basis of the March resolution. In reality, matters were different. Since the March resolution, it was precisely in the field of the NEP that there had been the most extensive return to pre-June, 1953, and even to pre-December, 1951, conditions.

I do not take up the question of the NEP because it was another area in which sharp attacks had been directed against me. Such attacks actually occurred only on one or two rather unimportant and not fundamental points. I take up the question because I do not agree with the policy that the Party leadership has been following with regard to the NEP since the March resolution.

According to Lenin's teachings the guiding policy of the NEP is to ensure victory over the capitalist elements to the proletariat in power, and the building of socialism through

* New Economic Policy, first announced in the Soviet Union in May, 1921.

economic solidarity based on the exchange of the goods between the working class and the small peasants. In the interest of the latter, the economy uses even the capitalist elements, so that they will be overcome and a socialist economy be built through the market and by use of the market rather than through direct exchange (barter) of goods, or without a market simply to avoid a market.

Thus the NEP is the specific means and form for building socialism, and is absolutely necessary in every country where there is a significantly large number of small peasants. Consequently, during the transitional period, the NEP is the basis for our entire economic policy. This means that the elements of the NEP are not operative to the same extent throughout the entire transitional period, but wither away to the extent that the building of socialism proceeds and to the extent that the socialist sectors of the economy develop.

The question that must be asked is whether the NEP was utilized in the spirit of Marxist-Leninist teachings.

A. During the period of the Three-Year Plan, the main task of the NEP—to establish the economic solidarity of socialist big industry and the small peasants—was on the whole successfully accomplished despite some smaller or larger mistakes in the field of free-market sale and trade.

B. The second period of NEP, from the beginning of the Five-Year Plan to June, 1953, was characterized by the liquidation of private retail trade, i.e., the substantial elimination of private small industry, and also by increasingly serious violations of the basic principles of NEP in the economic consolidation of socialist industry and the small peasants, particularly after December 1, 1951. The origin of the errors was the excessive rate of industrialization and the extraordinary speed aimed at creating an integrated socialist national economy. This showed up first in agricultural production, and principally in the neglect of aid to private peasant farmers; frankly speaking, in antipeasant policies. It turned out that with the too rapid development of heavy industry, the material resources of the country did not prove sufficient to give new impetus to agricultural production. A few statistics will demonstrate this quite clearly. According to the original Five-Year Plan, only 15.7 per cent of total investments were to be expended on the development of agriculture. However the augmented Five-Year Plan reduced this to 12.7 per cent, and even this allotment was further reduced to a considerable extent during the execution of the plan.

At that time, my opponents justified the rapid rate of development of heavy industry mainly on the basis of mechanization of agriculture. In actual fact, however, agricultural machine production did not keep pace with the large-scale development of our machine building as a whole; the ratio of agricultural machine production to machine production as a whole was reduced considerably. Tractor production, for example, was reduced to such an extent that in 1952 it did not cover replacement needs. Consequently, the agricultural tractors available not only failed to increase but decreased.

C. During the period before June, 1953, NEP was seriously violated by accelerated collectivization, which shattered the security of peasant production; less and less help was provided for the peasantry; the ever increasing state deliveries reduced sharply the quantity of goods that could be sold by the peasantry on the free market, thereby simultaneously reducing the actual material interest of the peasantry in producing as well as their desire to produce. As has already been mentioned, this loosened considerably the economic basis of the worker-peasant alliance, which is the main force for building socialism. Added to this, similar errors were committed in the field of retail trade and small industry; errors that similarly restricted the NEP and even eliminated it in numerous fields.

During the period between 1950 and June, 1953, the economic policy of our Party came into sharp conflict with the NEP, which is the basis of building socialism during the transitional period. This policy repeatedly violated NEP principles so seriously that in this period, especially in the year 1952, preceding the June resolution, in contradiction to Marxist-Leninist teachings, building of socialism in our country continued essentially *without* NEP. And yet Lenin had told us, with strong self-criticism, the errors committed in the Soviet Union with respect to the NEP:

We, who were raised high by waves of enthusiasm, who aroused the fervor of the people, first in the general political field and later in the military field, thought that we could also solve equally great economic problems directly and with enthusiasm. We counted on the fact—or perhaps more correctly, we took it for granted without sufficient consideration—that the proletarian state could directly, by command, organize in our country of small peasants all state production and state distribution of products on the basis of Communist principles. Experience showed that we were mistaken. There is a need for many transitional periods, during which state capitalism and socialism are needed to prepare —through long years of work—for the actual transition to Communism. Let us work first of all to build sturdy little bridges that will lead our small-peasant country to socialism through state capitalism: otherwise we will not arrive at Communism.

The conduct and views manifested among the highest leadership of our party in regard to the application of the NEP and in the matter of correcting the serious errors committed in this field is leading to renewal of old mistakes, instead of better understanding the lessons of the past, and is downright foreign to the spirit of Lenin's teachings and the system of self-criticism. Taking all of this into consideration, we can rightfully say that the June, 1953, resolution of the Central Committee also opened a new period in the application of the NEP in Hungary. Of course this did not go easily. The opposition was very strong in this area also, but we achieved important results anyhow. Without enumerating the results that were achieved through use of the New Economic Policy during the following one and a half to two years, we can conclude that the reinstatement of the NEP was the most significant fact of the June economic policy from the viewpoint of principle and practice. We will understand this if we know that, in accordance with the teachings of Leninism, the fundamental question in building socialism is the economic association of the working class and the working peasantry, primarily through the exchange of goods. This is the essence of the NEP.

Inasmuch as the NEP is the basis of economic policy during the transitional period, the collaboration of the working class and the working peasantry is of necessity the focal point of the NEP.

In connection with the NEP, Lenin unequivocally expressed his view that in order to be victorious, we must secure the relations between the working class and the peasantry, and between socialist industry and peasantry, through trade between city and village developed in every way possible—because, as Lenin frequently said, the small commodity producers will tolerate no economic ties to socialist industry except ties through merchandise, which normally result in trade. This arises from the fact that the peasantry wants to deal entirely freely with as much of its produce as possible. The peasantry wants to accomplish this not through direct exchange of goods but through the market.

According to Lenin's teachings, the NEP represents a certain degree of compromise, but a compromise without which socialism cannot be victorious. This is the kind of compromise, as Lenin said, that is necessary because it is the only guarantee of slower, but at the same time surer, progress.

Lenin also pointed out very often that the utilization of the NEP requires unusually varied and most distinct methods, which must be developed on the basis of experience. "The more varied our methods are, the better and richer our experience will be, and the surer and quicker the success of socialism."

On the basis of the June, 1953, resolution of the Central Committee, we successfully utilized these Leninist guides for a year and a half to two years in every field of the national economy to which they apply: in economic relations between the workers and the peasantry, in socialist industry and the production of small peasantry, in private trade, artisan trade, the turn over of goods, and the market.

The resolutions passed since the June, 1953, session of the Central Committee took a basically correct position on the questions of the practical application of the NEP, and had results too. Essentially, we corrected the serious errors committed in the earlier period. Nevertheless, the failure to clarify completely the theoretical problems of the NEP, along with the special circumstances and methods under which they would be

put into effect in Hungary during the transitional period, was
a serious omission and one for which we paid dearly later.

In wide circles, principally in the ranks of the Party membership, there was and remains a high degree of ignorance and confusion on this matter.

The March resolution of the Central Committee does not
even mention NEP, which is the fundamental instrument of
building socialism during the transition period. The criticism,
moreover, which was directed against NEP's most important
economic and political precepts, and described by them as opportunist right-wing deviationism, promoted within the Party
leadership the rise of anti-Marxist views, which also appeared in
disguised form in Party resolutions and according to which application of the NEP was an opportunist right-wing policy and
a "distortion" of Leninism-Marxism. This explains why the
"rectification" of the supposed "distortion" and right-wing deviationism committed in various areas of the national economy
is directed essentially and primarily against the application of
the NEP. Actually, instead of making baseless accusations, it
would have been more proper to learn from past experience, to
search for the roots of the errors, and to listen to Lenin, who as
we see courageously revealed the errors in economic policy and
pointed to the need for courageous application of the NEP.
Lenin dealt a great deal with questions of the NEP. "The small
farmer, as long as he remains a small farmer," writes Lenin,
"has need for such stimulation, prodding, and encouragement
as will conform with his economic basis or that of a small-scale
independent farm."

Elsewhere Lenin points to the fact that the NEP's "significant
and main task above all others is to establish solidarity between
the new economy which we have begun to build and the peasant economy which is the basis of subsistence of millions and
millions of peasants."

Lenin also emphatically called our attention to the fact that
"we must be free to use, and we must be able to use, every form
of economic transition whatsoever if it is at all needed to
strengthen the relations between the peasantry and the proletariat . . . for the promotion of industry and for the facilita-

tion of other large-scale or more important moves such as electrification, for example."

From the above, we can see that our party leadership did not apply, in the spirit of Leninism, and at present applies even less, the NEP policy, which constitutes the basis for building socialism.

Fear of the free market, fear of the development of the peasant farms, fear of the revival of capitalism as a result of the NEP policy—in other words, underestimation of the power of authority of the People's Democratic government, a disguised lack of faith in the concept of federation between peasants and workers —this is characteristic of the representatives of the extreme "left-wing" agrarian policy, who incline somewhat more toward "militant Communism" than toward a properly developed and continued NEP policy. Yet, in Lenin's words, the most dangerous fault of the "left-wingers" is that "they think of their desires as objective truth."

Unfortunately, it appears that our "left-wing" extremists are suffering from the same dangerous error. It is worth calling attention to the warning Lenin gave on May 27, 1919, to the Hungarian workers, especially to Hungarian workers having leftist tendencies. Lenin spoke of a rather prolonged transition period from capitalism to socialism. This period was necessary to break the power of habits of a petit bourgeois economy. This warning should not be forgotten, as it was in 1919 that an attempt was made to make socialized agriculture the predominant sector of agriculture within a period of four or five years.

These facts indicate that, in putting into effect certain theoretical precepts of Marxism-Leninism, some extremists ignore not only the special characteristics of the development of the Soviet Union, but of their own country as well. Yet Marxism is not a dogma but a guide to action.

Even before the March resolution of the Central Committee, opinions were being expressed to the effect that the practice of NEP should be curtailed. The old, incorrect, anti-Marxist thesis that in the worker-peasant alliance the economic link between worker and peasant should be strengthened during the transition period through the socialization of agriculture, rather than through a broadening of market connections, came into prominence again. This false, anti-Marxist theory is nothing but the theoretical formulation of the liquidation of NEP. It means that they want to lay the foundations of socialism by restricting market connections, or actually NEP at first, and finally by eliminating it altogether. It means further that socialism can and must be built without the political cooperation, alliance, and agreement of the working peasants and the peasant masses. But it means also that they intend to split apart the two interdependent main tasks of agriculture which are required by the basic law of socialism, as well as by the law of systematic, well-proportioned development as applied to the development of agriculture. These two interdependent tasks are: the simultaneous development of the production of the independent peasants, and the organization and development of the production of the producer cooperatives. By splitting these tasks, they intend instead to force the development of the producer cooperatives alone, at an increased speed and in excessive number. The attacks on NEP appearing in articles in the Party press since the March resolution of the Central Committee, plus a whole series of economic measures initiated since then by the government and the economic organs, all show that the actual implementation of the anti-NEP, anti-Marxist-Leninist, extreme leftist line that has become predominant in the Party leadership is being rapidly carried out. This seriously endangers the entire future of our building of socialism. The restriction of artisan trade, the increase in limitations on the market, the drastic reduction in the amount of produce that the peasant may dispose of freely, the introduction of compulsory delivery of cereal grains and corn, the increase in the mandatory sowing of many types of crops, the constantly increasing excesses in the field of contractual production, the reduction in the financial incentive of the producer, and many other regulations that discriminate against the small producer plainly show the attempts to liquidate the NEP.

The situation is similar in the case of artisan and retail trade. The instructions that have been issued are of such a nature and so far-reaching, and their implementation leaves so much room for excesses, that they will lead and have already partially led to a great reduction in the activity of tradesmen.

It is indisputable—and I am in agreement—that in the field of implementing NEP mistakes occurred after the New Course of June, 1953; extremes occurred, which must be—should have been—remedied somewhere along the way. However this cannot affect the basis of NEP's theory and its practical implementation—it cannot mean the restriction of NEP on the present course, when the principal task in this field is the broadening and expansion of NEP. What has occurred in the field of NEP since the March resolution of the Central Committee has far surpassed the necessary correction of the mistakes and has in essence prepared the liquidation of NEP. I do not agree with the Party's policy that NEP precipitates that serious condition, recovery from which was made possible in the spring of 1953 only by the bold and wide-ranging implementation of NEP. I consider the above policy to be harmful to the people's economy and dangerous to socialist construction, where it pertains to the agricultural, political, and social fields. In relation to NEP, it would have been inconceivable that they would have missed the opportunity of directly accusing me. Even though they are not saying it openly, they are pinning NEP upon me as a harmful rightist deviation. Gyorgy Csatar volunteered for this role. In the June 17, 1955, issue of *Szabad Nep*, under the title "For the Strengthening of Labor Discipline," he wrote that, upon the personal instructions of Comrade Imre Nagy, the respective state organs ordered that "industrial permits must be issued without any restrictions to anyone on request, even though he wasn't previously an artisan." This declaration by Csatar, like all the others, is a blatant lie, which he uttered with the knowledge that he could do it without any reservations, because no one except I would hold him responsible, and I could do so only behind closed doors and without effect. The slanderers can utilize the Party press at any time, which however is not at my disposal to refute the trumped-up charges. Since the editorial staff of *Szabad Nep* did not even bother to get the evidence from Csatar, I am forced to ask him to publicize the evidence upon which he based his malicious lies. My demand is all the more justified because it is Csatar and his companions, who are birds of a feather, who were and remain the vanguard of extreme "leftist" economic policy; they were the chief opponents of the June economic policy; it was they who sabotaged the issuance of industrial permits by every possible means. It was the subversive resistance of the Csatar type of subradicals that had to be broken so that we could validate NEP policy in the field of artisans and issue industrial permits to all those artisans who were entitled to them according to the government resolution, and to those who at that time, as a result of harmful anti-Marxist policy, were successfully deprived of the practice of their trade, so vital to the public, by the work of Csatar and his companions.

Chapter 17. The Problems of the Worker-Peasant Federation and People's Front

According to the March resolution of the Central Committee, "some individuals within our Party misinterpret the problems of the Worker-Peasant Federation. They forget that this is a class distinction that has, as its aim, the building up of the socialist society and the complete abolishment of exploitation. It is a federation that is led by the working class."

From the text, it is not clear who those "individuals" are. It is possible that I am also among them, for in essence the entire March resolution is directed against me. Since I do not wish to make it appear as if I am trying to evade the question, I must make my viewpoint known briefly. During the past twenty-five years, I have been so active in the theoretical and practical problems of the Worker-Peasant Federation, in various social systems and in various stages of its development, that, to obtain a clear picture of my viewpoint, there should be no great problem for those who actually wish to scrutinize my statements concerning the problems of the Worker-Peasant Federation.

I consider it unnecessary to reveal my activities in this respect, because in connection with the problems of the Worker-Peasant Federation, or problems of our relation to the middle peasants, no criticism or praise was directed toward me prior to the March resolution. But during the debate that developed at that time, my viewpoint was criticized on two counts. One statement was that my viewpoint—that the economic basis of the Worker-Peasant Federation during the period of transition to socialism is the city and town through the market exchange of goods between socialist industry and the small producing peasantry—was incorrect. With the theories taken from the classical teachings of Leninism and Marxism, in the previous chapter, I believe I have succeeded in proving that, considering the theoretical basis of the problem, my viewpoint is correct. The formula expounded was included in the Political Committee's resolution, and later in the resolution worked out on the basis of the Moscow discussion, without proper theoretical analysis.

The other count was that I allegedly had remained silent on the role of leadership of the working class in the Worker-Peasant Federation. I could prove the contrary by a mass of quotations, but I merely wish to quote from one of my most recent speeches, which will verify my standpoint:

> The Worker-Peasant Federation is the basis of our People's Democratic state. In our People's Republic, the social system depends on the cooperation of these two classes. The main strength of this state-creating federation, the possessor of power, is the working class, which has increased in number during socialist construction; has been heavily concentrated with the development of heavy industry; and has acquired class consciousness as a result of party and trade-union work.

This single quotation, from among many, clearly proves that I properly determined the role of leadership of the working class in the Worker-Peasant Federation.

Otherwise, I have dealt in detail with the problems and with the significance and tasks of the Worker-Peasant Federation in my report on "State Administration and the Tasks of Councils" at the Third Party Congress. This was unanimously adopted and made a resolution without any changes. No comments or objections to my report, on the portion relating to the Worker-Peasant Federation, have since been raised to contradict the views I expressed there.

During the June, 1953, meeting of the Central Committee

many serious accusations were made on the subject of the establishment of the Worker-Peasant Federation. It was said that the rapid pace of collectivization, the extremely difficult farming conditions of peasants, the large-scale redistribution caused by forced development, the mass encroachments and abuses, the wholesale violation of socialist legality against the peasants causing large-scale uncertainty in landholding as well as in farming, had brought about widespread land offerings and abandonments, which, as we know, covered approximately one million cadastral yokes.* The peasants lost their desire to produce, and by limiting their farming, or by total capitulation, they sought to earn a livelihood elsewhere. All this alienated them from us and caused the large mass of the working peasants —principally the central element of agricultural production, the middle peasantry, with which a lasting federation should have been established—to oppose us. The foundation of the Worker-Peasant Federation has been shaken and it is threatened with disorder. On the basis of the Central Committee's resolution of June, 1953, the Party and the government were forced to formulate urgently effective measures to eliminate these troubles and prevent further mistakes. The measures taken and the results are known. Party resolutions established that the peasantry's feeling of security had been restored; that its disposition to produce has increased; that it had begun the cultivation of so-called reserve lands; that it cultivated and paid more attention to the land; that it replaced and supplemented its equipment; and that it has increased its livestock and its investments in every branch of cultivation. There are facts, which have been widely documented statistically during the past two years. These results represented one of the most solid bases for raising the working people's standard of living. These were not empty promises but actual facts, based on fulfilling the promises made to the peasants in the government's program. To call these facts and results demagoguery and deception of the people is in itself nothing more than cheap demagoguery and deception of the people.

The results attained by the implementation of the June resolution are responsible for the fact that the Worker-Peasant

* The Hungarian yoke (*joch*) equals 1.07 acres.

Federation was again consolidated and further strengthened, and that it reached its new international stage and became as powerful and strong as it was only during the 1945 period of land redistribution. The period following June, 1953, the so-called New Course, must without question be considered as one of the most significant political successes. The results attained by the June policy in re-establishing the Worker-Peasant Federation established the role of leadership of the working class in practice. The leftist extremists hasten to divert attention from the success of the June policy with charges, in an attempt to discredit the results attained, or to turn them upside down. The simplest method to do this, for those who bear the gravest responsibility for shaking the Worker-Peasant Federation, is to brand all persons who adhered strongly to the Party's resolutions and extricated the stalled Worker-Peasant Federation from the tangled mess into which it had been led by the leadership prior to June, 1953, as rightists, Party enemies, and opportunistic deviationists.

According to the March Central Committee resolution, some individuals denied the role of Party leadership in the Patriotic People's Front, in which the strengthened rightist deviation appeared. "The establishment of the Patriotic People's Front (PPF) by our Party was followed by rightist endeavors to suppress the significance and leading role of the Party so that PPF would become the power to supervise the state and Council organs." For the sake of truth and historical accuracy, I must note that within the Party, I initiated the establishment of the PPF; and I prepared for the Political Committee the resolution that comprised an important part of my congressional referendum plan, and which after debate was unanimously adopted by the Political Committee. The debate centered around whether the new PPF should be patterned after the Bulgarian PPF or established on a different basis; whether it should be a mass organization or mass movement; and whether there should be individual membership or whether its membership should be made up only of mass organizations. Prior to the Third Party Congress, the Political Committee wrote the following in its letter addressed to the Presidium of the Soviet Communist Party:

In connection with the Party and government resolutions of last year, the Worker-Peasant Federation has become substantially stronger, as has the relationship of the intelligentsia and the middle classes with the People's Democracy, whence the need arose to activate the PPF in a manner that will broaden the mass base more than heretofore. We wish especially to obtain the more active political cooperation of the intelligentsia and peasantry through the reorganization of the PPF. The Political Committee considers the activation of such a people's front necessary—to begin this fall with a National People's Front Congress after proper preparation. The Congress would coincide with the election of local councils, which is scheduled for December, and serve as a political introduction to the elections. Debate was only held on the question of whether the PPF should have individual members in addition to member organizations, as in Bulgaria. In the end, it developed that individual membership was not desirable.

In the debate, several members of the Political Committee, including myself, were in favor of the Bulgarian type of PPF, in which the membership of the PPF includes individual members as well as mass organizations. The result of the debate, as established by the letter, was that our new PPF should be a mass movement generally without individual members; the Political Committee announced this in a unanimously approved resolution. In the meantime, I must note that even though we did not generally accept individual membership, we did provide that individuals of prestige and influence, whose cooperation in the PPF was desirable, could become members of the PPF if they so desired or on the basis of an invitation. This is the fact and the truth. On the other hand, it is contrary to the Party line that individuals, principally Rákosi, brand opinions expressed during a debate within the Party organ for the purpose of clarifying a question as rightist deviation, and to present the question in a distorted manner, as if I had taken a stand against an already established Party resolution.

At the Third Party Congress, the problem of the PPF was the subject of broad discussion. The report of the Central Committee, which was presented by Mátyás Rákosi, contained a brief text based on my proposal. However, on the basis of a theoretical foundation, I dealt with the problem more effectively in my report, the guiding principles of which I disclosed at a meeting of the Central Committee which preceded the Congress. The Central Committee approved the guiding principles. The Congress, which debated my report, unanimously approved and adopted it as a resolution in its entirety without any changes, including the part pertaining to the PPF.

In my report to the Congress, I expressed in detail my views on the PPF. Lenin very often and emphatically stressed that the enemy can be conquered only with the greatest effort and the wisest utilization of power. As he said, we must exploit every possibility, however small, so that we attain a federation that is supported by the masses. He pointed out clearly that one who doesn't understand this, doesn't understand even a minute portion of Marxism or the scientific socialism of our day. In my speech to the Congress, I said that Marxism must fulfill this precept through the People's Front policies of the Party and through the national unity embodied in the People's Front, in accordance with the teachings of Lenin. In our specific situation, under the conditions of the class struggle, the creation of a mass base wider and more extensive than the Worker-Peasant Federation is greatly aided by the fact that, by reason of the nature of our revolutionary development, the aspect of dictatorial violence became less evident, and the peaceful tasks of economic development and social and cultural activities became more evident. For the rest, I explained in detail that the new PPF must be a militant movement, not just a constructive one; that a front actually must be created to protect our attainments, our People's Democracy, our freedom, our independence, and our national sovereignty against internal and external reactionary imperialistic intrigue, to protect the peace, and to prevent war. The new PPF then would be the army struggling for these great aims, provided it takes deeper root in the masses of the Hungarian people. The intellectual content of the new PPF must be enriched. The idea of independence and freedom and our centuries-old traditions, which are a powerful force for moving the masses, must be fused with the concepts of democracy and socialism. In refutation of Szecsödi's lies—he brought the fabricated charge against me that, in the evaluation of our national past and our traditions, a serious rightist nationalistic deviation is perceivable—behold, here is the answer: our national traditions must be tempered with the concepts of democracy and socialism. In the social and political mass work of the PPF, the idea of patriotism and friendship of peoples (this isn't nationalism, but perhaps proletarian internationalism) must be promoted with greater emphasis. The heroic actions of the resistance movement and the traditions of the independent anti-Fascist front must be told more widely and courageously than heretofore, I asserted in my report before the Congress.

I stood for these Marxist-Leninist views as set forth in Party resolutions then, and I stand for them today. Policies that I developed were embodied in Party resolutions, yet some individuals are attempting to accuse me of distorting the resolutions of the Party, claiming that I personally distorted my opinions and views. At the Third Party Congress, they distorted the PPF policies and the resolution pertaining to the problems of the PPF, and furthermore they bypassed the PPF. However, this was not my doing, but the doing of those who have previously relegated several PPF's to a similar fate and who, from the beginning, opposed the new PPF and were only looking for an opportunity to eliminate the immature, though very promising, People's Front—in such a way, however, as to place the responsibility on rightist deviationists—in essence, on those who were in the vanguard of the PPF. With actually existing problems, or by exaggerating the alleged problems of the PPF, they hastened first to fabricate charges against me. One of these charges was that I wanted to place the PPF above the Party and state organs and to subordinate them to the policy and supervision of the PPF. My views on the role of the Party and state and their relationship to the PPF, as expressed before the Congress, refute this charge. It was stressed that the logical realization of our Party's new policy is a prerequisite for the successful emergence of PPF politics. This means that the PPF must be placed in the service of Party policy, not the reverse, and not that the Party be under the PPF, as they accused me of desiring it, although not by name, in the March resolution.

The charge was also often made that some individuals, rightist deviationists, attempted to discontinue DISZ * and make the PPF responsible for the organization of youth. It appears as if they are holding me responsible for all the views and activities of those individuals. Prior to the March resolution of the Central Committee, I was the first and only one of the members of the Political Committee and of the Central Committee who definitely and openly stood for keeping DISZ independent, and who opposed those who proposed to disband DISZ and allow it to be absorbed by the PPF. In my speech at the council election meeting, sponsored by DISZ headquarters and held in the Parliament Building on November 18, 1954, I stressed that "the task and responsibility of utilizing, through its own organization and work, that large opportunity and assistance which the PPF movement affords to youth, devolves upon DISZ. This is how DISZ gains strength; this is how the PPF obtains strong support among Hungarian youth. DISZ, therefore will not merge with the PPF as an impartial organization because it would lose its significance and importance and could not fulfill its mission of representing and solving the problems of youth."

I believe that the above facts prove that I stood in support of DISZ and spoke out against attacks on it. After the meeting, the leaders of DISZ acknowledged this with great satisfaction. In the March resolution, and afterward, all this was refuted. The spinelessness of several DISZ leaders, particularly of Szakali, was best indicated by the fact that after the March resolution, he not only kept silent on all that I had said in the interest of DISZ, but by his lies he himself endeavored to support and prove the trumped-up charges against me.

Undoubtedly there were faults in the PPF movement during its preparatory stage, as well as in the implementation of the resolution. We know, too, as could be anticipated, that the enemy also attempted to infiltrate the movement and utilize it for its own purpose. The Political Committee discussed this problem on several occasions and unanimously adopted resolutions to eliminate these hostile efforts and to correct preliminary faults. The trouble, the errors, the dangers began with excesses, with the exaggeration of rightist deviation, with which I did not agree because the situation and facts completely con-

* The Communist Hungarian Youth Organization.

tradicted this. I could not agree with Mátyás Rákosi, who classified the PPF, lock, stock, and barrel, as the revived activity of the enemy. At that time, I opposed this several times in the Political Committee. It is also certain that in some areas attempts were made in the PPF movement to make it independent of the Party, or, in other words, to raise the PPF above the Party and Council organs. In spite of these improper views and endeavors, the work continued successfully, and these efforts were restricted to only a few instances. Yet this was exaggerated to the point of calling it a national danger. I must point out that I also spoke up against these improper practices in the Political Committee and presented a satisfactory proposal, which was accepted by the Political Committee. It can be verified in the records of the Political Committee that, in the interest of ensuring the Party's leading role, I proposed that the vigorous progress apparent in the work and organization of the PPF had to be curbed, and at the same time the rural, mainly the village, Party organizations had to be strengthened, so that the expanding PPF movement could be kept under control and be assured of Party leadership and guidance. I pointed out several times, during the Political Committee meetings, that the chief task during the transition is not the further expansion of the PPF but the consolidation of the existing movement and of the results already attained, the development of cooperation with mass organizations on a sound basis, and, most important of all, the political and organizational assurance of Party leadership.

I discussed these same problems with the chairmanship of the National Council and emphasized that measures must be taken immediately against all persons and activities that attempt to utilize the PPF against the Party, and that the principal point—that the PPF stand on the theoretical basis of Party policy—must be adhered to in all operations of the PPF.

This and many other facts indicate that I struggled for the proper and complete realization of the Party's policies within the PPF movement. For this reason I cannot agree, and I consider it to be unjust and contrary to Party principles, that they are charging me with the entire responsibility for the mistakes and difficulties of the PPF, which generally are unavoidable in the preliminary stages of all mass organizations. Therefore I must make clear that, with respect to the problems of the PPF, neither my ideological views nor my actual activities were opportunist, anti-Marxist, or rightist deviationism, because I executed the Party's resolutions correctly and directly in the spirit of Marxism and Leninism.

The March resolution of the Central Committee states:

> It is the opinion of our Party Central Committee that we must
> continue our efforts to expand agricultural production. However,
> at the same time, the fulfillment of civic duties is required, for
> only in this way can the material bases of the people's economy
> —including the development of agriculture—be established.

I hold the resolution correct and am in agreement with it.
In the wake of the March resolution, press comments on this
question also began to appear, suppressing all that I had written
or said about these problems and all that I had done in practice
to work them out while Premier. With the aid of lies, they first
of all charged me with right-wing deviation.

In the interest of establishing the facts and to disprove the
slander against me, I will cite several sections of speeches I delivered during the past twelve to eighteen months. In my semi-
annual report on the business activities of the government,
given at the January 23, 1954, meeting of the National Assembly, I said the following:

> Legality is the firm foundation of our People's Republic and
> our government. Unlawful deeds undermine the power of our
> people. Therefore, they must be struck down with the full force
> of the law in every case. The local councils can count on the
> ultimate support of the workers in their efforts to ensure legality.

The task is twofold: the councils must realize that not only abuses in the application of laws but also failures to fulfill civic duties are illegal. Therefore, ensuring legality also means that the fulfillment of civic obligations must be enforced in every field, in the payment of taxes, in produce collection, and elsewhere. In the field of tax payment and produce collection, the government has assured large-scale advantages by reducing taxes and quota obligations. We linked the advantages to the prompt fulfillment of obligations, which we exact with increased severity. This application of the law is not only a right, but a state obligation of the local councils.

I dealt intensively and in detail with the related questions of state discipline, the fulfillment of civic duties, and legality, and I also pointed out the practical problems for state organs at the Third Party Congress in my report on "State Administration and the Duties of the Councils." In this connection I said, among other things:

The basis for the operation of our state and administrative organs is socialist legality, which is founded on state discipline and the fulfillment of civic duties as well as on the guarantee of civic rights. Legality and law are always the will of the ruling class, and the protection of the social order is its duty. Socialist legality, under the direction of the working class, is the broadest expression of the will of the masses, and a very powerful tool for the building of socialism and the protection of the People's Democratic system. Socialist legality must find its expression through the unconditional and strict adherence to and maintenance of the laws and other rules of the People's Democratic state by all state and social organs, officials, and citizens. There are even safeguards for this in our People's Democracy. One is the broad participation of the working masses in the work of the state, and in the sphere of the exercise of power and of administration alike.

The second safeguard is that here, and in the People's Democracies in general, laws and other rules are not forced on the people from outside, but express the will of the overwhelming majority and correspond to the interests of the workers; legislative power is even exercised directly by the people through the central and local organs. Every state employee, particularly the workers in the local councils, must keep this always in mind. This is the firm theoretical base which prevents all wavering in questions of legality, and no situation will arise in which the leaders of local councils, as is often said, do not know when they are transgressors and when they are opportunists. As if laxity or encroachments could only be committed in connection with law enforcement! They do not even think that it is possible to enforce the laws well and properly. Our local councils must keep this in mind above all else in their work, especially because this is an important condition of socialist legality. The exact enforcement of laws, however, demands strict state discipline. In this sphere, serious encroachments can be observed in the work of leaders and employees of local councils. Socialist legality cannot succeed if state discipline is lax. This is the root of the trouble. As long as the council leaders and employees do not personally fulfill their lawful obligations, they cannot expect others to observe the law.

Strict state discipline protects local council leaders and workers alike from error, laxity, and abuses. There is no other solution. Therefore, the most important task before us in the work of our local councils and other state organs is the strengthening of state discipline. This is the decisive link in the work of the entire state, and by adhering to it we can eliminate all weaknesses in the work of our councils and can increase the authority of our executive power.

The primary task of the local councils is to establish completely the validity of the laws in the sphere of both rights and duties in every area of state, social, and economic life. With regard to legality, experience shows that serious uncertainty prevails in the application and observance of laws in our local councils, chiefly with regard to the fulfillment of civic duties. They interpret legality in a one-sided fashion, exhibiting concern only with the protection of legal rights and not insisting on legal duties; they apply neither the provisions of the law nor punishment for negligence, as is clearly indicated by the lag apparent mainly in the field of tax payment and produce collection. Heads of local councils, responsible functionaries, and subordinates alike should realize that not only must encroachments in the application of the laws be considered as legal abuses, but negligence in the fulfillment of civic duties is also a legal abuse, against which one must act with no less severity than against encroachments. After the uncertainty, it is time to restore matters to full legality, for the sake of the consolidation of state authority. It should be understood that insistence on the observance of laws does not weaken or ruin the relationship between the councils and the working masses; rather, it strengthens the councils and improves that relationship, and increases the authority of the state. Weak, lax, and irresolute state organs have no authority in the eyes of the working masses, and this paves the way for the undermining of our council machinery. Not laxity, but the just and strict application of legality, places the majority of our working people and our working peasants in the villages at the side of our local councils. The people's sense of justice demands this of the council leaders and employees. The faith placed in the council and in its just and legal operation can be no more effectively shattered than by our council organs and workers retreating before illegality and ignoring neglect in the fulfillment of duties.

I very explicitly raised the question of legality at the Greater Budapest Party rally on July 11, 1953, where I said the following:

Being aware of this, it must be emphasized time and again that he who responds to the good will and far-reaching assistance of the government with a disregard of state and national interests, by violating the law, has no one to blame but himself. He will be confronted by the laws of our People's Republic, which we apply strictly to everyone who violates them. Nor can they count on being accorded the long-range rights and privileges in preparation for all. They do not deserve it. Whoever listens to the words of the enemy instead of the Party or government, whoever takes the path of illegality instead of the path of law, should not count on the help of the Party and the government. This applies to all our measures and to everyone. This includes those who, instead of waiting for October—the end of the financial year—want to leave the producer cooperatives in the middle of the summer when there is so much work, or who want to see them partitioned now instead of abiding by these laws in the manner and [for the] period ordered by the government. It also includes those who think the expansion of their rights and freedoms and of help and privileges means that they now have absolutely no obligations toward the state—neither the payment of taxes nor delivery obligations—instead of complying with these obligations. It applies no less to those kulaks who respond to government orders to put an end to illegality and violence with anti-Party anti-government, and anti-People's attitudes, with violations of the law, and with violence against the working people. They should be shown no mercy, and they will find that we apply the full severity of the law to them.

My standpoint on questions of state control, the fulfillment of civic obligations, and in general on legality, is precise and clear, and my practical activity was conducted in this spirit. I consider my standpoint and activity in these matters to be proper, and I do not accept the charge of opportunism.

The laxities revealed in the matters that have been touched upon are a consequence of past mistakes, but the fact that our Party and state organs fell into the other extreme as a result of the change also figures in these laxities. Therefore the leadership of the Party and of the state alike, in which I participate with them, are responsible. But to make the mistakes appear to be a result of my right-wing deviation is partly an evasion of responsibility and partly fraud.

The March resolution of the Central Committee says the following on the question of produce collection:

Certain people in our Party also have taken an erroneous stand in the question of collection. It is because of this right-wing viewpoint and the intrigues of the kulaks that the collection plan, which was duly reduced by the Party and government, was not fulfilled in 1954. The importance of the delivery obligation was not emphasized and the relaxation in collection discipline was accepted with passivity.

Since this charge is also directed primarily against the "right-wing viewpoint" and since, according to the March resolution, I was the primary representative of this, let us see what my opinion was in the problem of collection and what I did to put it into effect. As Minister of the Food Industry and Collection, and then Deputy Premier, when I was the responsible director for collection for approximately three years, I indicated on countless occasions, orally and in writing, the role and importance of collection in the building of socialism. In my actual work, the results of collection proved that I executed the resolutions of the Party and government successfully, even when I did not agree in many respects with the resolutions, as I pointed out at the time to the Party and state organs concerned. Thus in the past my expressed opinions on collection show that I represented a correct viewpoint in both principle and practice.

In my speech, "Several Economic Problems in the Transition from Capitalism to Socialism in the Countries of the People's Democracies," at the Hungarian Academy of Science, I said the following in my theoretical discussion of the significance of produce collection in the people's economy:

> During the current period of transition in Hungary, as well as in the other People's Democracies, the proportional role of independent farms is most significant in the production of consumer goods. Compared to it, the socialist sector is lagging. One of the characteristics of the period of transition in the field of production and trade of consumer goods and raw materials derives from this fact. One part of the consumer goods and raw materials needed by the city is produced by the state and cooperative sector, but an overwhelmingly greater part of it is produced by the independent small holder sector.
>
> Consequently, the supply of consumer goods and raw materials for the cities rests decisively with the independent small holder and not with the socialist sector of agriculture. However, the unplanned nature of production by the independent farmers, as well as their sale of surplus goods, makes uncertain the regular and planned supply of the city with consumer goods and raw materials. The importance of obligatory state collection during the current period of transition in Hungary and in the People's Democracies is therefore significant, because it is designed to smooth the conflict existing between socialist industry and independent small-scale agriculture in supplying the city with consumer goods and raw materials.
>
> State collection must procure that quantity of products with which the state can overcome the uncertainty stemming from the unplanned nature of independent peasant production in supplying the city with food and raw materials, and it can assure a regular supply. In this way, our view is that state collection has a very important role in the consolidation of economic cooperation between city and town and its further development, in the regular supply of goods for the inhabitants, and in an increasing implementation of the socialist principle of "from each according to

his ability and to each according to his work" in the distribution of goods.

This is also greatly helped by the fact that the city is no longer the center for exploiting the village, but is now an inexhaustible source of assistance, development, and socialist reorganization in the village, which is an important factor in strengthening the worker-peasant alliance and ensuring the leadership role of the working class.

I believe that my opinions on collection can in no way be classed as anti-Marxist right-wing deviation. In the question of collection, who among the members of the Political Committee and the Central Committee did represent the proper Marxist viewpoint, and when and where did they express it? To my knowledge—nowhere. But when responsibility is under discussion, they try to shift the blame entirely to me, even forgetting that there is a Minister for Produce Collection, on whom responsibility probably falls first if there are problems in this field. But the records of the Political Committee meetings should be examined, which show that in questions of mistakes, laxities, or violations in the field of collection, I participated in the debates on every occasion and made proposals much more actively than did many other members of the Political Committee, who now, forgetting all else, are helping to contrive the charge of right-wing deviation against me. At the conference held on January 25 for the Megye executive committee chairmen, it was I who, several days before I became ill, mobilized the council for the most important and most urgent problems of collection, indicating the tasks to be done. The day-long conference was attended by Andras Hegedus, who then had charge of produce collection, and Antal Apro, who supervised the council executive committees, and the problems of this area pertained to them. At the conference, which took up problems of livestock collection, chiefly the lagging hog collection, neither Hegedus nor Apro was willing to speak. I requested permission to speak, and in a speech of approximately half an hour I indicated the tasks of the council and collecting organs. If necessary, I can make the text of my speech available.

After this, one can justly ask what was done in the interests of produce collection by those who now accuse me, saying,

"The importance of collection was not emphasized and the slackening of collection discipline was viewed idly." If examined, it will become apparent that among the leaders many did nothing, and some few did far less than I for the enforcement of collection.

We also must discuss another aspect of the problem of legality. Much was said about this, and important conclusions were reached in the resolution and in the June, 1953, meeting of the Central Committee. The judicial and state security systems were not under the democratic control of the masses, which unavoidably caused these institutions to become bureaucratic organs, as the June, 1953, resolution states. These organs ensured neither legality nor law and order. The essence and strength of the constitutional theory and government of the People's Democracy depends on the preservation of a viable relationship with the people and on their control of that theory and government. However, we have deviated from these Leninist principles, and herein are the roots of the gravest evil of our state life, the damage to legality and to law and order, which ultimately stem from the separation from the masses.

In this respect, we are coming dangerously close to the situation of the spring of 1953, when extraordinary measures were required. Because of the mistakes of the Party and government leaders, we are again in a position in which our state apparatus, local councils, organs of justice, police, and national defense commit a series of illegalities with regard to the people, especially to the village inhabitants. They pass serious mass judgments that have no foundation in law. The number of people against whom legal proceedings have been started or carried out runs into the tens and tens of thousands, not to mention the abuses and other illegalities committed in the field of produce collection, tax collection, the regrouping of farm plots, and the organization of producer cooperatives. The dissatisfaction of the people is increased by the fact that even otherwise proper, necessary, and legal measures are executed in a cold, unfeeling, unpopular way. Besides impairing legality and law and order, all this has already greatly disrupted the very foundation of our statehood, the Worker-Peasant Federation. All the more frequent signs point to the degeneration of the dictatorship of the proletariat. During the past six months, the hazard of right-wing deviation has taken on dangerous proportions—not in the form of views that are a right-wing deviation from Marxism, but in the form of the shift to the right by the broadest masses of people, the ever more pronounced turn against the Party and government, and the spread and increase of a reactionary, counter-revolutionary atmosphere. In this regard, the situation today is more serious than in the period prior to June, 1953. The cause of this is extreme "leftism," expressed partly in the March resolutions but mainly in our actions, which is driving the masses into the arms of the enemy. The Communists have an immeasurable responsibility to recognize and prevent the impending danger and to indicate the way out of the danger, which can only be done by fully enforcing the principles laid down in the June resolution and the resolutions of the Congress.

Chapter 19.   Culture, Literature, and Art

The April resolution of the Central Committee asserts, *inter alia*, that "the anti-Marxist, anti-Party views . . . of Comrade Imre Nagy constitute a coherent system and encompass also the most diverse areas of cultural life."

The sense of this statement is that the Central Committee resolution holds me responsible for the right-wing manifestations appearing in cultural life also.

I hardly was able to engage—I am sorry to say—in cultural, literary, and artistic problems, except, for the most part, in discussions of proposals or reports concerning such matters that came up at the Political Committee, or in connection with concrete recommendations submitted to the Council of Ministers for decision. I was not involved in theoretical, literary, artistic, or cultural policy questions. Not one word appeared in the Central Committee resolution of March, 1955, about my responsibility for right-wing mistakes in this field. It would appear, however, that this did not keep them from condemning me for right-wing mistakes in this field too in the April resolution.

I concerned myself with literary questions in my petition addressed to the March session of the Central Committee, in which I wrote the following:

> I cannot remain silent on what is happening among the writers and in literature. Undoubtedly serious errors have been com-

223

mitted by certain writers in the literary field. They have written bad, improper verse and other works; they have used exaggerated criticism; mainly, they have looked for failure in everything, and so on. For this they must be censured, and we must help them find the correct road. This is in order. But I am unable to agree that certain comrades, and here I am thinking particularly of Mihály Farkas, should interfere crudely in literary questions, sometimes without knowing anything about them, thereby compromising not only themselves but also the Party. Not infrequently they have set the writers, or a considerable number of them, against the Party, injuring their self-respect, impugning their reputation as writers and as individuals, and questioning their Communist character in consequence of some mistake.

This, honored comrades, cannot be the policy of our Party with regard to literature; these cannot be the methods of our Party in dealing with the writers, who, despite small or even serious mistakes, having corrected these mistakes, serve the People's Democracy with honor, and, aside from mistaken writings, add to the progressive literary work of socialist realism with splendid compositions.

I judge this view of mine correct and support it now. In neither the March nor the April resolution is there any concrete reference as to when and in what way I committed mistakes that could justify the very serious statements in reference to the cultural field made in the April resolution. For just this reason, I must consider what I said about the tasks confronting the government in the cultural field as correct, until the alleged mistakes are clearly disclosed. In the government program on July 4, 1953, I said, *inter alia,* the following:

It is necessary that distinguished members of the intelligentsia of our People's Democracy be active in the field of their endeavor and that they occupy positions worthy of their talents—be they teachers, engineers, lawyers, doctors, agronomists, or something else. Everyone must take cognizance of the fact that talent and knowledge bring greater esteem in a People's Democracy than ever was the case in the old world of class distinction. This esteem must manifest itself in a broad work potential and material appreciation.

Later, I said the following in connection with education:

We have practically enforced college education with huge sacrifices. Efforts in this field must now be considerably more modest. At the same time, much greater attention than heretofore must be devoted to the people's schools; investment must be increased, and the number of schools, classrooms, and teachers must be augmented. . . . More attention, care, and financial resources must be devoted to the schools on the farm, in the village, and in the working quarters. This will be a considerably more democratic school policy.

More tolerance must be evidenced in religious problems too. The use of administrative tools in this field is inadmissable . . . in this question, the government must use tolerance, the tools of which are enlightenment and persuasion.

At the January 23, 1954, parliamentary session on our educational system, I said the following:

The maximum effort and material sacrifice must be made in our educational system for the improvement of the general schools. . . . The government must take up the material problems of the teachers, particularly those in the villages and on the farms. The general schools, however, must be provided with new instructional material as well as with building improvements. . . . It is here that, in the spirit of socialist patriotism, we must lay the foundations of the Hungarianism and higher culture level of the growing new generation. We must try and we must succeed in basing the cultural development of our youth on general school education.

In the same speech, I said the following about the problems of our cultural policy:

The major task is comprehensive, systematic work in every area of cultural life, and to eliminate cultural deficiencies by means of the tools of science, literature, [and] art, not the least of which is our film art. The democratization of culture and its far-reaching educational role must be ensured. . . . A major task is the fostering of Hungarian classical literature. . . . More fairy story books and novels for youngsters must be made available to our children and young people. The popular and national character of the theater must be more emphasized. Special attention must be devoted to the fate of Hungarian drama. In the sphere of the graphic arts, we must take great steps to convert such art into a tool for beautifying our life and for educating the masses.

Is this an incorrect, mistaken, right-wing, anti-Party view?

In order that my opinion about the symptoms appearing in cultural life and about deviations one way or the other be clear, I want to assert the following: After the new government program, great discussions began in cultural circles about the application of the June resolution of the Party. These discussions were generally productive and brought results; they approved the program calling for cultural democratization, a comprehensive study of our people's cultural requirements, and increased concern with the satisfaction of the cultural needs of the working people. The promotion of local initiative and the increase of independent activity in mass cultural work helped to deepen our cultural revolution.

A correct effort arose from the policy of our Party, an effort to strengthen and mobilize patriotic forces in artistic life. We must help the writers and artists in their work—the writers and artists who belong to us or who are drawing near to us. We must draw them closer in debates on principles; we must reach courageously for our progressive traditions and the rich inheritance of world culture. The ambition of our writers and artists to surpass the results so far achieved, their search for new forms of expression, is a proper ambition, which will help in the solution of the tasks confronting us.

The results achieved as a result of the June policy in the areas of a freer atmosphere for cultural work, of a marked decrease in the excessive degree of centralization, and of the elimination of bureaucratic methods had a favorable influence on cultural life. The activities of our artists and writers increased, and new achievements were born.

A greater creative liberty and the strengthening of independent activity in cultural work, and our efforts directed at an increase in national unity, would have helped to achieve additional results. Greater liberty and the increase in democracy demand greater political and ideological aggressiveness, increased efforts to correct errors, and a struggle against bureaucracy and schematism. However, care must be taken lest the struggle against bureaucracy and schematism and the freedom of criticism change into a denial of our cultural and political achievements.

The debate concerning the problem of old people and young people that has developed in the wake of the article of Peter Veres in *Irodalmi Ujsag* is a real contribution to a clarification of the future paths and tasks of our literary policy. The contributions of Tamas Aczel, Tibor Deri, Sandor Erdei, and Gyula Hay are real steps forward in the clarification of important questions of principle in Hungarian literature. I agree with their views and with their standpoint on principles. They are most competent to point out the paths and tasks of literary policy. Among other things, Comrade Gyula Hay wrote as follows concerning these problems in his article entitled "Freedom and Responsibility" (*Irodalmi Ujsag*, September 10, 1955):

> Perhaps the most characteristic aspect of the immediate situation in our literature is the positive, unified effort and approach of the great majority of Hungarian writers. No question but that this is a most heartening and healthy symptom, and it satisfies one of the most pleasing requirements of literary policy: the national unity of literature. The immediate aim of this unity is also especially heartening: the effort for the freedom of literature. A socialist society guarantees possibilities for the freedom of literature of which earlier societies could hardly dream. However, the possibility does not mean automatic realization. It is the duty of the writer to create a free literature and, in so far as it already exists, to defend it. . . . The existence or nonexistence of socialist literature depends on this: that the ideal of the freedom of literature be realized—or more precisely, that the outmoded bureaucratic, administrative obstacles that inhibit free literary creation and that are against the spirit of Party and People's Democracy be abolished. This is the most important goal: the development and progress of literature toward the creation of a deeper, more complete truth, toward the serving of the future— and this development can be reached only by eliminating all obstacles. . . .

Thus, there is emerging from our united struggle for the freedom of literature—the most important task from the standpoint of the future—the liberation of literary trends based on Marxist-Leninist ideology from various obstacles, which developed from the dialectic of things, not from hostile desires, but which nevertheless stubbornly persist.

Comrades Aczel, Deri, and Erdei wrote in the same spirit. They all gave expression to their aspirations for unity and liberty, which are the surest pledges for the future development of Hungarian literature.

We must turn to the question of partisanship also, a question that is being sharply revised these days in connection with the work of our writers and that is usually raised incorrectly and in a deceptive manner. Laszlo Szecsödi dealt with this question most recently in the October 2, 1955, issue of *Szabad Nep*, in his article entitled "Against Bourgeois Objectivism—for Proletarian Partisanship." Szecsödi defines proletarian partisanship in the passage that follows, and I consider his definition basically correct:

Thus, responsible representation of the class interests of the proletariat requires the frank and undistorted revelation of the truth. This is the most important demand of proletarian partisanship: a more correct recognition of the truth, and proper activity supporting that recognition in the interest of the proletariat and the entire working people.

I also agree with Szecsödi's statement made earlier in connection with the demands of partisanship:

The true Party Communist standpoint here is also the basic recognition and study of existing achievements—and their use in suitable areas of the social life of our People's Democracy. Those who see big words and phrases in partisanship seriously err and come into conflict with the most fundamental demands of partisanship.

All this is correct and true, and if Szecsödi had stood on these principles and fought for a Party socialist-realist literature he would have rendered a great service, together with our [other] writers, to the attainment of the great goals now crystallizing out of the literary arguments—national unity, freedom, and partisanship of literature. However, Szecsödi turns against the principles that he had himself set forth and gives a false interpretation of them, an interpretation that markedly deviates from the true essence of partisanship and from the Marxist-Leninist definition of it. It develops from his line of argument that partisanship is the approval, the affirmation without reservation, of the policy of the Party. Indeed, Szecsödi goes even farther, and though he doesn't actually say it, it can be inferred from his reasoning that partisanship is the affirmation of the March, 1955, resolution of the Central Committee and its realization in literature. But a stand taken on the policy announced in June, 1953, or on its approval, is opposed to partisanship. Szecsödi does not say why a stand in literature for the March resolution is correct partisanship, or why approval or defense of the June policy is antipartisanship. Therefore, because the essence of partisanship is not defined by the correct views of principle that Szecsödi expressed above, it is neither true nor a frank exposure of reality; rather, the leaders of the Party establish, for the moment, what conforms or does not conform to the Party line in literature and in art. This precludes the determination of reality, the search for truth, the exchange of ideas—and most of all it precludes criticism.

In the period preceding June, 1953, the Hungarian writers looked upon the events around them on the basis of this false, warped interpretation of partisanship, and it turned out that they were seriously in error. They distorted reality and truth with this warped partisanship; literature, art, and music became a distorting mirror in which the people did not recognize in their true proportions the great problems of their lives that needed answers. The workers of Hungarian literature were shocked into dismay by this after June, 1953, and they want to use this great experience—it is not excessive to say this historic experience—extensively as a basis for the consciousness and emotional atmosphere of the present generation, for the molding of a new, socialist type of man. How far Szecsödi deviates from a correct definition of the demands of partisanship is clearly shown by the following part of his article:

For example, it is remarkable that, prior to the March, 1955, resolution of the Central Committee of our Party, the rightest deviationists stated that errors, negation, and mistakes were the chief characteristics of the ten years of development of our People's Democracy. This pessimistic view of the development of our People's Democracy, this magnifying of errors and suppression of achievements, was one of the most typical manifestations of rightist deviation. The Parliament speech of Comrade Imre Nagy at the time of the June, 1953, resolution of the Central Committee distorted this resolution in the direction indicated, and this view—primarily on the basis of the speech—became widespread, especially in our literary and artistic life; soon the press echoed it also.

According to these statements it was the distortion of the June resolution—which I perpetrated in my Parliament speech —that caused the Party stand for the June policy to be opposed to partisanship. Szecsödi is launching his charge of distortion —and not for the first time—without being acquainted with the June resolution. Nor are the Hungarian writers acquainted with it. It is absolutely necessary for the sake of Hungarian Communists, and not just Communist writers, that the June resolution be made public property, so that the question of partisanship can be clarified and properly interpreted; so that Hungarian writers can take a Party stand; and so that new errors can be avoided.

The June resolution is the cornerstone of a socialist-realist Hungarian literature and art true to the Party. Without knowledge of it, our writers and artists are groping in the dark. Knowing it, they would be strengthened in their conviction that faithfulness to the principles of the resolution is an important factor in the partisanship of a socialist-realist literature and art and in the future development of a socialist-realist literature and art. Szecsödi's analysis does violence to the views he professes concerning criticism of the Party. He notes this himself when he writes, "Let us not err, criticism of mistakes is necessary." These are the words. However, in practice not only is criticism regarded as unnecessary, it is not even allowed. It is superfluous to cite examples of this. If we remain in the area of literature, it will suffice to refer to the orders executed

against some writers and all editorial staffs, and to the confisca-
tion of the September 17, 1955, issue of *Irodalmi Ujsag*. And
finally, as to the high-sounding phrases and lies to which
Szecsödi very correctly objected, they are a dangerous symptom
in Party and public life, in the press, and in propaganda. This
really is not compatible with partisanship; it is against just this
that one must resolutely fight in the name of partisanship,
which is today the outstanding reality in our literature and in
the behavior of our writers, the surrender of which would
mean great damage to literature, music, and art, and to the
entire moral foundation of Hungarian public life. Therefore
the steadfastness of the representatives of Hungarian literature
and art means also the defense of the moral foundation of our
social life.

I know only from hearsay—as it was not put at my disposal I
am not able to quote from it—the report of Mátyás Rákosi that
was given at the April 14 meeting of the Central Committee,
in which he mentioned that I summoned Jozsef Darvas and
took responsibility for his article, "Concerning Overbidding."
For the sake of the facts, it must be stated that if Jozsef Darvas
so informed Rákosi, he did not speak the truth. I did not sum-
mon Darvas; rather, he asked for a conference with me with
reference to important questions concerning his ministry. And
this happened at least several weeks after the appearance of his
article, at a time when, despite the statement of Rákosi, there
could have been no question of my wanting to speak to Darvas
about writing his article. On the other hand, it is true that I
said to Darvas, straight off and without beating about the bush,
that I did not agree with his article, which I consider incorrect;
it overstates the questions and thereby has caused confusion in
the ranks of the Party as well as in wide circles outside of the
Party. I disapproved it also because if the article really needed
to be written, why should Jozsef Darvas write it, particularly
since it could be felt from the article that he did not write it
on his own initiative or of his own free will? I told him this.
However, Darvas then protested most emphatically that he had
never discussed the article with anyone. It was only after the
April resolution that it became apparent from the report given
at the meeting that Jozsef Darvas had told me a lie when he

denied having discussed the article with anyone in the Party. On the contrary, Mátyás Rákosi stated that my conduct as regards the article was all the more serious because the article in question had been discussed with various comrades in the Party. However, I hardly can be held responsible for the consequences of Jozsef Darvas' false information.

Chapter 20.   Nationalism and
Proletarian Internationalism

With reference to the problem of Nationalism and Proletarian Internationalism, the following can be read in the March resolution of the Central Committee:

> One of the most dangerous manifestations of rightist deviation is nationalism and chauvinism. The Central Committee considers a ruthless ideological battle against every manifestation of nationalism and chauvinism to be an absolute necessity.

I agree completely with the statements of the resolution, indeed it repeats a well-known theorem of Marxism-Leninism when it states that one of the most dangerous manifestations of rightist deviation is nationalism and chauvinism, and further when it demands a ruthless ideological battle against such manifestations. However, the resolution does not specify how this has manifested itself among us or who is identified with this most dangerous manifestation of rightist deviation. However, what the resolution did not establish was provided by Laszlo Szecsödi in his article entitled "We Must Ruthlessly Expose Every Manifestation of Nationalism and Chauvinism" in *Szabad Nep*. In this article, which is replete with fabrications and anti-Marxist, unscientific views, Laszlo Szecsödi goes beyond the March resolution and names me as the chief representative of nationalist-chauvinist manifestations. If this were so, if this lie were true, then the March resolution of the Central Committee would have stated it. Instead, Szecsödi took the burden of the statement upon himself. I do not know whether the Central Committee authorized Szecsödi to do this work for it, so that he, rather than the Central Committee, should raise the charge against me on the question of nationalism and chauvinism. Still, it must be established as a fact that newspaper and magazine articles went much further than the resolution of the Central Committee in every question taken up in resolution of the Central Committee. Thus, it should be clarified whether the questions taken up in the resolution of the Central Committee represent the charge against me, or whether those writings that went beyond the resolution, drawing far-reaching conclusions and bringing up numerous new problems, leveled the whole array of charges against me.

In the article in question, Laszlo Szecsödi first declared that as a consequence of the activities of rightist deviationists, hidden and open manifestations of nationalism had revived in our homeland. Then he went into the officious, recondite aspect of Marxist and nationalist interpretations of national unity; and naturally he was a Marxist, and I was a nationalist. According to him, I am the proponent of national unity at any price. He writes as follows:

> For example, on October 24, 1954, in his speech at the congress of the Patriotic People's Front, Comrade Imre Nagy spoke without any reservation about the unity of the entire nation and the united hearts and minds of 9.5 million Hungarians, in favor of the goals of the People's Democracy.

Here follows a long, theoretical discourse on what actually is hidden behind this. He attempts to prove with simple-minded fabrications that my view of national unity is built on a class peace. Szecsödi writes: "Every attempt made for class peace must be exposed as a damaging, reactionary, nationalist theory." He derives his "class peace" national unity from the 9.5 million Hungarians because this makes up the entire population of the country, including several tens of thousands or hundreds of thousands of kulaks, reactionaries, or holdovers from the old regime. This is Szecsödi's "Marxism," and "class war" or "class peace," and national unity based upon population figures. Even here his logic is faulty, because the country has a population of some 9.8 million, which is some 300,000 people more than the 9.5 million Hungarians I mentioned. Thus, there is no question of class peace on a basis of Szecsödi's theory of Marxist class war because there still remain 300,000 class enemies, reactionaries, kulaks, etc. for the "class war," according to Szecsödi.

But Lenin destroys with much more serious arguments Szecsödi's heedless talk concerning the interdependence of national unity and class war. Lenin has shown that in the course of the construction of socialism, the social nature of the working class, the peasantry, and the intellectuals changes; those elements that previously separated them die out. Thus these social groups draw together in economic, political, and intellectual relationships. This has already shown itself in the formation of a popular unity wider than the worker-peasant federation, i.e., the dictatorship of the proletariat cannot be restricted to the Worker-Peasant Federation. According to Lenin:

> The characteristic form of the dictatorship of the proletariat is a class federation of the proletariat, of the vanguard of workers, and of the large number of workers of the nonproletarian strata (petty bourgeoisie, smallholders, peasants, intelligentsia, etc.) or the majority of them; it is an anticapital federation, a federation for the complete destruction of capital, for the complete repression of bourgeois resistance and attempts at restoration, for the final creation and solidification of socialism.

Marxism places special emphasis on the fact that the working class, after the consolidation of power and as the opportunity arises, will win over to its side the powerful petty bourgeois strata of the population, including the majority of the peasantry.

Lenin emphasized on innumerable occasions and with special force that the enemy could be defeated only with the greatest exertions of strength and with the most basic, careful, circumspect, and competent use of strength. As Lenin said:

> We must use every possibility, however minute, to bring about a federation that the masses will support, even if this federation

is temporary, unstable, unsure, untrustworthy, and conditional. He who does not understand this does not understand one iota of Marxism or of our scientific socialism in general.

This was Lenin's opinion, and this was the spirit in which I wrote and spoke concerning the necessity of national solidarity, concerning national unity, and concerning the Patriotic People's Front. Szecsödi could have found all this, if he had wanted to find it, in my report to the Third Party Congress. Indeed, he would have found much more there, but then he would not have been able to tell such a pack of lies. My views on the question of national unity are correct, they agree with the teachings of Marxism-Leninism, and they are free of the reactionary, nationalist "theories" concocted by Szecsödi. Besides, my entire report to the Third Party Congress, including the theoretical parts, in so far as it dealt with questions of the dictatorship of the proletariat, the worker-peasant alliance, national unity, and the People's Front, was adopted unanimously and without change and was actually made into a Party resolution. Thus the charges of Szecsödi really are an attack on the Party resolution of the Third Congress.

What Szecsödi has said, in the name of Marxism, concerning the characteristic development of a People's Democracy and the progressive traditions of our nationalist past was a mockery of Marxism-Leninism. His word for the "characteristic" development of the People's Democracy is "nationalism."

"The most frequently exposed manifestation of rightist, nationalist views has been a distortion of an interpretation of our nationalist past," writes Szecsödi, and goes right into accusing the "rightist" deviationists, which naturally means me first of all, because "they neglected to expose the contradictions of our nationalist past and wanted to obscure the inconsistencies in our history and in the development of our culture."

I do not want to defend rightist deviationism, or those who fell into these errors and oppose Marxism-Leninism wittingly or unwittingly, or those who actually stray into nationalism. It would be madness to deny that there are such people and that ideological battles must be waged against them. But to raise the charge that the rightist deviationists neglected to expose the contradictions of our nationalist past means, according to Szecsödi, that the rightist deviationists should have accomplished in one and a half or two years what the Marxists did not accompish for decades. In other words, it means that all responsibility for the oversights of the past must be borne by the rightest deviationists. To take up the question in this manner is nothing more than to distort and warp the actual situation. It was and is necessary to consider the negligence of Marxist workers in problems of our national culture. This is a serious negligence, but it is not rightist deviationism. Such negligence, unfortunately, is characteristic of all our ideological work and applies to every area of such work, and if the stigma of rightist deviationism must be fixed, it applies to those who did not attend to such work in the past decade.

If Szecsödi were going to concern himself with the interdependence of national traditions and nationalism, he should have indicated that prior to June, 1953—the date he gives for the beginning of rightist deviation—cosmopolitanism, i.e., a form of nihilism opposed to all respect for the values of our national culture and traditions, and extreme left-wing views that deprecated and opposed those values (and were therefore anti-Marxist) were dominant. The chief task after June, 1953, was to liquidate these harmful, incorrect views, which would have given birth, day after day, to those nationalist, chauvinist views against which we now must struggle as a direct consequence of the mistakes of the past. Szecsödi is actually, even today, at least in the article cited, the spokesman for these "leftist," anti-Marxist views. He puts forward these "leftist" views as Marxism and considers all other explanations of the questions at hand as rightist deviation.

This is how the situation is shaping up: Those who most frequently and most loudly repeat the charge of nationalism are those whose anti-Marxist, cosmopolite views and policies make it necessary to fight today, while there is a danger of nationalism and while rightist views are appearing in the ranks of the Party. On the other hand, of course, we must fight with the scientific weapons of Marxism, with great tact and competence, lest we injure national self-esteem and feeling of pride; this has happened recently and frequently in serious ways in connection with judgments expressed concerning our national past and our cultural traditions. It is stupid ill will—the like of which is driving the mills of nationalism—to quote against me a line by Petöfi—"If the earth were God's hat, then our homeland is the bouquet upon it"—as if this were a manifestation of nationalism. I believe that our Party accepts the "nationalism" of Petöfi, together with the quoted line.

We have met with forms of nationalism that are much more serious than those cited and much more harmful in their consequences, about which the March resolution remains silent—and those responsible for them remain silent also. I will not deal with them exhaustively, but I will touch briefly on those questions which must be pointed up not only in their economic relationship but also from the point of view of Marxist ideology. What are these questions?

A. The economic policy aiming at economic national self-sufficiency was followed by the leaders of the Party and the economy prior to June, 1953, and is now being revived. At that time, that policy had already damaged our relationships with the Soviet Union and the People's Democratic countries, and it will do so in the future.

B. The development of relationships, along Party and state lines, with Czechoslovakia and Rumania. Before June, 1953, there were extraordinary tensions in economic relationships, and there are documents to bear witness to the fact that these were the result of serious errors of Hungarian Party and economic leaders, and that even today we cannot completely eliminate the consequences of these errors.

C. The extraordinary aggravation of our relationships with Yugoslavia over a period of seven years, which manifested itself in the most rudimentary forms of nationalism and chauvinism and served as its greatest source, and which was intensified to extremes by those who today repeat the charge of nationalism against me.

These are only the most blatant examples from the past. In the course of carrying out the June policies the task of liquidating via state means the open and hidden manifestations of nationalism fell largely upon me. The change in our economic policy in the spirit of the June resolution meant a turning point also in the area of re-establishing our friendly relationships with neighboring People's Democracies. By liquidating the mistakes of the past with the German Democratic Republic and the Czechoslovak Republic, our relationships improved substantially in the economic, political, and cultural areas alike. I personally took the first steps to re-establish the friendly relations that we had formerly had with the Rumanian People's Republic, which were of mutual advantage. This was made especially difficult by the sharp dispute over the Paris Peace Conference and by the subsequent estrangement between the two countries, which resulted in a new resurgence of nationalism. In personal conversations with Comrade Gheorgiu Dej and later in my letter, I made suggestions for the liquidation of this unfortunate situation. There were also substantial initial steps in the area of repairing our relations with Yugoslavia, liquidating the serious errors of the past and renewing our previous friendly relations. I had a part in these, and this was recognized in responsible Yugoslav circles.

I have already written about the hatred of the little peoples of the People's Democratic countries of the Danube Valley for one another, and about the need for a fraternal unification. This was on March 30, 1947, in the periodical *Kozgazdasag*. Let us look at a few quotations:

By and large, the same economic and political factors rule in the Danube Valley countries, and if there are differences among them in the levels of development attained, still the economic and political development everywhere is along popular democratic lines. We are a more industrialized country than Yugoslavia or Rumania, but Czechoslovakia surpasses us in this regard. In the area of agricultural production there are no great differences. . . . Harmonized cooperation and economic collaboration will increase the capacity, importance, and influence of the small economic units. The close cooperation of the Danube Valley countries in the area of agricultural production and marketing, and in other areas of the peoples' economy, must replace the competing or at best the divergent economic efforts that they have been waging with only the support of their own resources. . . . Only in this way can the small People's Democracies stand up economically, and only in this way can they protect their independence—they must mutually support one anothers' democratic economic structure. The triumph of the People's Democracies, the leading role of the working class in directing the economic and political life of the countries along the Danube, is making possible the first step in the realization of this concept. We can advance in these areas only through close cooperation with our neighbors and through the coordination of our economic plans.

One must also see a certain hidden manifestation of nationalism in that increasing estrangement that is perceivable today in numerous measures taken by Party and government, even at a time when there is greatest evidence of proletarian internationalism. A peculiar People's Democratic provincialism, an intensified estrangement in those efforts that are raising a veritable Chinese Wall, not only between our homeland and the Western capitalist countries but between the Hungarian People's Democracy and other countries in the democratic and socialist camp, is now developing. We have come to the point where Party members, even members of the Central Committee, cannot obtain the newspapers of sister Parties; the statements by Party and state leaders of other People's Democratic countries; the speeches or articles of Comrade Bierut or Siroky; or the resolutions of sister Parties. The same applies to numerous manifestations in culture, art, and literature, to the debates in People's Democratic countries, to the exchanges of ideas, etc. Indeed, we have come to such a point that members of the Central Committee cannot even obtain certain publications of the Communist Party of the Soviet Union. Thus, for example, the agricultural resolution of the Central Committee of the Polish Party is banned in Hungary, and so is the evaluation of this resolution by the official paper of the Party, *Trybuna Ludu*, and so is a study concerning relationships of Polish and Western literature and art, etc. In numerous areas of Hungarian economic, political, and cultural life there is a hermetic seal isolating the problems that friendly countries share in the same areas; this indicates a fear of criticism, and at the same time— and this is more serious—it furthers the intensification of nationalism and of attitudes opposed to the teachings of Lenin on the subject of proletarian internationalism.

Another serious consequence of this is that the leaders of the Party and the government, the members of the Central Committee and of the Council of Ministers, are not able to orient themselves properly; they are not as acquainted with international life or the events in the lives of friendly countries as are the common citizens who listen to the radio.

The moral is this: It is not enough to speak about the great and noble concept of proletarian internationalism, and at the same time to isolate oneself from all activities indispensable to the practical achievement of proletarian internationalism. It is in this area that we must seek the roots of nationalism, and not in the repetition of the words about "God's hat." It is not primarily the poet, particularly the line of Petöfi, but the policies of the Party and government in the areas of our social, economic, and cultural life and in similar areas of international life, that are to blame; it is cosmopolitism and the extremes of isolation that hide within themselves the dangers of nationalism and chauvinism. Therefore, those men must bear the responsibility who have adhered, and still adhere, to such anti-Marxist views and policies.

Since the days when I first participated in the workers' movement, and since I became a member of the Bolshevik Party and later of the Hungarian Party in 1918, I have never been a nationalist-chauvinist, and I have never represented such a view. The concept of proletarian internationalism has determined my views and my actions. I gave proof of this during the great trials and bloody battles of the Russian Civil War in which I participated as an internationalist, and during the Second World War when given a leading role in the work devoted to the preparation of proletarian internationalism. But I was also a representative of the ideal of Leninist internationalism in my writings of 1919 and the 1920's; I wrote articles at the time of the Russian Civil War; I published pieces in the Moscow Hungarian-language periodical *Uj Hang* in 1936–1940, when I opposed Hungarian revisionism and rose to the defense of the Czechoslovak Republic against the common enemy, German fascism. In June, 1938, I wrote an article for *Uj Hang* entitled "The Freedom Fight of the Danube Valley Peoples." Among other things, I wrote as follows:

Ominous clouds are accumulating over the Danube Valley.
After the crushing of the independence of Austria, German
fascism is preparing to ring the death knell over the national life
of the little peoples of the Danube Valley. The most immediate
danger threatens the people of Czechoslovakia, who are to be
crushed between a German military attack from without and a
Fascist *Putsch* from within.

"Alone, relying on themselves, not one of the little peoples of
the Danube will be able to withstand the common danger threatening them. The common danger, the common fate, prescribe that
the endangered small peoples must join together. In these
ominous times, the Hungarian people have a special responsibility. As Fate has it, the behavior of the Hungarian people may
be decisive for the destiny of the Danube Valley peoples.

After further analysis I wrote as follows:

The Czechoslovak Republic is the outpost of European democracy, the strong bulwark and defender of the peace and of the
independence of the little peoples of the Danube. For this reason,
an attack directed at the Czechoslovak Republic would involve an
extraordinary danger to all small democratic and peace-loving
little peoples, but especially to the Hungarian people. The
Hungarian reactionaries are trying to throw the Hungarian people onto the front line on the side of German fascism against the
Czechoslovak Republic. . . . The peoples of the Czechoslovak
Republic, including the Hungarian nationals there also, should
recognize this danger. The Hungarian minority has turned against
the "autonomist" attempts of the Hungarian reactionary party
of Slovakia, attempts that were aimed at destroying the unity of
the republic; and at the very time when the Hungarian Revision
League [Magyar Revizios Liga], under the leadership of Ferenc
Herczeg, was organizing mass meetings and demonstrations in
Budapest for the reacquisition of the Uplands [Felvidek], large
sections of the Hungarian minority in Slovakia were taking a
stand for the independence and integrity of the Czechoslovak
Republic and were rushing with all their strength to the defense
of the endangered peace, of liberty, and of democracy, and to the
defense of the Czechoslovak Republic. . . . The fate of the Hungarian nation will be decided with that of Czechoslovakia.
Therefore, it is not a matter of indifference to the Hungarian people that the Hungarian reactionaries are being driven against

Czechoslovakia while in the grip of German fascism; rather, it is in the best interest of the Hungarian people to take a stand with their brothers beyond the borders on behalf of Czechoslovakia. There can be only one choice for the Hungarian people: to rush with all their strength to the defense of the hard-pressed Czechoslovak Democratic Republic.

This is where I stood at the beginning of the Second World War, when the war machine of German fascism had started to crush the European peoples. I wonder if this stand should be called nationalism or Leninist proletarian internationalism? I wonder if there is anyone among the leaders of the Party who would, at that time, have expressed proletarian internationalism in such a manner, in opposition to their own bourgeoisie? I represented such a stand after the liberation also, in the area of theory as well as in my practical work. On August 19, 1948, at the inauguration ceremony of the Kossuth Academy, I said the following:

> In the spirit of the revolutionary lessons of 1848–1849 and in the spirit of the legacy of the grand policies of Kossuth, we should cultivate the most cordial friendship with freedom-loving peoples, especially with the country of socialism, the Soviet Union, whose people have sacrificed the blood of tens and tens of thousands of their best sons for the liberation of our country. Under the exalted concept of the brotherhood of freedom-loving peoples, you must be the standard-bearers of the great idea of our national development, of national unity, and be the vanguard of the national independence front built upon the worker-peasant alliance, which will unite every creative force of the working people.

This is how I expressed the ideal of the interdependence of national unity and proletarian internationalism. My declarations concerning our fraternal relations with the Soviet Union and the peoples of the People's Democratic countries have had a great deal of weight in all my speeches and writings. This can be checked, it can be looked into, and I wish it would be, all the more so because no one has raised the charge of nationalism against me prior to the March resolution of the Central Committee. Also, for this reason, I strongly protest against the use of the quotation taken from my welcoming speech at the People's Front Congress to prove the charge of nationalism.

At the same time, in order to avoid all misunderstanding, I want to emphasize that as a son of the Hungarian people and as a member of the Hungarian nation I am proud of my Hungarian past. I do not deny my Hungarian nationality and ardently love my Hungarian homeland and my Hungarian people. True patriotism, together with a love and respect for other peoples and nations, is the basis and essence of proletarian internationalism. This distinguishes and separates me, even today, from the cosmopolites and the "leftist" extremists who are foreign to the Hungarian people and to their ambitions—which are fused with the ideal and grand design of socialism—and who are also incapable of true patriotism. They are the ones who, in the past as well as in the present, have turned against the national feelings of the Hungarian people. It is they who sow the nationalistic and chauvinistic seeds of dissension, wittingly or unwittingly.

In closing, I will set down the following portion of the speech I made in November, 1954, at the meeting held at MAVAG, which will clearly answer all those who have raised the fabricated charge of nationalism against me:

Within our growing socialist society there is arising the indomitable spirit of the international revolutionary workers' movement, of the teachings of Marx, Engels, Lenin, and Stalin, and of the magnificient goals of the militant lives of Liebknecht, Rosa Luxemburg, Bebel, and others. As a result of the epic victories of the Great October Socialist Revolution, of the Soviet Union, and of the Red Army, these ten years of sacrifice and spirited work on the part of the Hungarian working class have changed the course of historical development. . . . It is a gigantic achievement, comrades, for the Hungarian working class, which hardly a decade ago was living through a most terrible time and which today holds power. It is a wonderful example for the working class and the revolutionary parties in capitalist countries, whose struggle in the spirit of proletarian internationalism, will receive a great boost as a result of this.

Chapter 21.   National Defense and Pacifism

The March, 1955, resolution of the Central Committee does not charge me with pacifism, yet I must still turn to it because Istvan Bata, alternate member of the Executive Committee, made this grave charge against me specifically. In his speech at the First National Conference of the Hungarian Voluntary National Defense Federation in 1955, Bata said, among other things, the following:

> I must say that some persons, seeing the results achieved and the successes realized, are inclined to delude themselves with pacifist illusions, believing that the danger of war has completely disappeared. The spread of such harmful pacifist views and manifestations was served by the views of the right-wing deviationists —Imre Nagy and his associates—who belittled heavy industry, the building of socialism, and national defense.

Bata knowingly is stating untruths, deliberately lying and slandering. He knows very well that I am not a pacifist. He knows exactly my stand on questions of national defense in the National Defense Council and before the responsible Party organs. I do not want to go into details. But whether the important questions of the equipment, personnel, or supplies of the army, war industry, or the modernization of national defense were concerned, I most emphatically supported the proposals of the Ministry of National Defense within the framework permitted by our political and economic possibilities. As a result of a more thorough knowledge of the actual situation, I went further and represented a more correct viewpoint in this field than did Mátyás Rákosi, who, as he used to say, had already burned his fingers once by fulfilling excessive demands. I have said enough on this subject. Details would touch on questions that I do not deem it proper to raise in public even before the Party.

That I am not a pacifist is evidenced by those countless speeches and articles in which I fully explained my viewpoint on the importance of national defense. This was not saber-rattling or aggressive boasting, but always a clear and decisive viewpoint as regards the organization of home defense. In the following, I quote from several of my speeches and articles. In my speech at Nyiregyhaza on May 1, 1948, I said the following:

> Our great purpose is the preservation of peace. For this reason we have established friendship and mutual aid agreements with our neighbors. But we should not depend only on this. The greatest pledge of our security is the increase of our own strength. The lot of the weak is slavery. Only the country whose people are strong and growing can be free and independent. Therefore we must augment and strengthen our country. Only the strong can protect peace, freedom, and independence. The lot of the weak is to be defeated. Therefore let us not be weak, let us be strong politically and economically, and for this purpose let us develop our industry and agriculture and raise our people's economic and cultural standard of living.

Continuing in connection with national defense, I said the following:

> We must attend to increasing the defensive strength of our country. We must see that the democratic Hungarian Army is the strong and unfaltering protector of the Hungarian people, the Hungarian working class, and the peasantry. Workers and peasants, working youth and peasant youth, place yourselves in command; be the officers, leaders, or soldiers of the democratic Hungarian Army. This will guarantee that no one will dare to raise a hand against us. . . . We must be on guard because international imperialism incites war. . . . The imperialists must not forget that a third world war would mean their ruin. The People's Democracies and socialism would emerge victorious from this struggle.

I quote the following from my speech made at the celebration of the first graduation of lieutenants of the Kossuth Academy on August 19, 1948:

> Our army was born in the storm of the 1948–1949 people's revolution and in the bloody storm of the freedom fight against foreign oppressors. The idea of popular freedom and independence inflamed and inspired it to those wonderful acts of heroism that elicited the unanimous admiration and appreciation of the progressive peoples. . . . Having completed your studies, take your posts as officers in the ranks of our army. Begin the work of creating a strong and glorious Hungarian People's Republic, peace and security, and a people's army of freedom and independence. I want your future work to be crowned with as much success as possible. If, however, in defending our true business, a peaceful life and freedom, we should be compelled by the imperialists to fight, may laurels of victory crown your banners for the glory of our country. Comrades, on with your work, living and if necessary dying honorably in peace or war for your country.

This is not pacifism, even if the Minister of Defense declares it is.

Recently, on December 21, 1954, on the occasion of the tenth anniversary of the forming of the Provisional National Assembly and the national government, I made an official speech at Debrecen, in which I dealt with the importance of national defense and the duties we have in that regard:

> The imperialist efforts aimed at resurrecting German militarism and establishing an aggressive German army warn us that we must increasingly look after the defense of our country's freedom and independence, our national sovereignty, our people's peaceful creative work, and the building of socialism. We must develop and perfect with greater sacrifice our people's army, whose predecessor, our glorious Hungarian Army, was born in the storm of the 1948–1949 people's revolution, the bloody storm of the freedom fight against foreign oppressors. . . . The people's power, which is lying at rest, has a decisive role in the modern development of our people's army through the worker and peasant federations and through the firm unity of the nation.

There was hardly an important event or an occasion when I did not, in speech or in writing, emphasize the importance of national defense. In my official speech given on the thirty-fifth anniversary of the Great October Socialist Revolution, I said the following on the subject:

And our people on the Hungarian front of world peace—more united than ever—have merged with all peoples of the world desiring peace and, under the leadership of the powerful Soviet Union, stand ready to fulfill the call of history and defend our freedom, independence, and our work of building peace. We surround with love, respect, and far-reaching solicitude our people's army, the dauntless protector of the peaceful work of our working people, to whose ranks we give our best sons in order that our army may be a worthy follower of the heroic Soviet Army, the most powerful guardian of world peace.

Bata knew then and knows now of all these and countless similar correct Marxist—not pacifist—viewpoints and opinions that I have held regarding national defense. If he nevertheless spoke of the harmful right-wing pacifist views of "Imre Nagy and his associates," he obviously did it by falsifying the evident and well-known facts.

Chapter 22. The Question of the Relationship of Party and State

The April resolution of the Central Committee says among other things the following: "Comrade Imre Nagy . . . has tried to set the state organs . . . against the Party."

In the question of the relationship of the Party and the state, the June, 1953, resolution of the Central Committee drew attention on the one hand to the mistakes that had been made earlier in this area, and on the other hand it set forth the tasks along Party and state lines confronting us in this area. Unfortunately I do not have the June resolution at hand; therefore I will quote the pertinent parts of the reports made at the meeting, which faithfully reflect the position taken by the June resolution in the question of the relation of Party and state. Let us look at the following:

> The unprincipled and un-Partylike leadership of the Party has brought with it a violation of the fundamental principles of the People's Democracy, as regards the relation of Party and state and of state and the masses. . . . The fault is that the Party has excessively dominated the state and economic leadership of the country; the Party not only has made the rules and the decisions but to a large extent it has also executed the measures prescribed. The Party is not suited, either in its organizational structure, its operation, its make-up, or its social character, for attending to state functions, nor is this its job. Nevertheless, it has interfered excessively in the execution of state tasks, thereby

violating the independence of state organs, paralyzing their operations, and discrediting their reputations. . . . Added to this is the fact that Comrade Rákosi combined in his own person all the power in the country—he was First Secretary of the Party and Chairman of the Council of Ministers [Premier], and he took the State Security Authority [AVH] under his immediate direction. He has committed serious errors, both in his leadership of the Party and of the state and in the work of the AVH, errors that contain within themselves great dangers. . . . We can assert that the government was in reality a shadow government, which approved Party resolutions that had already been passed, and that the authority and responsibility of the ministries was also greatly curtailed. . . . Such governmental organs and methods are not suitable for absolutely guaranteeing legality in all aspects of state and economic life. Here are the most serious evils of our state life, the roots of the violation of socialist legality, which, in the last analysis, derive from a separation from the masses. . . . It must be stated frankly that, owing to the errors of the leaders of the Party, we have deviated from the principles of Lenin as far as our popular democratic state is concerned.

These reports set clearly before us the task that we had to accomplish in the area of correcting Party and state relations in the period that followed the June resolution.

It should further be known that the question of the relation of Party and state was also discussed very sharply in the conference held with the Soviet comrades prior to the June, 1953, meeting of the Central Committee, and in the spirit represented above. At this conference Comrade Malenkov pointed out that, in May, 1953, they had discussed with Mátyás Rákosi the personal questions also that concerned the separation of Party and state leadership. "We asked, 'Whom do you recommend as your deputy?' He could name no one. He had objections to everyone whose name was mentioned; he had something against everyone. Everyone was suspect except he alone. This appalled us very much," said Comrade Malenkov. Comrade Molotov declared that Mátyás Rákosi had said that he did want a Premier, "but he wanted a Premier who would have no voice in the making of decisions." Comrade Khrushchev noted, "The matter involved was that the leadership of the Party and the state should not be concentrated in the hands of one man or a few men; this is not desirable."

We prescribed the relations of the Party and state on the basis of the principles worked out at the Moscow conference and laid down by the June resolution of the Central Committee. This was not very easy—in several respects it did not work at all —and the results achieved were soon defeated because of the resistance on the part of Mátyás Rákosi within the top leadership of the Party. It was he who from the outset saw that by regulating the Party-state relationship in the spirit of the advice given in the June resolutions and at the Moscow conference, the Party would be forced into the background and would be made subordinate to the organs of state. This is the source of the often repeated but baseless charge against me that I allegedly undervalue the leading role of the Party, and that I raise the state organs above the Party. Mátyás Rákosi considered the actions taken in the spirit of the June resolution of the Central Committee concerning the relation of Party and state to be an undervaluation of the leading role of the Party, and he could not conceive of solving the problem except in the pre-June fashion. The March, 1955, resolution revived this notion, and what has occurred in practice since then in this area proves that we are returning to the pre-1953 state of affairs in the questions of the role of the Party and the relationship of Party and state, a state of affairs that the June resolution condemned and that was held to be in need of change.

One also must remember that Mátyás Rákosi did not always hold this view concerning the role of the Party in the question of the relationship between Party and state. There was a time when he did not think that placing the state in the foreground was rightist deviation and an undervaluation of the role of the Party. It is well known among Party leaders that when Mátyás Rákosi became Premier he alluded to Stalin in voicing the view within the Political Committee that it was necessary to increase the role of the state vis-à-vis the Party; that it was necessary to place the government more into the foreground, in the interest of wider and more direct connections with the masses: this, according to him, was required by the new situation. He indicated that placing the state and the government more into the foreground and increasing respect for them was an important task of the Party when the Council of Ministers came to the fore. I believe that there is no need for commentary on this. However, this is not a theoretical stand on an important question.

In his speech at the April meeting of the Central Committee, Mátyás Rákosi allegedly said that he felt heavy responsibility for the fact that I had become Premier on July 4, 1953, thereby suggesting that he at least "recommended" me for Premier. For the sake of truth, it must be stated that it was not Mátyás Rákosi, but the Soviet comrades—Comrades Malenkov, Molotov, and Khrushchev—who recommended what Comrade Rákosi and all members of the Hungarian delegation accepted with approbation. Thus Rákosi is innocent in this question; there is no basis for his remorse, because he bears no responsibility at all for my nomination as Premier.

In connection with the question of the relation of Party and state one must turn to several important problems of ideological significance:

A. Prior to June, 1953, the oppressive functions of the state were unduly in the foreground, although it would have been better, because of the nature of the development of the revolution, to bring into the foreground the peaceful tasks of economic development and of social and cultural activity; tasks toward which the main efforts of the state were directed from June, 1953, until the March resolution of the Central Committee. This could not at all mean, nor did it mean, that we would have abandoned for one moment the necessary vigilance and oppressive functions directed against the class enemy.

B. The Party exercises direction and control over the state organs. But expropriation of the functions of state organs is incorrect and harmful, as was clearly shown by the practice prior to June, 1953. In that period, the activities and role of the Party in the area of state functions represented a swing toward degeneration of the dictatorship of the proletariat. In the course of the preceding eighteen to twenty-four months there had been some success in combating this danger and in placing state functions on the firm basis of Marxist-Leninist state theory. Since the March, 1955, resolution of the Central Committee, the old errors have been reborn from the displacement of the functions of state and Party and from the serious "leftist" distortion of Marxist state theory; errors on the basis of which our popular democratic system is being attacked.

C. In practice, the theory of class struggle has been distorted. Sectarian, extreme "leftist" deviation concludes from the theory of class struggle that there is a need to incite class struggle—as we have seen in the past and as has again come into the foreground since the resolutions of March, 1955. In the theory of class struggle, we disregarded the fact that there can be various degrees of acuteness and that it is not absolutely necessary under our present domestic and international circumstances for our class struggle to take as sharp a form as that of the class struggle in the period of the development of the Soviet Union, which was then isolated and encircled by imperialism, and whose internal and international circumstances were different.

These views led me to a correct Marxist determination of the relationship of Party and state. In neither my theoretical nor my practical work did I expound activities deviating from Marxist-Leninist teachings. At the Third Party Congress, for the first time in the life of our Party, I dealt exhaustively and in detail with Marxist state theory and with its practical application to the conditions unique in Hungary during the period of transition. I explained the relationship of Party and state, the role of the Party, and its functions in our popular democratic system. I dealt in detail and exhaustively with the operation and chain of command of the state apparatus. In my report, our entire state machinery and administration were placed for the first time on the solid ideological basis of Marxism-Leninism. Together with other arguments, this bears heavily upon the statement that the charge that I tried to set the state organs against the Party is groundless.

Chapter 23.   The Evaluation of the Party's Role and Achievements

The March resolution of the Central Committee asserted the following about the Party's role and its achievements:

> The strengthened right-wing opportunist deviation also was evidenced in the disparagement of the leadership role in the Party. Some individuals denied the Partys' leadership role in the Patriotic People's Front. The establishment of the PPF, which our Party initiated, was followed by rightist activities aimed at suppressing the significance of the Party and its leadership role and making the PPF the power that would supervise the state and council organs.
>
> One of the basic characteristics, reflecting the rightist line of Comrade Imre Nagy, was evidenced by the fact that he denied and disparaged the victories gained through the Party and consistently remained silent on the subject of its accomplishments.

As we can see from the first part, which mentions the Party's leadership role, they generally emphasize that "some individuals denied" and "disparaged" the Party's leadership role. However, they interpret the "disparagement of the victories and achievements gained by the Party" as a manifestation of my "rightist line." Let us consider this charge systematically.

What the resolution establishes in respect to the Party's leadership role, as related to the PPF, is not in accordance with the facts. I have covered this in detail in the section dealing with the PPF. As far as the Party's leadership role in the councils is concerned, its significance and realization, etc., I was the first in the history of the Party to define it, and I did so correctly, in the spirit of Leninism, and with the unanimous approval of the Third Congress, before which I read this report. Therefore I have nothing to correct in these matters, which clearly indicates that the portions pertaining to this in the March resolution are out of order, and I do not agree with them.

In my speech of August, 1947, I described our Party's role and activities as follows:

History will verify the inestimable service rendered to our national rebirth and our future generations by the Hungarian Communist Party, which in these difficult times withstood the onslaught of the dark old world and with a strong hand guided forward the ship of the People's Democracy with the infallible compass of a farsighted policy. Only a party that is actually the entire nation's party, that can place national interest before party interest, and that unites within itself our traditions and the public creative power, is capable of solving these gigantic tasks. The Communist Party has been such a Party, and it will continue to remain such.

According to the teachings of Lenin, as I wrote in my book entitled *One Decade:*

Our Party's strength lies in the maintenance of a lively relationship between the millions of Party members and the non-Party masses—the better this relationship, the more lasting are the results. In the ocean of the masses, writes Lenin, we are merely a drop, and we can govern only if we properly express that which the people have accepted. Without this, the Communist Party will not lead the proletariat; the proletariat will not carry along the masses.

The basic question is how one interprets and sees the realization of the Party's leading role. Quoting Stalin on this subject, I wrote as follows:

The Party is the military General Staff of the proletariat. The Party, however, cannot be solely a vanguard. Once and for all, it must also be the vanguard of the *class,* an integral part of the class, with all the roots of its existence closely tied to the class. The Party cannot lead the class if it has no connection with the non-Party masses, if there is no cooperation between the Party and non-Party masses.

I wrote further:

> For this reason the most important task is to ensure and strengthen the leadership role of our Party, and this can be realized only by the establishment of a close and lasting relationship between the Party and the widest possible segment of the no-Party masses. The weakening of the tie between the Party and the masses is the greatest danger threatening the Party.

This is the way I interpreted the leadership role of the Party on the basis of the teaching of Lenin and Stalin. That was my viewpoint in 1949 when I wrote the above, and it has remained my viewpoint ever since. There are indispensable conditions tied to the leadership role of the Party, and their neglect or violation deprives the Party of its ability to fulfill its leading role.

The leadership of the Party does not come about automatically; it is not created by some higher opinion.

Consequently, it is the greatest possible mistake if some leaders confuse their wishes in this regard with objective reality. Therefore the role of the Party's leadership can and must be evaluated, primarily on the basis of the Party's influence on the masses and on its relationship to the non-Party masses. It was in the light of the scientific findings of Marxism-Leninism that I interpreted, or where necessary criticized, the Party's fulfillment of its mission.

In this question, a basic difference exists between myself and those whose interpretation of the Party's leadership role forces the Party to adopt aims and methods that isolate it, turn it against the working masses, and deprive it of the absolute confidence necessary to leadership; in short, who undermine the Party's leadership role.

After the year of the change, this danger arose rapidly and spread in the Party. In 1949, I wrote that it was indispensable that our Party functionaries change their behavior toward the non-Party masses for the purpose of ensuring our Party's influence on the masses. Subsequently I quoted Stalin:

> Let the Communist learn to treat the non-Party member as an equal treats an equal: he should not give orders but listen with attention to the non-Party member so that he will not only instruct the non-Party member but also learn from him. . . . The problem of the mutual relationship between Party members and non-Party members is a very important problem in our Party practice. Lenin defined this mutual relationship in two words: mutual confidence. But we cannot expect confidence from a non-Party peasant if we cannot treat him as an eqaul treats an equal. In these cases, distrust rather than confidence arises, and this usually leads to the alienation of the Party from the masses.

The neglect of serious, purposeful, and consistent Party work, and its replacement with catch-all phrases, unavoidably goes hand in hand with arrogance and the issuance of orders. This kills initiative, criticism and self-criticism, and Party discipline, and undermines Lenin's basic democratic principles of our Party life.

This interpretation of Party leadership was called "Revolutionary Saxon paternalism" by Lenin. He asked for "less inflated catch-all phrases, more simple everyday deeds, less political chatter, more attention to the most simple but actual facts of the building of Communism."

In the evelution of the role of the Party's leadership, I was guided by these ideological viewpoints, which I never violated in my actual work. I opposed the radical "left-wing" deviationists who distorted the role of Party leadership and replaced it with Party dictatorship, which had been emphatically condemned by Lenin and Stalin. The "left-wing" extremists ignored the teachings of Marxism-Leninism; I protested against this in 1949 because the danger became apparent at that time that they would alienate the Party from the masses and the working class and cause serious harm to the Party and also to the People's Democracy. Prior to the June resolution, during the years 1950–1953, we saw a great deal of proof of this, and we experience it to no lesser degree today as a result of the implementation of the March resolutions.

In spite of all charges, I did not damage the role of the Party's leadership either in the past or in the government program. During the June 11, 1953, meeting of Party activists in Budapest, I stressed the significance of the Party's leadership role in practically my entire speech. There, among other things, I said the following:

> Those splendid results and dazzling successes that our Party has attained in its thirty-five years of existence are the safest assurance that our Party will also perform its new tasks successfully.
>
> During the dark years of Horthy reactionism, and during fascism, our glorious Party, in costly struggles at the head of the working class, showed the people the road to liberation. It was our Party that, fused with the people and at the helm of our heroic working class, upset the exploiting rule of the upper classes and placed all the power in the hands of the working people. With the guidance of our Party, we crushed the landlord system and uprooted the old feudal bourgeois Hungary. Who assigned the task? Who guided the struggle? Who lead our working people to victory over capitalism? It was our Party. Out of the ruins of the country, crushed by the criminal fascist war, our Party developed the creative strength of the working class, of the entire working people, and outlined the tasks for rebuilding the nation. The Party instilled strength and self-confidence in our working people. At times, transitional difficulties and serious mistakes obscured our magnificent achievements, yet how much work, exhaustion, and sweat—how much value there is in these magnificent creations, which all belong to the working people. We must cherish our achievements still more because without this, the recognition and correction of mistakes cannot progress along the proper road.

Who can say that this is a disparagement of the Party's leadership role and of our achievements?

I have nothing to explain; therefore I do not consider it necessary to quote all the passages in which I wrote or talked about the role of Party leadership. Nevertheless, I still consider it necessary to call attention to one or two facts for the purpose of exposing the fabricated charges, and because the "left-wing" extremists do everything within their power to cover my statements on the role of Party leadership with the veil of oblivion. Although they have banned my books and writings, the transcript of the Third Party Congress is still in public circulation, and my introductory speech, in which I spoke about the significance of the Party and the role of the Party leadership, can be read there. From this, I quote the following:

> This Party, which has met to discuss the fateful problems of our free country, is the Party that, in the more than thirty-five years of its heroic past, has spent a quarter of a century amidst cruel persecution, making great sacrifices in its fight against the oppression and exploitation of the Fascist system, believing in and struggling for the noble cause of the liberation of the Hungarian working class and our working people. This Party now beginning its national discussions is the Party that, for nearly ten years at the helm of our magnificent working class, steeped in the trust of our working people, depending on the impregnable Worker-Peasant Federation, has consolidated the People's Democratic system, and now, with the power in its hands, is successfully establishing the basis of socialism in our country. We are here gathered for the Congress of that Party which is the most magnificent embodiment of our national endeavors and under whose leadership our country has made unparalleled progress in the past decade.
>
> This Party which begins its discussions today is the Party that has done more for the country in the interest of independence, national sovereignty, and the welfare of the people than any other political party. It was with the leadership of this Party, our Party —the Hungarian Workers' Party—that Hungary began and progressed victoriously toward the magnificent and certain future, toward socialism. It is an inspiring feeling to be a member of this Party, and those of us who were sent to the Congress as representatives with the trust of its members are filled with pride.

That is what I said among other things, in my introductory speech at the Third Congress. It can be ignored, but it cannot be denied as something that never occurred; even less can it be called a disparagement of the Party and its achievements. At the Third Party Congress, in my report on "The Tasks of

State Administration and Councils," the portion on the role of the Party was significant. Among other things, I said the following:

The Party is the leading force of our People's Democratic system and of our entire social and state life. The Party can successfully perform the gigantic task that falls upon it because it is the vanguard of the working class and, hardened in the crucible of class struggle, it unites all those great and valuable experiences that it obtained in the course of decades, in its costly struggles to overthrow capitalism.

Subsequently, in the following, I pointed out:

The Communist Party stood at the helm, from the every beginning, in the difficult struggle for the new power of the people. The first buds of the new power of the people, the National Committees that were established as a result of the people's initiative, came into being through Party leadership. The Party revived and directed the large-scale mass organization of national unity, the Hungarian National Independence Front, which is the successor of the Magyar Front that was established during the struggle against fascism. Our Party revived and led the massing of democratic forces which, after difficult and successful struggles, eliminated step by step the representatives of the reactionary capitalistic classes from Parliament and government. The basis of the decisive victories of the democratic people's power was the large-scale support of the masses for the Party's policy; they considered it their own and struggled for it. Our Party's successes were enhanced by those magnificent results that we have achieved since the year of change in establishing a socialist economy, national industrialization, the socialist reorganization of agriculture, and state organization.

I wonder whether this can be construed as disparagement of the Party's role and of our achievements?

In November, 1954, in my speech at the MAVAG, I also singled out the leadership role of the Party, beginning with a review of its past struggle and emphasizing its magnificently fulfilled role in the building of socialism:

Emerging from dangerous illegality during the past ten years, strengthened by the building of the country and the relentless political struggle against class enemies, the unified Marxist-Leninist Party of the working class, the Communists, i.e., the Hungarian Workers' Party, has become the leading force of our People's Democratic system, the director of our political, economic, and cultural life, the organizer of our victories.

On December 21, 1954, the tenth anniversary of the Provisional Parliament and national government, I also praised the role of the Party leadership in my speech at Debrecen. I said:

The rebirth of our nation is an outstanding accomplishment of the Hungarian Communist Party. It is the achievement of the Party that spent a quarter of a century of the thirty-six years of its heroic past struggling against an exploiting, reactionary system, to liberate the Hungarian working class and our working people; of the Party whose leadership has enabled our country's development, in one decade, to surpass any other in our history. During its ten years of struggle, the Hungarian Communist Party has obtained the respect and acknowledgement of our people and our country's leaders through its magnificent achievements in the building up of the country. Today, on its anniversary, the Hungarian Workers' Party is enjoying the unlimited love and trust of our people. It is joined solidly with the people, and the Hungarian working society sees in it the security of our country, our future, and our destiny.

With these few quotations I merely want to point out the actual facts, in contrast to the charges made against me with regard to my views on the Party's role. In addition to the quotations cited above, it is essential, before accepting slander, to become acquainted with my other speeches and writings to which I cannot refer here because of lack of space.

Lenin interpreted the Party's leading role by saying that the Party convinces the majority of the working people of the soundness of its policies and thus realizes its aims.

The "left-wing" extremists pay no attention to whether or not the majority of the people or the majority of the Party membership agree with their policies. They give orders and commands; those who disagree with them are pushed aside, placed in economic difficulties, or even, in many cases, dropped from the Party. According to Stalin, this type of leadership is "syndicalism, anarchism, bureaucratism, anything but Bolshevism or Leninism."

This explains why many of the Party functionaries do not heed the words and opinions of the masses; not only non-Party members but many Party members are afraid to speak, let alone criticize anything, because they know that a few "left-wing" extremists, making a mockery of the Party's organizational statutes and the Leninist principles of the Party's inner life, can harm them in many ways. Thus it occurs that, being alienated from the people, the Party leadership is not aware of and does not understand their grievances and problems; it becomes arrogant and self-contained; it cannot properly express, and even less represent what Stalin called "that which the people acknowledge as truth."

The leadership role of the Party is expressed chiefly in the Party's activity in its assumption of leadership, in the designation of tasks, and in the supervision, guidance, and organization of their implementation.

The facts prove that, from the resolution of June, 1953, until the resolution of March, 1955, the Party did not fulfill its leadership role in the manner required by the complicated economic and political tasks. This stimulated opposition, especially in the economic organizations, and the opposition was intensified by the economic apparatus under the leadership of sectarian "left-wing" deviationists. It was this apparatus that, during the period prior to June, forced upon the nation the economic policy that subsequently proved to be so costly. With these deeds the "left-wing" deviationists critically injured the authority of Party leadership. They intentionally forced the Party into the background and kept the Party membership in uncertainty, in order to reduce its activity and to discourage it. This is how the matter really stands, if we compare the pretentious phrases with the facts in respect to the Party's leadership role.

In the resolution of March, 1955, as I pointed out at the beginning of this chapter, they also charged me with disparagement of achievements. It would certainly be a serious mistake if I had actually disparaged achievements. For this reason, it is worth while to scrutinize this charge more closely. Who doesn't recall that up to June, 1953, it was Mátyás Rákosi, "Mighty Ernö [Ernö Gerö], and other "left-wing" extremists who consistently disparaged achievements; who were never satisfied with them; who strained production and collection alike to such an extent that the matter of socialist building in our country all but arrived at a dead end. However, a complete change of attitude occurred in June, 1953, as the disclosure, ventilation, and criticism of past mistakes got under way. Thereafter, all their endeavors were aimed at concealing their mistakes and ending criticism as soon as possible. It was not without reason that Khrushchev said in June, 1953, that "Mátyás Rákosi practiced self-criticism so that he would not be criticized any further." After June, 1953, the persons who began to "appreciate" Party achievements were the very ones who previously were the least satisfied with them. They began to demand, ever more forcefully and vociferously, that we must speak more about our achievements. Their aim was to hush up past mistakes and to divert public attention from themselves. They outbid everyone in this field, acting as though the Party had been obliged to make the drastic change in June, 1953, because we had failed to value properly the achievements of the preceding period, rather than because we wanted to eliminate the effects of their detrimental policies. After June, 1953, the Party's chief task was certainly the thorough revelation of mistakes, without which it could not undertake the correction of the mistakes and attain results. Therefore, when the "left-wing" extremists began their vociferous claims about past achievements and began to air their charges about the disparagement of achievements, they attempted by a deceptive maneuver to divert the Party's attention from the principal task. In essence, this was the hidden motivation behind the charges of "disparagement of achievements." Disparagement of achievements, as I have already noted, would have been a serious mistake, but the "left-wing" deviationists distorted the matter so that disclosure of mistakes became synonymous with the disparagement of achievements, which is anti-Party, right-wing deviationism. Under these circumstances, the charges about the disparagement of achievements actually amounted to the hushing up of mistakes and the suppression of criticism. This is the manner in which they created the impression within the Party that the guilty ones were not those who actually committed the mistakes prior to June, but those who, after June, spoke about these faults and not about achievements. Quite without justification, I was the first to be listed among these by the March resolution. It is true that I criticized sharply the serious mistakes of the past and the men who committed them; but I did this on principle and in line with the Party's policy. At the same time, however, I did not fail to speak about the achievements, nor did I disparage them.

There is hardly an article or a speech made by me in which I did not stress the subject of our achievements in some manner. I did this in the government program, and later in Budapest, at the meeting of Party activists on July 11, 1953. Since then, during more than one and one-half years, I have often written and spoken about our successes. I will mention my words spoken at the meeting of the Hungarian Academy of Science on May 23, 1954, concerning the achievement of science during the decade:

During the ten years since liberation, our scientific life and its heart, the Hungarian Academy of Science, has actually been reborn. Historically, ten years is too brief a period for evaluating events, yet one decade is sufficient for us to measure the scientific achievements of our People's Democratic system. These achievements, of which we can justly be proud, indicate that the development of Hungarian science is boldly progressive and has fulfilled its tasks in both of its fields. In many respects it has effectively cooperated with the nation's economic and cultural development, and, on the other hand, it has contributed in numerous fields to scientific knowledge on a world-wide scale.

It is also worth quoting several parts of my speech made at the MAVAG:

It is only a decade, yet it is nevertheless an entire historical era. In our history we cannot find another generation similar to ours, which was so fortunate as to accomplish the most magnificent national tasks. There has been no other generation that has solved the historical tasks falling upon it as successfully as we have, and that has shown so many successes in uplifting the nation and people as our generation has shown. The Hungarian working class has earned everlasting merit in these magnificent victories and achievements. . . .

Comrades, the last ten years have brought about deep-rooted changes in every phase of economic, political, and cultural life. They have established the basis of socialism: a new society. And now, when we look back upon the road we have traveled and begin to take stock, we look with satisfaction upon the success of our struggles; our achievements, our socialist industry and progress in agriculture, our growing cities and towns, our cultural and scientific organizations, our new literary and artistic creations taken together—the work performed in laying the foundation of socialism. . . .

The power of the people under the leadership of the Party has brought about and consolidated, in the Constitution of the Hungarian People's Republic, the human rights for which Hungarian organized labor has struggled in vain for decades; for which the best fighters suffered persecution and prison terms; and for which the streets of Pest were often red with blood. These are historical achievements that must not be allowed to be obscured, and least of all forgotten. Let us preserve and safeguard them. It is through the memories of previous struggles that we can really value the freedom that became the property of the working class which, liberated from the yoke of capitalism, has been enjoying its blessings for ten years now.

In my Debrecen speech on December 21, 1954, I did not disparage; on the contrary, I noted the magnificent achievements of the last ten years. Let us quote a few parts of this speech:

During the past ten years there has been a very notable change here. We can look upon the work completed during the past ten years . . . in our people's economy, in every field of our social and cultural life, with heads erect. Today, our economic resources are greater than ever before. During the past ten years our industry has achieved results that were inconceivable under capitalistic conditions and can be attained only in a country where the instruments of production are in the people's possession, and cannot become instruments of exploitation. And now, in drawing up our balance sheet, we can say that we have a socialist industry and an expanding agriculture as a result of our work. The producer cooperatives have been solidified, and their strength is increasing. We have new literary and artistic creations which glorify our work in the field of establishing socialism. The struggle and achievements of the last ten years in the consolidation of our People's Democratic system and socialist building prove that the working class is the properly qualified possessor of power. The following factors have had an inestimable role in this: in the past decade, since the beginning at Debrecen, our country has been engaged in the building of socialism, in the development of socialist industry and trade, in the socialist reorganization of agriculture, in the promotion of large-scale cooperative farming, in furnishing far-reaching aid to our working peasantry, in deepening our cultural revolution, and in making our magnificent achievements public property.

This is the way the charges made against me and established in the March resolution appear in the light of actual facts. It is apparent, even from the few brief quotations, that I did not remain silent and I did not disparage our achievements. Would it have been possible to speak about them more frequently? Very definitely. But let us weigh everyone on the same scale; let us determine whether it was I, of all the members of the Political Committee, who spoke and wrote least about our achievements; whether it was I who consistently disparaged them. This is necessary because these charges were made only against me, and against no other member of the Political Committee. But the facts clearly prove that the majority of the members of the Political Committee did not speak up nearly as much as I did on the role of Party leadership or on the significance of our achievements. Therefore, why do they charge me with rightist deviationism? They do so because it is more difficult for them to admit their errors than it is to criticize me. This, however, is not in line with the principles of the Party and is incompatible with Communist morals.

In the first place, the proper evaluation of achievements springs from furnishing information systematically and sincerely to the Party membership and the public. In relation to this, it is a basic prerequisite that the nation be given a clear picture of its economic problems. This is a part of the responsibility that the Party and the state leadership owe to the members of the Party and to the entire working people, who have the right to know the actual state of conditions. This, however, cannot be said to be the case today; an evaluation of the currently prevailing situation and atmosphere, and the methods used, resemble the years 1951–1952. As in those days, the leaders of the Party and the state are again giving out in speeches and writings, in propaganda and agitation, that we are following the proper road and that the Party's policy is reaping one success after the other and clearly indicates the only road to the building of socialism.

Then, as now, they spoke of achievements in the economic, political, and cultural fields, ignoring and distorting facts. Contrary to the actual facts of everyday life and the public opinion of the nation, they presented a rosy picture of the economic situation as well as of the outlook for the future. This accounts for the surprise caused by the June, 1953, resolution of the Party and the government program, which established that the Party's line was in error; that we were not following the proper road; that the serious mistakes could cause grave political and material losses to the People's Democracy and lead the nation to the brink of catastrophe.

Articles that attempt to prove that we are on the proper road and that the Party resolutions are correct, and the propaganda that attempts to depict achievements and conditions in a rosy light, are dark forebodings of a return to the past. It is to be feared that, under the influence of our own propaganda, we may arrive at the brink of national disaster before we become aware of possibly catastrophic mistakes.

Innumerable times they charged me falsely with being the "people's enemy." This brings up the question of who is actually the people's friend and who are the enemies. It is most proper to listen to the people themselves. The opinion of the entire nation is not concealed, and it is ignored only by those who are indifferent toward the people's grievances and problems, those who confuse the people's voice with their own. The working masses, which determine who their friends or enemies are on the basis of their own experiences, by the improvement or deterioration of their condition, do not classify me as their enemy. The charges that I am an enemy of the people are false;

they are slanderous utterances and writings; they cannot shake the confidence of the Hungarian people. The people consider the slanderers as their enemies. Let the slanderers ask the people who they think is their enemy! They will hear the answer, and it will not condemn me.

Chapter 24. The Opposition: Its Methods, Forms, and Effects

The March, 1955, resolution of the Central Committee makes absolutely no mention of the opposition which was condemned by both the Third Party Congress and by several resolutions of the Central Committee, and for the elimination of which it was found necessary to take a number of urgent steps. The complete ignoring of the opposition at the March meeting of the Central Committee cannot be considered accidental. The explanation is simple: the "left-wing" extremists, who openly or covertly organized and directed the opposition to the implementation of the June resolution, considered it their most important task to declare that right-wing deviation was the source of all the trouble, and not the opposition, which had actually been obstructing the implementation of the Party resolution and the government program for almost two years. Consequently, the March meeting of the Central Committee directed its fire at extreme right-wing deviation rather than at the opposition, which was the actual cause of the trouble. How could the Central Committee, whose October resolution—had it been carried out—would have greatly advanced the successful implementation of the June policy in our Party and government life and in the building of socialism, have reversed thus itself? How can it be explained that, instead of blaming the obstruction of the "left-wing" extremists, they suddenly claimed that right-wing deviation was not only gravely endangering the building of socialism, but was the cause of all the troubles and mistakes of the past, which the Congress and the Central Committee had previously blamed on the opposition? At the March meeting, the Central Committee simply removed the blame from the "left-wing" opposition and placed it all at the doorstep of right-wing deviationism.

However, this did not in the least alter the facts or the responsibility of, and the serious harm done by, the opposition. No amount of scheming and calling things right-wing deviation can make me responsible for the damage done by the harmful economic policy pursued between 1949 and 1953, or for the nonrealization of the June policy, which was aimed at repairing this damage.

It was foreseeable that the persons who for years had been piling mistake on mistake would not give up their extreme "left-wing" viewpoint, and that they would obstruct the implementation of the June resolution and government program in one way or another. I considered it necessary to bring up this question as far back as at the July 4, 1953 meeting of the National Assembly:

> It is evident, respected National Assembly, that it will not be easy to carry out these tasks and that they certainly will not take care of themselves. It is plain that the best guarantee of success lies in the active participation of the great masses. However, it is plain also that there will be some who cannot or will not refrain from arbitrary conduct and antipopular abuses, who do not want to stop using administrative devices, and who will attempt in one way or another to obstruct the quick and successful carrying out of the measures taken for the good of the masses.

Thus the question of the fight against opposition arose on the very first day and remained on the agenda till the October, 1954, meeting of the Central Committee; in fact, as opposition increased, it became more sharply defined. The speech of Mátyás Rákosi at the June 11, 1953, meeting of Party activists was already a sign that opposition from the Party as well as the state and economic organs would have to be reckoned with. The struggle for the implementation of the June resolutions had begun. In countless statements to Party functionaries,

Mátyás Rákosi showed over and over again that he did not agree with the June policy. His behavior encouraged the believers in the old, mistaken policy, the "left-wing" extremists, to obstruct the June resolution, and mainly the government program, with impunity. Mátyás Rákosi, as First Secretary of the Party, evaded all attempts to hold him responsible. In October, 1953, the Central Committee was already calling attention to the dangers and harmful consequences of opposition:

> The attitude that the comrades of the "left-wing" sect are taking with regard to the resolutions of the Central Committee is extremely dangerous and immeasurably harmful. These comrades fail to realize that their behavior is obstructing and hindering those proper regulations aimed at increasing the welfare and standard of living of the working people and particularly the industrial workers. This attitude makes it apparent that such comrades look down on a healthy relationship with the working masses and do not consider it important. Unless such behavior is vigorously dealt with, there is the danger that the Party will become isolated from the workers in the village and the city, among workers, peasants, and intellectuals alike.

By the end of 1953 and at the beginning of 1954, it had already become evident to the Soviet comrades, too, that there was opposition to the June resolutions, and for this they blamed primarily Mátyás Rákosi. Comrade Malenkov said, "The faults we noted in June are being remedied very slowly. Rákosi has not taken the lead in remedying the faults." Comrade Khrushchev also noted, "Gerö has no words of self-criticism or feeling or responsibility for the serious mistakes of the economic policy; at best he admits, 'It is possible that Comrade Nagy is right in feeling that I am held back by the old economic policy.' "

The result of these warnings and of more forceful action here at home was that double-dealing became the chief method of the opposition. This explains how, despite the fact that the Third Party Congress, the Central Committee, and the Political Committee enacted any number of resolutions for ending the opposition, these resolutions had no effect. Thus, for example, when Mátyás Rákosi gave his report on the Central Committee at the Third Party Congress, he said among other things:

We have noticed that there is opposition to the change that has become necessary, and that this opposition has not ceased entirely even to this day. This opposition is not always conscious; frequently it assumes the form of a "we'll get around to this later" attitude among persons who should be taking certain timely steps after farsighted, considered, and systematic work. Others exaggerate the difficulty of realignment and of the regrouping of forces, and, using these difficulties for excuses, they fail to meet the deadline for certain measures.

It must be emphatically stated that such behavior is non-Communist and unworthy of responsible state officials. Persons who adopt a "let George do it" attitude or react with undue coldness toward implementing the resolutions designed to raise the standard of living of the workers cannot hold a responsible Party or government position. Then there are some, though fortunately few, who agree verbally with the policy of our Party and government, but who try to do exactly the opposite in practice. These are double-dealers, or the enemy itself, or persons under the influence of the enemy, who must be ruthlessly called to account.

Such were the words; but the deeds that Mátyás Rákosi heralded remained undone. Nobody was called to account. This was double-dealing.

Thus, despite the resolution of the Third Party Congress, opposition could not and did not cease. It did not even diminish; on the contrary, it continued to grow and become dangerous. To arouse panic and to justify and make their proposals for undermining the June policy acceptable, opposition elements at the head of organs directing the Party, the government, and the economy began predicting inflation and unemployment—in a very misleading manner, as events proved. These proposals called for a general reduction of industrial output; a large-scale cut-back in social provisions for the workers; a great reduction in the standard of living of persons living on wages and salaries; and an increase in the burdens of the peasants. The anarchistic and inhuman manner in which rationalization was carried out contributed to all this and embittered a large section of the intelligentsia in the government. All these measures were so timed that their implementation would have occurred at the time when the local councils were holding elections and PPF committees were being set up. In this way the "left-wing" opposition would have succeeded in turning all sectors of the population against the Party, the People's Democracy, and mainly the government. This was what they were getting ready to do; but the wide-scale political activity arising from the resolutions and from the October stand of the Central Committee succeeded in preventing this to a great extent.

However, the October, 1954, meeting of the Central Committee and its resolution could prevent these plans only temporarily. At the October meeting of the Central Committee the report of the Political Committee had the following to say about the opposition:

> The Party Central Committee pointed out the dangerous consequences of the opposition that revealed itself with regard to the realignment as early as October, 1953, and Congress has also called attention to them. However, we have not waged a sufficiently forceful battle in the field of ideology against the improper point of view that sees nothing but a pro-peasant policy in the vigorous development of agriculture. At the same time, in the fields of practical work, we have failed to take strong measures against those who implement the Party and government resolutions concerning the realignment of industry and the development of agriculture indolently, under protest, and slowly.

The resolution of the Central Committee, which was unanimously accepted, stated clearly:

> The Party will wage an unremitting battle against all distortions of the resolutions passed in June, 1953, and at the Third Party Congress, and against any deviations from this line. . . . The Political Committee must carry out the regrouping of cadres in the economic organs as required for this purpose, and must initiate organizational measures against those who refuse to accept sincerely the resolutions of the Third Congress and the Central Committee, and who are incapable of carrying out the policy of the New Course.

The situation prevailing before the October meeting of the Central Committee made clear that the Central Committee's main task was the elimination of opposition. The unanimity and decisiveness of the stand taken by the Central Committe in October, its courageous support of the June policy, and its determination to liquidate opposition, temporarily defeated the "left-wing" opposition, which retreated. The position taken by the Central Committee and the staunch way in which it abided by its principles plainly showed the "left-wing" deviationists that if the Party and government should succeed in carrying out the October resolution, there would be no hope of a return to the extreme "left-wing" policy. After the October resolution of the Central Committee there was confusion in the ranks of the "left-wing" opposition and an increase in double-dealing. This is reflected in the speech made by Ernö Gerö in Szolnok, in which he stated:

> If there are some who are unable to understand the Party's policy and the demands of the New Course, and if they persist in clinging to the old way, they must be removed, no matter how loyal they are to the Party. And if there are some who are deliberately obstructing the Party's policy, they must be swept aside.

Then, speaking of the Party's most important task, raising the workers' standard of living, he said:

> This has been and will continue to be the policy of our Party after the meeting of the Central Committee; this policy is the policy of our working class, the policy of all our people. The enthusiasm with which our people support this policy and with which they are now participating in the work of the PPF proves that we are following the only correct way.

Thus spoke Ernö Gerö in Szolnok. But he spoke quite differently on this same subject in the spring of 1955, not to mention his actions, which were diametrically opposed to the economic policy of our Party and government and were aimed at liquidating the June resolution.

After the October meeting of the Central Committee, Mátyás Rákosi tossed aside the reins of Party leadership. The Budapest Party Committee did not process the October resolution of the Central Committee for a long time. According to the report of the Party and Mass Organization Department, some of the Party cadres did not approve of what we had been doing since June. The result of the elections of leaders of primary organizations showed the low grade of the Party's political work; in many fields the Party organizations were still firmly following the old policy. The weakness of mass work and the low political level of the leadership also indicated that the Party organization had failed to adopt either the June Party resolution or the new work style. These and similar facts prove that Mátyás Rákosi, the Party's First Secretary, did not want to direct the Party during this period that was so crucial from the point of view of the implementation of the June resolution and the liquidation of the opposition to said resolution. Instead of carrying out the October resolution of the Central Committee, he felt the time had come to take a stand against them, for false and misleading reasons. He evaluated the international situation improperly, expecting first of all an increase in war tension. He exaggerated internal political and economic difficulties, claiming to see only trouble and mistakes since the inception of the New Course in June, 1953. He deemed the situation worse than it had been in 1952. He spoke of economic and political crises, claiming that the enemy had become more powerful in the country and that the PPF was in the hands of the enemy, and that a hostile right-wing wave was sweeping the country. All this was said immediately after the October meeting of the Central Committee, which had established that quite the contrary was true. It was said at a time when the strength of the Party was growing and developing; when its influence and closeness to the masses was increasing; when the social basis of the People's Democracy was becoming firmer than it had been at any time during the preceding five years, as the October resolution of the Central Committee had clearly stated. Mátyás Rákosi's stand was directed against the resolutions of the Central Committee. He denied the importance of the success achieved at the elections of the local councils and in the establishment of the PPF committees, whereas these plainly proved the correctness of the October resolution. As a result of Rákosi's stand, the "left-wing" opposition began openly attacking the October resolution of the Party and the political principles evolved there; actually they were attacking the consistent implementation of the June policy. With this, the die was cast.

The opposition, as is known, assumed the most varying guises in the field of Party, state, and economic life: prevention of the disclosure of pre-June mistakes; the enforcement of a passive attitude in Party, state, and economic organs; the creation of uncertainty and confusion within the Party; the obstruction of the implementation of measures; the exaggeration of difficulties; frequent changes in economic plans; attempts to decrease output; evasion of the organizational regulations aimed at controlling the opposition; drives to enact antipopular regulations; etc. As a result of the opposition, the Party and government organs concerned failed to evolve a concrete program for the realignment and simultaneous development of industry.

Since the October meeting of the Central Committee last year, the "left-wing" extremists have caused unusually serious economic, political, and moral damage. The most serious was the alienation of the masses from the Party and the government. The solidarity and decisiveness of principle manifested by the Central Committee at the October, 1954, meeting frightened the "left-wing" opposition. In March, it was the Central Committee that flinched before the onslaught of the "left-wing" extremists. The Central Committee of the Party must have sufficient strength, power, and courage to carry through the will of the Party and the Marxist-Leninist principles within the policy of the Party, despite either "right-wing" or "left-wing" deviationists.

From the Party resolutions and the press articles appearing in connection with the resolutions, and in the discussion of various problems, it appears that they are attempting to hold me personally responsible for the opposition and its consequences. If I am responsible for anything in this regard, then it is only because we failed to break down the opposition in time, resolutely and with forceful regulations. However, without the help and support of the Party apparatus, it was impossible to accomplish this through purely Party methods, to which I have always adhered. For this, however, not I, but Mátyás Rákosi is responsible, who from the start had two irons in the fire as far as opposition was concerned.

Hiding behind the opposition were primarily anti-Marxist, anti-Leninist ideologies: ideologies that have often been exposed and branded by the classicists as extreme "left-wingism," which represents a crude violation and distortion of the basic principle of Communism and the legitimacy of our development as a People's Democracy.

But we find also fear of disclosure of mistakes and of being held responsible. We know that the sincerity of a party can be measured primarily on the basis of the party leaders' attitude toward their mistakes. Some facts, very unpleasant to the "left-wing" deviationists, have come to light since the time of the June resolutions, although far from everything has become known. They were and are aware that these facts reveal them as falsifiers of Marxism-Leninism. The only way they can defend themselves, even if only temporarily, is by preventing the disclosure of their mistakes and by nipping all possibility of criticism in the bud. They fabricate charges because this is always easier than standing up and conducting a debate along the lines of Marxist-Leninist reasoning.

The debate, which requires at least two participants, has been entirely one-sided so far: they have made loud accusations, while I was obliged to listen in silence. But it was also one-sided because they have made serious charges without proving anything. Yet it is an elementary requirement that he who accuses must be able to prove his accusations. Nevertheless, the situation to date has been that they have accused me without any sort of evidence, and I am obliged to prove that the charges made against me are false.

Chapter 25.   Adherence to the Rules of Party Life and the Question of Rehabilitation

The pre-June Party leadership, which the June, 1953, resolution of the Central Committee branded as "clique leadership," had serious consequences in the internal life of the Party too. This legacy, which had to be liquidated and replaced by Leninist principles in Party life, was very onerous and became the biggest problem of the new Party leadership.

The decisions arrived at and the resolution made at the June, 1953, meeting of the Central Committee disclosed the anti-Marxist views and anti-Party methods that were disrupting the internal life of the Party, and particularly the higher leadership of the Party. But at the same time, the resolution indicated what had to be done to overcome these faults.

The faults for which Rákosi, as leader of the Party, was primarily responsible stemmed from the fact that under his leadership the internal life of the Party had failed to conform to fundamental Marxist-Leninist principles and had violated them through its directives and activities. It did not adhere to the organizational principles of the Party; its actual direction was not in the hands of the elected organs of the Party but was seized by Gerö, Farkas, and Róvai, led by Rákosi. In fact, even this small group became narrower, so that state leadership was actually in the hands of Rákosi and Gerö. They failed to inform the Secretariat, and still less the Political Committee, of important matters. They made decisions and took steps in affairs beyond their jurisdiction. They formed opinions on the various questions in advance, and then had the opinions passed as resolutions. They did not consider the other members of the elected organs of the Party their equals; they looked down on them.

Thus, instead of being led by elected Party organs, the Party was actually led by a clique. This inevitably resulted in lack of principles and violation of the Party line, and became the source of serious mistakes.

The replacement of collective Party leadership by clique leadership could lead to nothing but a series of mistakes and was the chief origin of the mistakes. It was also the origin of the personality cult and of "Führerism."

In Führerism, the role of the individual is enlarged in an idealistic, anti-Marxist sense, which exaggerates the role of the "elect" or the "predestined" individual as the shaper of history. The extreme danger of this idealistic point of view is that it makes no attempt to win the confidence and support of the people; it denies the creative power of the masses. Another harmful and dangerous aspect of Führerism is that it generates no initiative or activity in the masses but only an attitude of waiting with folded hands, because it is the leader or leaders who are expected to act. Both the personality cult and Führerism are alien to our people and can lead only to estrangement from the masses; and that is what happened in this case.

Rákosi and the Party leaders, Gerö, Róvai, and Farkas, impaired seriously the effectiveness of the Communist principle of criticism and self-criticism within the Party and the government. They generally considered criticism from below as the voice of the enemy and acted accordingly. They did not criticize one another but shielded each other from criticism. They took even the mildest form of criticism as a personal insult. According to them, mistakes could be made only at the lower echelons. They themselves were infallible and could do no wrong. At the same time, they were all the more outspoken when dressing down comrades called in on official business to attend meetings of the Secretariat and the Political Committee.

Fear of self-criticism or criticism from non-Party members is the most dangerous disease in the Party; lack of a critical spirit and the suppression of criticism and self-criticism play a big part in it. The responsibility for this falls on the Party leaders, especially on Rákosi. Our Party was permeated with Führerism and the spirit of noncriticism, which spread from the leaders down through the ranks.

There is every reason to ask why such serious mistakes in Party leadership occurred. Lenin's saying gives the exact answer: The best policy is a policy of principle. However, a policy of principle cannot be carried on without theoretical-ideological work. This is the root of the trouble. Where there is no theoretical work, no ideological debate, and no unfolding conflict of opinions, there it is possible to engage in politics without Marxist-Leninist preparation, and to practice Führerism. Where theoretical work is poor, lack of principle, which produces confusion and errors, takes over. Until we change this, there is and can be no assurance that we will not make even more serious mistakes.

The resolution of the Central Committee makes even more serious statements concerning the responsibility and anti-Party methods of the Party leadership.

Our Soviet comrades quite correctly stated that one of the greatest shortcomings of the old leadership was that "in Hungary, a true collective leadership failed to develop because Rákosi is incapable of working collectively." "He has lost the self-confidence required to correct mistakes, and it can happen that proper leadership will come into being over his head, which is a catastrophe for a leader," said Comrade Khrushchev at the May, 1954, conference in Moscow.

Comrade Malenkov, too, found that we were slow in correcting our mistakes in Party leadership and that Rákosi, as Party First Secretary, was not doing the job well. Rákosi was incapable of taking the lead in correcting mistakes. Each time we were in Moscow, the Soviet comrades noted that Rákosi's reports on our problems failed to make mention of the main questions, the urgent problems connected with Party life. The Soviet comrades were the ones who had to bring up the matter of Party unity and collective leadership. They found that their criticism and advice had led to no action.

During our visit preceding the Third Party Congress, the Soviet comrades emphasized:

Comrade Rákosi must take the lead in the fight to correct previous mistakes and to implement the resolutions of the Central Committee. He must put a final end to the mistakes of the past, bravely, manfully, and like a Bolshevik. He does not have to put the blame on Beria, the international situation, or anything else. Rákosi must promote Party unity by fighting consistently against the mistakes.

Our Soviet comrades pointed out that all mistakes must be disclosed, regardless of whom they involved:

Franker and more theoretical debates, Party-type criticism, and intra-Party democracy must be ensured. Lack of experience or training must not be looked down upon. Divergent opinions and possibly mistaken points of view must not be capitalized on politically to the detriment of those who hold them. There is no highest and lowest man in the Political Committee. Much more care must be devoted to the complete clarification of the principles involved in the questions. This is the only quick way to dispel the duality existing on certain points within the leadership.

They went on to emphasize:

The policy of airing grievances must be terminated, and the remnants of Führerism, of disdainful, insulting, and offensive conduct must be eliminated. The Party leadership needs Comrade Rákosi, but he must know and realize that he will have to merge into the collective leadership because that is the only way in which he can do his work well.

In connection with the well-known Kovacs letter, which discussed and called to the attention of the Party the problems of dualism in collective leadership, Party democracy, criticism, and self-criticism, and in attitudes toward principles, the Soviet comrades found it necessary to emphasize that Rákosi's report had side-stepped and failed to clarify the question of the unity of Party leadership, whereas debate on the Kovacs letter would have given him opportunity to do just that. It was not a debate of principle. It lacked Bolshevik frankness and got off on the wrong track, ending up as it did with a compromise of principle. The Political Committee was afraid to face the duality in leadership and its true cause. The matter was made more serious by the Political Committee's evaluation of the situation, which stated that there was an improvement in unity of leadership and that duality did not exist.

The Soviet comrades also considered it wrong that the Political Committee had taken up the matter of the Kovacs letter during my absence, whereas it was I who requested that the discussion be postponed for a little while.

The discussion of the Kovacs letter and the resolution of the Political Committee, both of which occurred during my absence, were the first crude attempt by Mátyás Rákosi to place the blame for the troubles arising from opposition to correcting old faults on the New Course and on me personally. The Central Committee's resolution concerning the Kovacs letter, which the Soviet comrades said was "lacking in Bolshevik frankness and deviated in the direction of compromise of principle" and which the Political Committee was obliged to change, willy-nilly, after it had been published, showed the true motives of Rákosi; even before the Third Party Congress, he tried to achieve what he did achieve in the spring of 1955. In short, assisted by baseless contentions, he used my absence enforced by illness to make the Political Committee accept a resolution condemning the policy of the New Course and putting the blame on me. Not only did Rákosi have this matter discussed at the Political Committee in my absence, but he wanted to go to Moscow without me. The Soviet comrades felt this would be wrong and refused to give him permission. Thus Rákosi's attempts in May, 1954, were a fiasco. He was obliged to admit both in Moscow and before the Political Committee that he had made the Politial Committee accept a resolution containing unfounded and misleading statements concerning collective leadership, unity of principle, and Party democracy, and that he had informed the Soviet comrades in this vein. The disclosure of this matter revealed the unethical political campaign directed against me, which had already started at that time.

From the beginning, Rákosi was opposed to the democratic principle regulating internal Party life. He was unable to adapt himself to collective leadership. He was unable to accept the principle of the equality of the members of the Political Committee. In connection with the June resolution criticizing Party leadership, he argued that the "foursome" was actually a small collective, so that there could be no talk of individual leadership. In any case, he continued, Stalin alone was leader in the Soviet Union, compared to which our "foursome" was a collective. A person who evaluates the mistaken leadership of the past in this manner, and who views the essence of collective leadership in this light, is incapable of remedying past faults or of adapting himself to collective leadership on the principle of equality—as events have proved.

Owing principally to Rákosi's obstructive attitude, the Political Committee began and continued its struggle to combat the deterioration of Party life amidst great political vacillation. One manifestation of this, which I have already mentioned, was Rákosi's July 11 speech to the Party activists of Budapest. This speech left the Party inclined to feel that there was no need for great changes in Party life, leadership, and policy; that actually the old policy could be continued. Even the Political Committee was unable to keep Rákosi from this endeavor.

The other manifestation took the form of directives issued by the Political Committee at the end of August, 1953, concerning the implementation of the June resolution. Fundamentally, these also omitted making mention of either the political and theoretical mistakes or the anti-Marxist, anti-Leninist methods of the Party leadership. This confused the Central Committee, the leading Party functionaries, and especially the secretaries on the lower levels, all of whom interpreted the directives as meaning what Rákosi had already convinced them of in his July 11, 1953, speech, i.e., that the Political Committee had made basic changes in the June, 1953, resolutions of the Central Committee. Actually the Political Committee was against such endeavors, but the directives had already been issued by the apparatus of the Central Committee and it was too late to make amends. All this shows that in implementing the June resolution the Political Committee, under the influence of Rákosi, vacillated a great deal in the matter of replacing the dictatorial methods practiced in inner Party life with democratic methods that would be in keeping with Party rules. It neither eradicated entirely the old anti-Party methods nor created new ones with any degree of consistency. This benefited only the "left-wing" extremists, the opposition, which was not in favor of the Party policy in any case. This led the Central Committee to declare in its October, 1953, report on the implementation of the June 28 resolution that some of the comrades continued to work sluggishly and squeamishly, and that unless they supported and promoted the resolution of the Central Committee quickly and without reservation, they would do great damage to both our Party and our people. This situation in the Party arose as the result of the behavior of Mátyás Rákosi. Yet, hardly a year later, despite the evidence of repeated Party resolutions and of facts, Rákosi attempted to bring the very same charges against me and to put them on record in the resolution of the Central Committee.

In June, 1953, and later, more than one session of the Central Committee established that Party resolutions were not being carried out in the spirit of Leninism as regards criticism and self-criticism either. Lenin states:

> A political party's attitude toward its own mistakes is one of the best and most certain criteria of the sincerity of the party, and of how it is actually performing its duty to its class and the working masses. A sincere party is characterized by its readiness to admit errors openly, to discover their causes, to analyze the situation responsible for them, and to debate by what means they may be rectified. In this way, the party fulfills its obligations; thus it trains and teaches first the *class* and then the *masses*.

The Central Committee pointed out that before 1953 certain comrades were little given to practicing the virtue of self-criticism, and had become unaccustomed to taking criticism, especially from below, from simple Party members. They had become alien to the fresh, invigorating atmosphere of Party democracy, to the procedure of collective leadership. Now, after June, 1953, when they came up against criticism, when their errors were disclosed and rectification demanded, a number of them went about their work with distaste, with reservations, and without real impetus. This was another serious error of past leadership. The Political Committee and I have made great efforts in the past two years to eradicate this attitude, to bring about criticism and self-criticism in the spirit of Lenin, and we have had some success. In the meantime, as I have already said, there were some mistakes and some extremism, but on the whole we made real progress in the crucial matter of internal Party life. By developing and ensuring intra-Party democracy, the June resolution made criticism possible.

However, it must be stated that in the wake of the March and April resolutions of the Central Committee there was a recurrence in the Party of the pre-June Party methods, adopted under the pretext of combating right-wing deviation. Criticism was stifled, and there was a return to terrorism and reprisals, both of which are a flagrant violation of Party democracy, run counter to the principles of Lenin, and are actually a return to the old mistaken practices of Party leadership. Criticism was again classified as either the "voice of the enemy" or more moderately, as a slander of the leaders. In this atmosphere, persons who continued to criticize and to disclose errors regardless of who committed them, who considered it not only their right but their duty on the basis of Party regulations to criticize, were usually abused and often suffered material, moral, or political setbacks, such as loss of their jobs and disciplining by or expulsion from the Party. Terrorism and fear of reprisal killed the sincerity of Party members and compelled them to keep their opinions to themselves. Their behavior and statements showed ever increasing duality. Within the Party organization, at meetings and conferences, they remained silent or spoke with indifference, reserving their true opinions for discussion outside the Party; that is where they talked politics. Such things are danger signs of the dissolution of Party morale, life, and discipline, and are the consequence of the return to threats, terror, and the stifling of criticism. The Party leadership is seriously to blame for this, the more so because these are well-known facts in the Party, among the leaders and members.

During the nearly two years preceding the March, 1955, resolution of the Central Committee, the rules of internal Party life were endangered by the autocratic methods of the "left-wing" extremists. Today, this danger has again become a reality and has created within the Party a situation of a gravity unparalleled since liberation. Not only has it disrupted the unity and mutual trust re-established within the Party after June, but also the connection and trust between the Party leadership and the members, the entire organizational political life of the Party. These are facts that no distortion or falsification can alter, as some Party bureaucrats are now trying to do. In an article entitled "Let Us Strengthen Democratic Centralism in the Party," appearing in *Szabad Nep* of May 22, 1955, Tivadar Matusek attempts to give a false picture of the crushing of Party democracy:

> During the past months, Party democracy also has been suffering from a right-wing attack. The Lenin-Stalin sense of Party democracy was especially crudely distorted by Comrade Imre Nagy. His most serious error was to supplant the right to criticize with license to criticize. He has distorted the frank and profound self-criticism of our Party and slanders our Party and its leaders.

To prove this, he quotes the following passage from my article of October 20, 1954:

> The old economic policy gave socialism an entirely incorrect interpretation: it failed to take into account man and society; it narrowed the concept of socialism till it meant only a maximum increase in the production of iron and steel, and an excess of industrialization.

The quotation is a mild, but absolutely correct, criticism of the old economic policy, and I abide by my opinion to this very day; in fact, it needs to be expressed more strongly and openly. But it appears that the Party bureaucrats have become so unaccustomed to criticism that, seizing their axes, they must attack through me, in the columns of the central Party journal, all those to whom it may occur to criticize anything. And only these "left-wing" extremists dare speak of the Leninist-Stalinist interpretation of Party democracy, these persons who with their bluster, threats, and regulations would silence the Party members with their extreme "left-wing" interpretation of freedom to criticize.

But it was not only Party democracy, but also collective leadership, which was distorted by me and not by the "foursome," whose attitude toward collective leadership is well known. In the same article, Matusek writes the following:

Comrade Imre Nagy seriously violated the principle of collective leadership, too. He gave an improper and biased version of the June, 1953, resolution of the Central Committee, and at the National Assembly he presented his own government program, independent of the Party resolution.

He also mentions my speech to the PPF Congress and my article of October 20 as further instances in which I exceeded the resolutions of the Central Committee and presented my own platform. On seeing the slander in the foregoing few sentences, one is obliged to ask who is right—Matusek, or the countless Party resolutions that contradict Matusek's slander? Let us take things in order. To begin with, why does Matusek not describe the June resolution of which I supposedly gave a biased interpretation and explain in what respect the government program is independent of the Party resolution? Because he feels safe, he is safe in lying, since only the initiate are familiar with the June resolution. And they will not call him to account, far less expose him. Between June, 1953, and March, 1955, the Central Committee has held many meetings; in fact, our Party Congress has been in session too; great resolutions were formulated; serious criticisms were voiced; many articles were written and speeches made; but never, anywhere, has there been a word or hint to the effect that I distorted the June resolution or that I put forward my "own" separate government program. This proves again that Matusek is telling a brazen lie. Every Party resolution, dozens of articles and speeches, emphatically stressed that the Party resolution and government program were identical. Even Mátyás Rákosi maintained this up to March, 1955. Let them decide among themselves who was telling the truth and who was lying. Even if what Matusek alleges were true, I would stand by the government program, because the welfare of the people, the country, and the Party required it, and it served their interest to a very great extent. If the need should arise, under similar circumstances, I would say it again. There was no mistake in the government; the trouble was that the June Party resolution on which the government program was based should have been published first. But this is not my fault. I was all in favor of publishing the resolution of the Central

Committee. On the other hand, Mátyás Rákosi and other persons responsible for the mistakes of the past were against this, for understandable reasons. They were so much against it that neither the Party members nor the people ever had a chance to become familiar with the June, 1953, resolution of the Central Committee. It is through this June resolution, which is being kept secret, that Matusek is attempting to charge me with violation of Party democracy and collective leadership. It is not difficult to show up these machinations. All that is needed is to make the June, 1953, resolution of the Central Committee available to the Party members and let them judge for themselves who distorted the June resolution; whether the government program is at odds with it; and whether present Party policy is based on the June resolution.

In my petition to the March meeting of the Central Committee, I found it necessary to comment on the relationship existing between Party bureaucracy, the Party apparatus, and the elected organs. Since then the situation has become still worse; the Party apparatus has become predominant, which, for one thing, proves the correctness of my contentions; and, for another, makes it necessary to bring up the subject again. At that time I wrote:

There are many indications of a gradual return to old, incorrect, un-Partlylike methods in Party leadership, in the work of the Party apparatus, and in the internal life of the Party. At meetings of the Political Committee, I have pointed out more than once that the leadership is slipping slowly from the Political Committee to the Secretariat, and that consequently the Party is not under the leadership of the elected body but of the Party apparatus. Thus collective leadership is nothing but a principle, having no practical reality. This among other things has contributed to the Political Committee's loss of prestige. Due to the predominance of the apparatus, officials of the apparatus have come to symbolize the Party. They speak and make statements in the name of the Party; their opinion is considered the opinion of the Party. Two types of Political Committee members are coming into being: those who hold posts in the Party and those who do not. The prestige of members of the Central Committee depends on this also.

The predominance of the apparatus and the eclipse of the elected organs, with a resulting increase in administrative methods in Party leadership, is nothing new in the life of our Party. It was typical of the pre-June methods of Party leadership. We were unable to alter this, which was particularly bad because the Soviet comrades, and especially Comrade Khrushchev, on many occasions called our attention to the danger: to the fact that the apparatus is leading us and is overpowering the Party. The growing pressure, terrorism, and browbeating in the field of intra-Party democracy and criticism and self-criticism, is closely related to the predominant role assumed by the apparatus and the increasing use of administrative devices in the internal life of the Party. It is undoubtedly true that intra-Party democracy and the right to criticize were abused in many places and used against the Party. Action must be taken against this type of abuse, but it should not be replaced by the mistaken attitudes of the past, which responded to criticism with browbeating and terroristic tactics. Yet, unfortunately, these are beginning to spread to a dangerous extent, and the harmful consequences of such tactics are already becoming apparent in Party life and in the behavior of Party members.

Viewing the matter in retrospect, I still feel I was right in raising the question. The rise of bureaucracy and the predominant role assumed by the apparatus, the overshadowing of the elected organs, combined with the financial dependence of the Party leadership and most members of the apparatus, play a significant role in the distortion and suppression of the Leninist spirit in Party democracy, collective leadership, and criticism and self-criticism. These factors played a crucial part in the turn of events owing to which Party policy was set back on a pre-June footing, after the groundwork for the turnabout had been completed in March through opposition to the policy of the New Course.

The April resolution of the Central Committee, without any cause, explanation, or reference to positive facts, accuses me of resorting to "factional" tactics. I classify this as common slander. The charge of factionalism stems from distorted views concerning the rules of the internal life of the Party. Every political statement of the Party members looks like factionalism to persons who deny the fundamental right of Party members to dis-

cuss Party problems and to debate and exchange opinions; who
believe that Party members may discuss Party life, political, economic, cultural, or international questions only in the presence
of the Party Secretary or under the surveillance of members of
the apparatus; who feel that discussions must be conducted according to specific rules or from a predetermined point of view
and within a limited scope—in other words, only under the conditions that the "left-wing" extremists and the Party bureaucracy are willing to tolerate.

Yet one must realize that Party rules guarantee every Party
member the right to take a stand in questions concerning Party
policy, to debate his stand, and to exchange opinions on this
subject with other Party members. In fact, Party members have
the right to move that sessions of the leadership, the electorate,
or even the Central Committee be convened; if necessary, they
may even ask for an extra session of the Party Congress, provided that the required number of Party members approve of
the motion. They have the right to do all this in an uncontested
fashion, and without being called factionists by anyone who
adheres to Lenin's interpretation of Party rules; who respects
the rights of Party members; and who is not motivated by dictatorial aspirations.

It appears that some people consider it a factional tactic that
I refused to tolerate the illegal and irregular resolutions of the
Political Committee that attempted to isolate and silence me
completely on the basis of the medical report composed by the
Committee. At that time, I was frequently obliged to write to
the Central Committee because of the irregular actions of the
Political Committee. In my letter of February 25, 1955, I wrote
the following:

> A week ago today, I addressed Mátyás Rákosi in the form of a
> letter and requested him to inform me about the Political Com-
> mittees proposals, resolutions, agenda, etc., as pertaining to the
> meeting of the Central Committee. I did not receive an answer to
> this request. The case was similar to the Saturday's "orientation"
> meeting, of which I was not notified. I am completely unfamiliar
> with the Political Committee's report on the problem that was
> presented there. . . . I consider this procedure unforgivable and
> irregular, and I object to it. It is apparent that they want to

conduct the Central Committee's meeting without me; without giving me an opportunity to express my views on the debatable problems; without allowing me to justify my standpoint. For my part, it is apparent that the Political Committee, which with numerous actions has actually stripped me of my membership in the Political Committee, does not wish to solve political differences of opinion on the basis of principle—or in the sphere of Party-like discussion—or with the assistance of the Central Committee, but through the use of various irregular Party methods. They wish to remain silent and are hastening to influence the standpoint of the members of the Central Committee by not telling them the whole story. I maintain this to be arbitrariness, contrary to Party principles and unforgivable in our Party.

I was absolutely right when I wrote this in my letter.

Prior to this, I also objected to irregular Party procedure in my letter of February 23, 1955; in this letter, among other things, I wrote the following:

As a result of my illness, it is apparent that for a certain period I must be dissociated from Party and state work. I will make allowance for this, but I cannot agree with those exaggerated regulations that on the pretense of my illness result in irregular Party measures against me. At present, the situation is that my membership in the Political Committee is purely nominal, so that the above-listed and other irregular measures have in fact terminated it, even though the Central Committee, elected at the Third Party Congress, sent me into the Political Committee as a full-fledged member. But, since they do not consider me as an actual or bonafide member of the Political Committee, I am turning to the Central Committee with this as well as with other problems.

My objection against the irregular Party procedure of the Political Committee was also in order.

Afterward, in my petition addressed to the March meeting of the Central Committee in opposition to the chain of abuses, I presented my standpoint as follows:

In recent days, I have turned to the Central Committee with a letter which I sent to the First Secretary of the Central Committee and to other members of the Central Committee so that they can present it at the meeting of the Central Committee. As I wrote in my accompanying letter addressed to Comrade Rákosi, I was forced to resort to this means because for weeks neither the Political Committee as a body, nor any of its individual members, nor the First Secretary of the Central Committee, has kept in contact with me on the pretext of my illness. He does not give me any answer whatsoever to my letters, my petitions, my requests, or my complaints, even though I objected to serious irregular Party procedures. At the previous meeting of the Central Committee, they went so far as to make known serious things about me and my political standpoint, without informing me. This was entirely one-sided; it was done without making known my objections and standpoint on those same problems, so that the members of the Central Committee were not given the opportunity to take the proper political stand with full knowledge of all information. With respect to all these irregular Party procedures taken against me, I request the Central Committee to exert pressure so that the clarification of the problems take place within the farmework of principle and Partylike procedure.

Therefore I most emphatically reject, with complete justice, the charges of factional methods. I did not employ factional methods—they were employed against me.

These methods, in addition to creating great uncertainty and confusion on principles in the Party and in the so-called politically misinformed Party membership (which lead to a serious rift between the membership and leadership), caused the widespread decline of the prestige of the Party leadership. This was not my doing. After the Central Committee meeting of October, 1954, I wrote in my article "After the Meeting of the Central Committee" in the October 20 issue of *Szabad Nep*, the following, which I still consider to be correct and worthy of emphasis:

> In everyday Party work, far-reaching implications must be drawn from the discussions and resolutions of the Central Committee. The meeting of the Central Committee was a magnificent display of the unity of principles of Party leadership. We must now take this further and manage to get the entire Party membership to speak as one. For this, however, the methods of leadership must be changed, and the improper views that have arisen about the role of Party members must be eliminated.

That Party members have an important role not only in the execution of tasks assigned by the virtue of leadership but also in the formation of the Party's policies must be vindicated. Without this there cannot be a healthy Partylike life within the Party; the leadership, floundering and alienated from the broad masses of Party membership, would lose the necessary power and momentum.One of the principal morals of the Central Committee's meeting is that this must be changed. We very properly pay a great deal of attention to the relationship between the Party and the working masses. But very little is said about the relationship of the Party leadership and the Party membership, and the unity of political principles. However, in the Revolutionary Workers' Party this is an indispensable condition of Party leadership. The close relationship between the Party and the masses cannot be realized without this. The failure to discuss Party principles and policy with the Party membership, as though this were the job of the leadership only, and as though the membership were concerned only with its execution, must also be changed.

We have not relied enough upon the members of the Party. We have not presented the problems of the Party's policies to them. We have brought to them primarily problems of production and daily economic tasks. In essence, we have treated them as though they were not of age. However, our power rests on the wide masses of our Party membership, on unified action and class consciousness. At the same time, a responsibility associated with Party membership is to support Party policy, to explain it, and if need be to defend it. Languid and indifferent conduct must be punished unmercifully. A harsh struggle must be continued against enemy propaganda, which at times finds acceptance among Party members.

As a result of the detrimental consequences that have appeared in Party life during the last half-year, the above viewpoints must be endorsed to an even greater degree today. The prestige of Party leadership must be restored and protected, mainly by virtue of the faultless conduct and operation of these organs from the viewpoint of exemplary and Partylike politics and morals. The restoration of the prestige of Party leadership demands the dismissal from Party leadership and public life of all those who with their criminal acts and misuse of authority during the past years have seriously harmed the demands of

Communist virtue and public morals—the constitutional rights of Party members and citizens. An end must be put to the ever increasing lies in the Party's leadership, in the apparatus, and in the press, and to errors committed by Party members contradictory to Communist virtue. Lenin spoke out very sharply against so-called "Communist lies." The Party members have found more than one Party leader engaged in this, but the broad masses also engage in such lies in both domestic and foreign politics and, last but not least, in connection with my troubles with the Party. This, however, cannot be continued very long without serious consequenes. They underrate Party members and workers when they choose to deceive them with malicious lies. The people have their own minds and like to use them.

Perhaps the greatest harm done and still being done to Party leadership authority is the ideological confusion and uncertainty prevailing in Party ranks, which was caused by the March and April resolutions of the Central Committee and the articles and tirades that followed them; a confusion evidenced in words and deeds, in resolutions and their implementation, in repetitious assertions about the June policy, and even in discussions on reversion to the old policy. Thus a lack of calm political activity, mainly in the Party leadership, a lack of solidarity and deliberateness, or in other words a lack of stability, is the decisive fault in Party policy. There is an almost continuous confusion in Party policy, a restlessness in the Party membership and in public opinion, and a pushing of masses from one direction to the other. Under the pretext of struggling against rightist deviation, this has completely upset the Party and the nation, and has undermined the prestige of Party leadership and the confidence placed in it.

The Party had to be and must be ideologically and politically armed for the struggle against rightist errors and views and against their threats. But at the same time it was and remains improper today to disarm the Party vis-à-vis "leftist" errors and dangers which have deep roots in the Party. But a struggle against "leftist" deviation cannot be expected from the "leftist" extremists who today have a decisive role in the ideological and political guidance of the Party. Yet the Party cannot continue the struggle on only one front. The mistake in this field was that after the June resolution of the Central Committee, we conducted the struggle against the "leftist" mistakes and dangers in such a manner as to neglect the struggle against rightist mistakes and dangers. The task should have been, and still is today, as far as I am concerned, that the struggle against faults and dangers must be carried on at both fronts. Instead of this, they led the Party to the other extreme (of fighting on one front only) which the Party membership did not and does not understand. In addition to increasing distrust, this caused indignation in the Party membership and in public opinion. The "leftist" mistakes and dangers came back to life with extraordinary strength and speed following the thorough assessment of the June policies and the return to the extremely "leftist" policies of anti-Marxism and anti-Leninism. These dangers came back to life more ominously, with more harmful consequences, and in a more serious form than ever before. The very thing that the Party should have guarded against, as its major task, came to pass.

The April resolution of the Central Committee also implemented measures, much less severe than mine, against Mihály Farkas because he had allegedly supported "my" policies for a long time. This qualification of Farkas' act does not stand up; it is not sincere—it is deceptive. A much more severe punishment is in order for Mihály Farkas, not on the basis of a motive prescribed in a resolution, but rather by the revelation of his criminal actions in matters of rehabilitation and of state defense. If anybody is burdened with responsibility because he supported the implementation of the June policies, it is not Mihály Farkas, of all people.

The ever widening rift between the Party and the masses of the Hungarian workers occurred because the masses were unwilling to follow the Party on the old, mistaken, antipeople political path, which had already proved a failure once, at heavy cost to the people of the nation.

On the problem of rehabilitation, they charged that I brought the question before the public, in my article in the October 20, 1954, issue of *Szabad Nep*, in such a way as to weaken the unity and the authority of the leaders. It was then and still is my opinion that it is not a matter of how the question is posed, but rather that the commission of the crimes in question was and is detrimental to the Party and to leadership authority. Experience shows that it would have been far better to attend to the problems in the autumn of the preceding year, instead of continually deferring them, as this caused serious uncertainty and tension among Party members and the broad masses of the workers. We long since could have worked out these touchy Party problems. Numerous circumstances, pointed out more than once by the Soviet comrades, hindered solving the problem with reference to the long-range interests of the Party. Comrade Khrushchev, at the first of last year, urged the rehabilitations, saying, "The detainees are being released slowly. This is Rákosi's fault, because he hasn't taken the matter in hand. Rákosi alludes to the fact that his nerves are bad. Nerves don't count. He has lost self-confidence in the correction of errors." On the occasion of our Moscow talks prior to the Third Congress, Comrade Khrushchev likewise said the following: "Rákosi is responsible for the arrests. Therefore he does not want to release these people. He knows that he is guilty and will compromise himself. It is not permissible to denounce men and to throw suspicion on them." Comrade Khrushchev advised that "the rehabilitations should be carried out so as not to destroy Rákosi's authority." But, so that his words would not be misinterpreted, he added, "We will protect Rákosi's authority only in so far as it is not prejudicial to Party authority.

"It may happen that on the pretext of protecting Rákosi's authority, the old policy will be reinstated and the freeing of the prisoners will not proceed. Of course, it is difficult for Rákosi to free the prisoners," Comrade Khrushchev said, "because he ordered the arrests. Despite that, what happened must be told. Neither silence nor glossing over will increase the authority of the Party; rather it will take frank discussion."

I represented this point of view from the beginning, and this is now my stand on the question of rehabilitation. I fought in the Political Committee for the vindication of my stand, just as I did in the Rehabilitation Committee, from which I resigned at that time because of rising opposition.

In my report addressed to the March session of the Central

Committee, I expressed my views, based on the above-cited viewpoints, about the rehabilitations and the related problems of state security. The evidence of the half-year since the March resolution, and Rákosi's recent speech at Csepel, indicate that Rákosi does not want to settle these matters—i.e., the great trials, principally the Rajk trial—frankly and thoroughly, but rather in a way to gloss over former mistakes and to hide crimes and criminals. Mátyás Rákosi's attempt to induce various comrades to help him hush up this affair regardless of the truth or of the facts is proof of that.

The denial of human honor, of Communist morality, and of socialist legality, however, brings grim retribution. Whoever acts contrary to this has only himself to blame and should not charge me with damaging the authority of Party leadership.

Epilogue

George Paloczi-Horvath

Imre Nagy completed this appeal to the Soviet and Hungarian Communist Party leadership at the beginning of July, 1956. A Russian translation was sent to the Soviet Ambassador in Budapest. The Hungarian manuscript was read by many members of the Central Executive of the Hungarian Communist Party. *At that time a political trial was in preparation against Imre Nagy.* The press campaign against him and his followers was renewed and it became more intensive than it had been in November, 1955, right after he was expelled from the Party.

When the Central Executive met on July 12, 1956, the First Secretary of the Party arrived with a carefully prepared new resolution. He suggested that the "Imre Nagy any-Party conspiracy" should be liquidated at once. He had a list of four hundred people whose arrest he demanded. The first name on the list was that of Imre Nagy. He suggested further that the Writer's Association, the *Literary Gazette (Irodalmi Ujsag)* and the Petöfi Circle of university youth should be banned. This resolution, soon after the Twentieth Congress of the Soviet Communist Party, would have meant a full return to Stalinism in Hungary, when in the Soviet Union the anti-Stalin line was still going strong. Several members of the Central Executive were strongly against the resolution. The debate lasted for several days. Some members of the Executive went to the Soviet Embassy and have reported that Rákosi's resolution, if carried, would provoke disturbances *within* the Communist Party. On the 17th day of July Mikoyan arrived by air, demoted Rákosi and made Ernö Gerö First Secretary. But for this last-minute Soviet intervention, Imre Nagy and his associates would have figured in a large-scale confession trial in Budapest.

In the pre-revolutionary atmosphere the demand for Imre Nagy's full rehabilitation grew stronger. He was readmitted to the Party on the 14th of October and became Premier again on the 24th.

Imre Nagy's role in the October revolution is well known. This book proves that his decision to renounce the Warsaw Pact, to declare Hungary's independence and neutrality, was not forced upon him by "counterrevolutionary" reactionary elements. He clearly stated in 1955 that Hungary should stay outside the power blocs, that for Hungary neutrality was the only possibility for national survival. These statements in the book are used now by the Soviet and Hungarian Communist newspapers to prove that Imre Nagy "conspired since 1955 against the Warsaw pact." A true Communist—these articles emphasize—cannot be neutral in the fight between the "socialist camp" and the "imperialistic camp." Consequently Imre Nagy had already committed treason against the Communist cause in 1955 when he suggested neutrality for Hungary. "A true Communist cannot call the 'socialist camp' a power bloc. Imre Nagy only pretended to be a Communist, in fact he was already in 1955 an imperialist agent," asserts the July 28, 1957, issue of *Nepszabadsag,* the official organ of the Hungarian Communist Party.

On the 4th of November, after the second Soviet attack, Imre Nagy with seventeen of his closest associates and their families took refuge in the Yugoslav Embassy in Budapest. On November 14, Prime Minister and Party Leader Janos Kadar told a delegation of Budapest workers (who had asked that Nagy should take over leadership of the government) that if Nagy left the Yugoslav Embassy "it would be possible to consult and reach agreement with him." Meanwhile negotiations were going on between the Kadar government and that of Yugoslavia about the future of Imre Nagy and his associates. On the 21st of November Premier Kadar signed an agreement according to which Imre Nagy and his associates could return to their homes in Budapest. The Hungarian government reaffirmed in writing *"the statement which has already been given verbally on several previous occasions that it has no intention of taking punitive action against Imre Nagy and members of his group because of their past activities."*

During the negotiations Premier Kadar offered to send a bus to the Yugoslav Embassy to take the Hungarian politicians to their respective homes. This was important because at that time there was no transportation in the city.

The refugees in the Yugoslav Embassy called up their friends and families on the afternoon of the 22nd and announced their arrival home for 7:00 A.M. that evening.

At 6:30 a large bus drove up to the Yugoslav Embassy. Imre Nagy and associates entered the bus with two Yugoslav Embassy officials who had the task of seeing them safely home. A few blocks from the embassy Soviet Security Police cars and tanks surrounded the bus and Soviet officers tried to board it. Imre Nagy and the Yugoslav diplomats protested in vain. The Yugoslav diplomats were forced to leave the bus, which, accompanied by Soviet armored cars, was taken to an unknown destination. The Yugoslav Embassy immediately protested against this breach of the signed agreement. Kadar and his Deputy Premier, Dr. Munnich, pretended that they knew nothing about the kidnaping. They might have spoken the truth because next day, on the 23rd of October, *Nepakarat* published the text of the already broken Hungarian-Yugoslav agreement and the safe-conduct given to Mr. Nagy and associates. The paper also reported that they had left the Yugoslav Embassy to return to their homes in Budapest.

On the afternoon of the 23rd, Premier Kadar declared that Imre Nagy had requested that he should be taken to Rumania. Two days later he justified the deportation on the ground that *"counterrevolutionaries might have murdered Imre Nagy as a provocation."* Nagy was therefore still treated as a possible victim of counterrevolutionaries, rather than as one of their number.

He is now in solitary confinement somewhere in the Soviet world. He is the most important prisoner of the international

Security Police network directed from Moscow. Since his abduction they have tried everything to break his resistance. The great rigged trial concerning the Hungarian revolution cannot be staged without his confession. And this rigged trial should be the final proof that the thousands of Soviet tanks did not fight last year in Hungary to squash the unanimous uprising of the Hungarian people, but to crush a counterrevolution staged by imperialist agents.

Prisoners in the Soviet orbit usually confess soon after a supreme Party resolution has indicted them. It is the task of the Security Police to obtain the confession. The joint declaration of the Soviet and Hungarian Communist Parties stated on March 28, 1957:

> The Nagy-Losonczy group of traitors had been hand in glove with the counterrevolutionary underground long before the October events, while falsely professing their allegiance to socialism. Over a period of many years that group had been shattering the Hungarian Working People's Party from within. . . . Imre Nagy and his confederates traveled a road common to all revisionists. Having departed from the principles of Marxism-Leninism, they quickly slid into a position of undisguised cooperation with counterrevolutionary elements and became the executors . . . of reaction.
>
> Incontrovertible facts and documents at the disposal of the Hungarian Government show that the armed action of counterrevolutionary forces in Hungary in October-November, 1956, was prepared under the direct guidance and with the participation of Western aggressive quarters.

In thirty years of Soviet practice such a Party indictment was usually followed by an appropriate confession trial. At the end of August, 1957, there was a clear indication from Budapest that plans for the trial were ready. The official spokesman of the Budapest Foreign Office, who had previously denied the rumors about the preparations for a trial of Imre Nagy, made the following statement: "I fully realize that bourgeois public opinion is quite excited by the possibility of an Imre Nagy trial. I am sorry that I cannot satisfy curiosity in this respect. I can state one thing though: The courts of the Hungarian People's Republic institute proceedings against everyone who endangers the rule of the working class."

And Imre Nagy is being almost daily accused with precisely the same crime by the Hungarian Communist press. His associates who were kidnaped with him and abducted to Rumania have been prisoners since early spring in the Fo Utca jail of the Budapest Security Police. His own whereabouts are not known. But it is more than obvious that a rigged trial is being prepared against him and his friends. All the Security Police want is their confession. But they do not seem to confess. Imre Nagy himself is in a very strong position. He is a mortally sick man. He had a serious heart attack before the revolution and his doctors have warned him that too much strain and excitement will kill him. So the usual methods of the Soviet Security Police cannot be applied in his case for fear that the next heart attack will take him out of reach of brain-washing.

Imre Nagy, sixty-one years old at the time of this writing, cares more for his historical reputation than for his physical existence. He realizes full well that by confessing to nonexistent crimes, he would besmirch the cause for which he fought. As one who spent five years in Security Police jails and went through fourteen months of brain-washing, the writer must, however, state this: Torture, sleeplessness, utter degradation, cold and hunger and the subtler means of brain-washing have a different effect on each individual. Many are those who have gone insane during this experience, many are those whose spirit has been completely broken, although they had been all their lives men of great courage and integrity. All one can safely state is that the sixty-one-year-old Imre Nagy by withstanding for more than ten months his tormentors proved himself to be of exceptional courage and integrity. There is no doubt that the Soviet Security Police network never had as important a task as the breaking of Imre Nagy. The staging of his trial is of supreme importance to the entire Soviet orbit. This rigged trial should disprove the report of the UNO Special Committee on Hungary; it should put a thick smokescreen around the ugly fact that Soviet tanks were fighting against the united working class of a socialist country.

How proud the Communist leaders were that in the Soviet

orbit they never had to fight with tanks and guns against "the simple working people." The East Berlin and Poznan risings were disquieting symptoms. But the Hungarian eruption represented deadly danger to the system.

In their own countries, in the so-called "free world," how often have they used tanks against the working people and the unemployed, tear gas, weapons, bludgeons, hundreds and thousands of policemen, gendarmes and soldiers against those who only asked for bread? . . . What wouldn't the "Voice of America" give to be able to cite just one example of tanks being used against the masses in a socialist country, one example where it had been necessary to use tanks and arms the way it occurs every day in the countries of the so-called "free world"?

So spoke Imre Nagy's treacherous adversary, Mátyás Rákosi, then dictator of Hungary. Imre Nagy's rigged trial should prove that thousands of Soviet tanks were not employed against the masses, but against counterrevolutionary capitalists, imperialist agents and fascist beasts. The Soviet and *colonial* press—because the word *satellite* gives an exaggerated impression of freedom— has concentrated for months on an all-out drive to falsify recent history. It has to be proved that the Hungarian revolution was a counterrevolution, instigated by Western imperialists and fought by Horthyites.

The Epilogue to Imre Nagy's book would be incomplete without a survey of this great drive for the falsification of the history of the Hungarian revolution by the Soviet and colonial press. In this drive attacks against Imre Nagy play an important part.

During the revolution, *Pravda,* the Soviet leaders, and Mr. Kadar had nothing to say against Imre Nagy. On the 30th of October, after Mr. Nagy announced the end of one-party rule, Kadar, who was a member of the Nagy government, referred to Imre Nagy in a radio broadcast as his "much respected countryman." He added that the presidency of the Communist Party *"fully approves of the decisions."* On the first of November Kadar made the following broadcast:

Hungarian workers, peasants and intellectuals . . . In a glorious uprising our people have shaken off the Rákosi regime. They have achieved freedom for the people, independence for the country, without which there can be no socialism. . . . We can safely say that the ideological and organizational leaders who prepared the uprising were recruited from among your ranks. Hungarian Communist writers, journalists, university students, the youth of the Petöfi Circle, thousands and thousands of peasants, and veteran fighters who had been imprisoned on false charges fought in the front line against the Rákosi-ite despotism and political hooliganism.

After November 4, the line changed. But at first there were only cautious remarks about counterrevolutionary elements exploiting the just uprising of the people. Imre Nagy was then treated as a weakling carried along by the "counterrevolutionaries" against his will. Thus Kadar said in a broadcast on November 11, 1956: "I, as a Minister in Imre Nagy's government, must openly state that to the best of my knowledge neither Imre Nagy nor his political groups meant knowingly to support the regime of counterrevolution."

The Soviet press did not attack Imre Nagy as a traitor to his country until January, 1957. It was admitted that the original uprising was caused by real grievances. *Pravda* stated on November 23:

The former Party and government leadership in Hungary mechanically copied the experience of the Soviet Union in the field of industrialization, regardless of the fact that the leaders of the . . . Hungarian Communist Party were frequently given comradely advice not to do so.

A long list of examples followed, ranging from the overdevelopment of industry and failure to provide more consumer goods and raise the standard of living, to the insistence that Hungarians should have their hair cut and their school lessons marked in the Russian fashion.

On January 5, 1957, Khrushchev and Malenkov visited Budapest. From that day on, Imre Nagy became a traitor, and two months later, an imperialist agent.

In November and December both the Soviet and the Hungarian Communist press blamed former Party dictator Rákosi and Gerö for everything. In the above-quoted article, *Pravda* stated:

> . . . There is not doubt that the former . . . leadership, headed by Rákosi and Gerö, is to blame, for . . . they committed gross mistakes both in general political questions and in the field of economic policy and cultural development. . . . In such circumstances dissatisfaction became increasingly bitter until finally it led to street demonstrations in Budapest on October 23.

Now, however, it has to be proved that there was no popular dissatisfaction, no general uprising; hence Rákosi and Gerö must be whitewashed in order to blacken Imre Nagy all the more. *Nepszabadag* wrote on March 7, 1957:

> The Imre Nagy group, which turned counterrevolutionary, simply cannot be bracketed together with the old leadership. However serious may have been the faults committed by Comrades Rákosi and Gerö . . . neither Rákosi nor Gerö concluded an alliance with the counterrevolutionary forces against the proletarian dictatorship.

The present rulers of Hungary called Rákosi a sadist criminal for the murder of Laszlo Rajk and his group. Now Imre Nagy and Geza Losonczy are accused of "arranging the funeral of Rajk and partners." In fact, at the time of the ceremonial reburial of Laszlo Rajk on October 6, 1956, neither Nagy nor Losonczy was a member of the Party leadership. The reburial was arranged by Kadar and his present associates. If anyone exploited the occasion to incite against Rákosi and his gang, it was the two principal speakers at the funeral.

Ferenc Munnish, at present First Deputy Premier, said: "He [Rajk] was destroyed by the sadist criminals that crawled to daylight from the swamps of the cult of personality. . . . It was in the swamps of that cult that the falsification of history, sycophancy, careerism, condemnation of tradition and trampling on laws grew and thrived."

Antal Apro, at present Kadar's Minister of Industry, said: "We have called and will call to account in the Party and state leadership those who have committed these shameful, illegal acts."

But both of them speak now of Rákosi as a comrade who committed some "errors," and of Imre Nagy as a traitor, who by arranging the Rajk funeral gave the last impetus to the revolution.

Within little more than a year of the Twentieth Party Congress, when Mikoyan denounced the "historical nonsense" written under Stalin, the Soviet and colonial public have been and are being presented with distortions at least as gross. But the falsification of that recent period of history, which is so desperately important to the Soviet leadership, cannot be achieved—so they believe—without the help of Imre Nagy and his principal associates. They have to confess, to make the case complete. And they do not confess. And Imre Nagy even from prison serves the truth. This book is the greatest obstacle to the success of the falsification drive. If Western readers perhaps find it hard to understand the full impact of this "dissertation," it is because it is couched in the usual Marxist terminology. But for readers beyond the Iron Curtain—and the attacks against it prove that it has many readers there—it is a most important indictment not only of Rákosi but also of his Kremlin masters.